PROTESTANT THOUGHT
IN THE TWENTIETH CENTURY

Whence and Whither?

THE MACMILLAN COMPANY
NEW YORK · BOSTON · CHICAGO
DALLAS · ATLANTA · SAN FRANCISCO

MACMILLAN AND CO., LIMITED
LONDON · BOMBAY · CALCUTTA
MADRAS · MELBOURNE

**THE MACMILLAN COMPANY
OF CANADA, LIMITED**
TORONTO

Protestant Thought in the Twentieth Century

⊱ *WHENCE & WHITHER?*

Edited by ARNOLD S. NASH

THE MACMILLAN COMPANY
New York: 1951

The editor makes acknowledgment to the following publishers
for the use of quoted material: to The Federal Council of the
Churches of Christ in America for Sanford: *Federal Council of
Churches of Christ in America* (Fleming H. Revell, 1949); to the
University of Chicago Press for Nichols: *History in the Theo-
logical Curriculum* (copyright, 1946); to *Christendom* for Van
Dusen: *The Issues of Christian Unity* (Spring, 1946); to
Abingdon-Cokesbury Press, for Van Dusen: *World Christianity
—Yesterday—Today—Tomorrow* (copyright, 1947).

The dogmas of the quiet past are inadequate to the stormy present: the occasion is piled high with difficulty, and we must think anew and act anew.

ABRAHAM LINCOLN
Annual Message to Congress
December 1, 1862

All great problems of life must be solved first on the religious plane and the new synthesis is the task of Protestantism for the future.

EDUARD SPRANGER

PREFACE

AMERICA today not only has "come of age," to borrow André Siegfried's phrase, but the American nation as a whole is accepting (the antics of Senator McCarthy and his cohorts notwithstanding) the demands of its political maturity in a fashion that is only credible because it has actually happened. Moreover, the role played by America in current political and economic affairs is one that has its counterpart in the realm of religion. That is true for Roman Catholicism, Eastern Orthodoxy and Protestantism alike. In the counsels of the Vatican no nation figures more largely when decisions are made and thought is implemented than does America; and the Communist jibe against the World Council of Churches to the effect that it is an instrument of American ecclesiastical imperialism in Protestant dress is a recognition of a fact even if it also involves a serious misrepresentation of that fact. Last but by no means least, it is America that provides in Archbishop Athenagoras, if not one of its native-born nationals, yet one of its citizens to become, as Patriarch of Constantinople, the spiritual head of more than a hundred millions of Greek Orthodox Christians.

To point out thus the role of America in the religious life of the world is, of course, to indicate that American life is based upon a unique experiment in cultural pluralism where what binds a nation together is not a particular religion but a certain attitude towards religion. Yet that fact, important though it may be, must not obscure its correlate, namely that the religious roots of American culture lie in Protestantism. A perfect symbol of that fact is that little more than a generation separated the epoch-making event at San Salvador on October 12, 1492, from those at Wittenberg on October 31, 1517.

This book, then, tries to explore what has been happening among Protestant religious thinkers in America over the last fifty years. But the year that sees the publication of this symposium is not only the one that begins the second half of the century in which we live, but that century is one which, it is well nigh universally recognized, sees the end of an age.

A book, therefore, that concerns itself with the question of where Protestant thought in America is going can only do so in the light of some understanding of the cultural crisis as a whole. It is for this reason that the opening chapter of the book considers the "Zeitgeist" of the twentieth century as it has influenced every realm of thought and action and what, consequently, has happened to Protestantism.[1]

In the light of this opening chapter, each of the authors of this symposium was asked to take as his starting point an interpretation of Protestant thought in his particular sphere of scholarship in North America when the century opened and then to proceed to give an analysis of the development of thought in that sphere both in the light of its own development and the impact of events upon it. The further suggestion made to him was that he should conclude by attempting the very difficult task of indicating the problems which in his particular field of study face us now and whose attempted solution, therefore, will dominate, so far as can be seen, the rest of the century.

However, in fairness to each author, I ought to state that these were simply suggestions to serve as guidance rather than a plan to be slavishly followed. In other words, each author was left free to pursue his task along those lines which he would find most conducive to its successful completion, granted the peculiarities of his own field of study and his own personal inclinations. He knew who his fellow authors were and he was left free to consult with them as he saw fit and appropriate, but that was left entirely to his own discretion. The book, then, is a symposium. It does not pre-

---

[1] It is, I think, relevant here to mention that the book had its immediate origin in an article on this very point which I contributed to the *Christian Century*, October 30, 1946. I am indebted to the *Christian Century* for permission to embody substantial parts of this article in the opening chapter of this book.

tend to furnish conclusions about which all the authors agree. They are all too much the children of Protestantism to think that such a hope would be desirable or even possible. Yet, having stated that fact, it gives me not a little satisfaction to have played as editor some part in presenting what is substantially a surprising consensus of opinion as Protestantism faces the future. Surprising, because no deliberate attempt was made to get authors representative of the different Protestant Churches who yet agreed with each other, and pleasing because they exhibit all shades—from Episcopalianism to "Unitarianism"—of the theological spectrum which emerged after the far from "white" light of medieval Catholicism entered the prism of the Reformation.

I should emphasize, too, that by Protestant thought I do not mean self-conscious thought about "Protestantism." Too much thought by Protestants, I know, is precisely that. Moreover, Protestantism is all too often conceived of simply as the opposite of "Catholicism." Rather, the book seeks to present Protestant thought *in action* in all the various realms of theological scholarship.

This book, I would also add, does not seek to give anything in the nature of a Protestant "solution" to the problems of the present age, but it seeks to present the ways in which Protestant thought in America has moved over the last fifty years as it has sought to make its message relevant to the modern era without submerging it under the spirit of that age.

Arnold S. Nash

CONTENTS

AMERICA AT THE END
OF THE PROTESTANT ERA

Arnold S. Nash

ARNOLD S. NASH, now *James A. Gray* Professor of the History of Religion and Chairman of the Department of Religion at the University of North Carolina, was born in 1906. Educated at the University of Liverpool, Ripon Hall, Oxford, and the London School of Economics, he holds graduate degrees in chemistry, philosophy and sociology, the connecting link in his studies being the nature of scientific method and the part played by science in moulding Western civilization.

In 1939 he came to the United States from England, where he had been Executive Secretary for the Student Christian Movement in the University of London to lecture on the relations between Christian theology, history and the social sciences at various American colleges and universities. He was editor of and contributor to *Education for Christian Marriage*, and he is the author of *The University and the Modern World* and various contributions to symposia and journals.

I

THE HISTORY of western civilization can be viewed as a great river formed by the confluence of its tributaries from Mesopotamia, Egypt, Palestine, Greece and Rome whereby they produced that mighty stream, *Pax Romana*. But this river of history, like the geographical rivers of the continents of the earth, has not always flowed placidly along. Rivers continually change their speed, their volume and even their course. Sometimes the changes are slow and imperceptible; sometimes they are almost cataclysmic. Then, all these factors just considered are changed simultaneously. Frequently the source of these overwhelming changes is a constituent part of the course of the river itself: such is the Niagara Falls for the Niagara. Often, as in the impact on the Mississippi of its tributary, the Missouri, the origin of these changes comes from a cause external to itself. So, too, the river of western civilization has in its course reached certain turning points after which every aspect of the life of man and his society have been revolutionized. In the history of western civilization during the Christian era there have been, until the last two decades of the twentieth century, two and only two such fundamental revolutions. The first of these occurred when the Roman Empire was destroyed in the early years of the fifth century. Ancient history then ended and medieval history began. The second was reached at the turn of the fifteenth century when medieval history came to a close and modern history was born.[1] Then feudal culture was no more. Manor and serf gave way to the entrepreneur and the wage laborer. Christendom as a theocratic political unity collapsed before the forces of nationalism to give the system of sovereign nation-states. Scholasticism as the

[1] As will be seen from what follows, I cannot agree with those who, like the Polish historian, Oscar Halecki, regard these distinctions as simply the product of the imagination of "a second-rate German scholar, Cellarius." See *The Limits and Divisions of European History*, p. 17 (New York, 1950).

pattern of correct thinking gave place to scientific method and historical study of origins as the correct methods for discovering truth.

All these victories were successes of a new social class who demanded, fought for and won a substantial control in the affairs of state. In achieving power they tore down all the fences based on the identification of privilege with the ownership of land as they successfully inserted contract in the place of status as the juridical foundation of society. When they had finished, no longer were the land-owner, the ecclesiastic, and the knight-errant symbols of social prestige. The banker and the merchant, later to be joined by the manufacturer, took their places. The members of this new class soon worked out its equivalent to the code of chivalry and system of canon law that had provided medieval society with its standards of value and its social mores. Whereas the feudal system of mutual dependence based upon personal loyalty harmonized with the medieval system of salvation by sacraments controlled by the ecclesiastical hierarchy, the merchants relied on written documents which, like the Bible, could be understood by all men. Like their medieval ancestors they, too, believed that "Where your treasure is, there shall your heart be also." But their treasure lay in a different place and so they evolved a code of conduct to govern economic affairs which sharply reversed long-established Christian teaching about the danger of money-making. Indeed, their entire ethical system was based upon the conviction that the life of business enterprise was not as spiritually hazardous as the medievalists had taught. Instead, they regarded it as the most appropriate field of operation for the saved soul, and the idea of credit in the bank available for the merchant of sound commercial standing replaced the medieval notion of stored merit in heaven under the control of the ecclesiastical hierarchy on earth. In short, the leaders of the commercial middle classes were Protestants.

However, just as ancient history and medieval history came to an end, so too "modern" history has reached its finale. All the differing realms of human thought and activity, politics, economics, and education are being basically transformed. The recent war simply hastened a process already begun and has thereby thrown into a clearer relief what was already to be seen by those who could recognize the signs of the times. In industry and commerce free enterprise is giving way to an ever-increasing measure of economic planning. We may no longer believe in the just price of the medieval canonists but notwithstanding that fact, we produce, in the idea of a "floor" for prices in time of depression and a "ceiling" for them in time of war, a secularized equivalent to it. In domestic politics virtually all of us, whether Republican or Democrat, now believe in the "welfare state." Only 14 votes could be mustered in the House of Representatives last October *against* the extension of social security, but 313 votes were counted *for* it. In the field of international politics, an awareness of the significance of the atomic bomb has persuaded the stubborn Anglo-Saxon mind, if not the Russian one, to recognize that the issue dominating all others is the need to limit the sovereignty of the nation-state by some appropriate international organization. The war in Korea has vividly underlined this truth to the point that both Democrat and Republican alike are willing to allow the American armed forces to serve in and under the direction of an international authority. That seems a small price to pay if we are to have freedom from the horrors of an atomic war.

The atomic bomb, indeed, furnishes a dramatic illustration of the contention that we have reached the end of our present era. The scientific movement since the days of Galileo has been based on a reversal of the medieval idea that in searching for knowledge the possibilities of evil were as real as those for good. The modern scientist believed until a few years ago that although his discoveries can be used for evil ends, yet ultimately they were a "good thing." Now, however, the scientist's faith in that dogma is severely shaken. Today he is much more acutely aware of the possibilities of immediate use of the atomic bomb for evil than he

is of its potentiality for ultimate good. The atomic bomb, moreover, has provided us with a perfect symbol of the intellectual
confusion of our times outside as well as inside the scientific
movement. Those scientists both in England and America who
have been shouting loudest for some years that we should change
our present methods of unplanned scientific research and substitute planned team investigation now argue for "free enterprise" both in the open publication of all results and in unfettered
investigation in the laboratory. At the same time the business men
who have been loudest in the praise of free enterprise in commerce
and trade do not wish to apply their doctrines to the atomic secret:
that should remain a closely-guarded federal monopoly.

Thus we see that all the characteristic features of a middle class
bourgeois culture—science, politics, economics—are rapidly being replaced by others more capable of meeting the demands of
the world now being so painfully borne. Have we any reason to
believe that Protestantism carries within itself anything of more
permanent worth than the culture, now disappearing, that has, historically speaking, been the vehicle through which the insights
of the Protestant faith have been made available for the Western
world? But before we do, let us examine what has been happening
to Protestantism as such. Even that simple fashion of phrasing
our task is an index to our confusion. We assume in our conversa-
tion and in the organization of our church life in the military
forces and out of them that the three religions of America are
Judaism, Roman Catholicism and Protestantism. Yet could there
be a more egregious error? I am not only thinking of the in-
accuracy of such categorizing if we include under Protestantism
the various branches of the Orthodox churches or even Episcopalianism. I am thinking of the ease with which we assume that
Martin Luther or John Calvin would recognize as Protestants those
who today willingly use the term as applicable to themselves.
The three typical figures of classical Protestantism, Luther, Calvin, and Cranmer, carried over into Protestantism a set of ideas
that today in North America we regard as medieval. They be-

lieved, for example, that membership of the Christian Church, even if baptism is required, is something, nevertheless, into which a child is born: if he was born in Saxony, then he was a Lutheran, if in the canton of Geneva, a Calvinist, and if in England, an Anglican. On the contrary, most Christians, who today in America would call themselves Protestants, believe that infant baptism is an appealing spectacle and that membership of the Christian Church is the result of a self-conscious act of decision whereby on approaching maturity the Christian elects to join a voluntary and exclusive fellowship. The Reformers believed that religion, in terms of a single type of worship within a particular territory as alone legal and maintained by the authority of the state, should dominate all other forms of cultural life, especially education. Protestantism in America would negate every proposition in such a proposal if it were to be made today on the grounds that it is contrary to the American way of life. The founders of the Reformation believed in the essential corruption of the human will; they believed that witches exist; and they believed that God somewhat arbitrarily interferes with the day-to-day functioning of the physical universe. We reject (whether rightly or wrongly is not the point) all such ideas as contrary to everything that "modern science" teaches.

The explanation of such profound differences between what the Reformers stood for and what the typical American Protestant stood for can easily be given. To use Ernst Troeltsch's classic distinction, the Reformers believed in the "Church" type of Christianity whereas—and to some extent this is true even of Roman Catholicism and Protestant Episcopalianism—we believe, consciously or unconsciously, in Christianity of the "sect" type.[2] It is true that those branches of the Christian Church in North America that stress the importance of episcopal orders have been

---

[2] This summary, of course, like all historical generalizations, needs severe qualification if we are to do full justice to the sociological complexities of American church life. For some penetrating observations in this direction see "The Ecumenical Issue in the United States" by Reinhold Niebuhr in *Theology Today*, Vol. II, pp. 525 ff.

better able to stand against the impact of a "sect" theology upon their thought and practice than have the other churches. But at many important points they, too, have succumbed. For example, an eminent Roman Catholic educationist recently sought to justify the study of religion at the college level on the quaint ground that religion, like mathematics, is a worthy cultural achievement. To Thomas Aquinas such a remark would have been quite unintelligible. It is a mark of the "sect" type of Christianity to protest against anything that looks hierarchical and so the Episcopal Church shies at the idea of calling its Presiding Bishop an archbishop even when, as now, he has been elected for the rest of his active life. Among Presbyterians the distinction between a presbyterial and a congregational conception of the minister is no longer effective. The modern Presbyterian has strayed so far from his Calvinistic heritage that he is immune against Oliver Cromwell's famous jibe:

"They claim a ministry deriving itself from the Papacy and pretending to that which is so much insisted upon—succession,"

or John Milton's tilt:

"New Presbyter is but old Priest writ large."

As for the Methodists: no branch of Christ's Church has been more insistent on the Protestant insight that the priesthood of all believers means the complete dismissal of the medieval idea that the "religious" life is somehow more pleasing to God than "secular" life. Yet in no church in the whole of Christendom is the minister more expected to be the moral model for the laity. Indeed, one might say that the requirement that a Methodist minister must not smoke while the layman may is a surprising yet exact parallel to the medieval notion that the priest should practise a more lofty ethical code than the laity. But it is not Archbishop Cranmer or John Knox or John Wesley who would exhibit the greatest surprise if he were to come back to earth and gaze with astonishment on his ecclesiastical descendants. That role surely must be reserved for Roger Williams, since no body of Protestants have gone quite so far as the Baptists have in departing from their traditional position. There are many Northern Baptist churches which have not seen a "total immersion" for years and in few is it considered an essential form of admittance to church membership. The Southern Baptist state conventions in many areas are rapidly building up a system of ecclesiastical control that represents a striking departure from the classical Baptist position. Conventions in Oklahoma and Arkansas have refused to seat "messengers" from congregations dubbed "liberal" and from others which permit nonmembers to participate in Holy Communion or which affiliate with the Federal or World Councils of Churches. As the *Christian Century* decisively pointed out, this policy "violates Baptist principles at three fundamental points. It sets up a creedal basis of fellowship. It runs counter to the Baptist emphasis on religious freedom. It brings into question the Baptist insistence upon the autonomy of the local congregation."

In short, Baptists, like the rest of their Protestant brethren, not only have strayed away from the characteristic doctrines of their forefathers; they have reversed them. The major reason is not far to seek. The Protestant fathers knew where they differed from the teaching of the Renaissance and its characteristic Hellenistic optimism; but we have lost our historical roots and, falling an easy prey to that optimism, we have ended up by making it the basis of our entire ideology. How much of contemporary so-called Protestant life and thought is explained once we recognize that behind them is the conviction that social harmony can be achieved if each person follows what he as an individual wants! [3] This fundamental belief expressed itself in science in the notion that freedom of research would lead to sufficient agreement to give sense to the idea that the word *knowledge* has no plural. It expressed itself in politics in the idea that freedom of discussion would insure sufficient accord for government to be stable and

[3] I would like to express here my indebtedness to Professor Paul Tillich for considerable illumination on this and on many other points. See his prophetic article, "The End of the Protestant Era," in *The Student World*, Vol. XXX, pp. 49 ff. (Geneva, Switzerland, 1937).

for law and order to be preserved. It expressed itself in international politics in the idea that somehow, out of the system of independent national states, universal peace would one day be achieved. It expressed itself in commerce in the idea that freedom of competition in trade for the individual would lead to the greatest economic good of the community. It expressed itself religiously in the notion that only by tolerating freedom of belief to the point of allowing atheism its right of expression can the world be converted to Christ. Today the optimism to which Protestant life and work is culturally and theologically so closely tied, has been so profoundly shaken in every aspect of human life that no Church which links itself to it can hope to survive, except as a vestigial remnant of a culture that has gone.

In short, the "Protestant" era really has ended, and we go forward into an age that many shrewd and informed observers call the post-Christian era. Others feel that that is going too far. In either case the question occurs. Has Protestantism any prophetic word to utter?

The medieval synthesis was born amidst great tribulation when the Christian Church as the residual legatee of the Roman Empire sought to impress law and order upon the wild barbarians from beyond the Rhine. Thanks to the incredible courage, audacity and skill of the missionary monks, the effort was successful and the barbarian hordes became the biological bearers of the spiritual inheritance of Athens, Rome, and Palestine. The result was the idea of Christendom embodied in a culture that for almost a thousand years shone forth brilliantly in art, in literature, in philosophy and all the arts of man. Its claim was to universality. Was there not a universal church, the Catholic Church? And a universal philosophy, Scholasticism? And a universal law, Roman Law? And a universal art in Gothic architecture? And a universal ethic, the code of Christ's commandments? And a universal code of manners, chivalry?

But this civilization was not as Christian in reality as it thought it was. It failed to realize, for example, how much its advocacy of the just price was in fact a subtle defense of the economic self-interest of a land-owning aristocracy of Church and manor. In short it was, to use Reinhold Niebuhr's adaptation, a Tower of Babel. As such it was built on sand and so, when the winds of a legitimate demand for justice and equality began to blow, it collapsed before the onslaught of a class whose religious badge was Protestantism. However, Protestantism, like Roman Catholicism, bears witness to a truth that transcends the historically conditioned movement that gave it birth. Hence for the coming new age the Protestant principle still has relevance; for Protestantism has a witness to make to the world even when the Protestant era has departed. The common conviction of the authors of this book—however divergent might be their individual expressions of it—is that the Protestant witness to this day and age can be expressed in three paradoxes:

(I) Within the context of the ecumenical movement, Protestantism must urge that the Word of God always transcends any form of either literary or ecclesiastical expression of its truth and that, just because that is so, there is always possible a living word to the Church and to individuals. Yet the Church cannot be the instrument of this Word unless she recognizes that in our present mass society that living word can be spoken only if it is in terms of symbols that relate man socially as well as individually to the Living God.

(II) To the world of scholarship and science Protestantism must urge that the source of our present intellectual confusion is not that scientists do not know enough nor is it that thinkers are not sufficiently acute. Instead, it lies in a spiritual self-sufficiency that was the inevitable outcome of an approach to knowledge that began with *cogito ergo sum*. Furthermore, the Protestant witness must gather up within itself all that modern science and humanism have stood for in their insistence that truth is always more than educational organizations or ecclesiastical assemblies can recognize.

(III) The Protestant witness in society must subject the political and economic foundations of contemporary culture to an independent criticism which recognizes that the remedy for the shortcomings of a Protestantism allied with the political right is not to identify it with the political left. Yet in seeking to criticize from a perspective that transcends both capital and labor or the Anglo-Saxon powers and the Soviet block, it must not hesitate to speak and act about concrete issues as they appear on the day-to-day scene.

The task envisaged by such a program is not an easy one. It is indeed one that Luther, Calvin and Cranmer, in terms of their day and generation, all tried to perform. They did not succeed, for it involves nothing less than obedience to Christ's implied commandment to be in the world but not of it. However, against gigantic forces they triumphed sufficiently in their day to furnish us in our day with our opportunity. Like them, judged by the test that they would approve, we too shall fail:

When ye shall have done all those things which are commanded you, say: We are unprofitable servants; we have done that which was our duty to do.

However, that kind of failure is the open door to salvation since we then seek justification not in what we have done but in what God through Christ can do for us and that is the essential timeless Protestant witness.

BIBLIOGRAPHY

Smith, Gerald Birney, ed. *Religious Thought in the Last Quarter Century* (Chicago, 1927)

Cavert, Samuel McCrea, and Van Dusen, Henry Pitney, ed. *The Church Through Half a Century* (New York, 1936)

Tillich, Paul, *The Protestant Era*. Eng. Transl. by James Luther Adams (Chicago, 1948)

Niebuhr, Reinhold, *Beyond Tragedy*, Chapters I, II, and XII. (New York, 1938)

Thomas, George F., ed. *The Vitality of the Christian Tradition* (New York, 1944)

Anderson, William K., ed. *Protestantism* (Nashville, 1944)

Fullerton, Kemper, "Calvinism and Capitalism," *Harvard Theological Review*, Vol. XXI, No. 3, July 1928

Laski, Harold J. *The Rise of Liberalism* (New York, 1936)

Tawney, R. H., *Religion and the Rise of Capitalism* (Penguin Edition, New York, 1947)

Carr, Edward Hallett, *Conditions of Peace*, Part I (New York, 1942)

Commager, Henry Steele, *The American Mind* (New Haven, 1950)

Sperry, Willard L., *Religion in America* (New York, 1946)

Sweet, W. W., *The Story of Religions in America* (New York, 1930)

THE STUDY OF THE
OLD TESTAMENT

George Ernest Wright

GEORGE ERNEST WRIGHT was born in 1909 and graduated from Wooster College, Ohio. He subsequently studied at McCormick Theological Seminary in Chicago, the American School of Oriental Research in Jerusalem, and Johns Hopkins University, where he took his Ph.D. in 1937. Before joining the faculty of McCormick Theological Seminary, where he is now Professor of Old Testament History and Theology, he served as field secretary of the American Schools of Oriental Research. He has been prominently associated with the Bible Study Commission of the World Council of Churches, attending meetings of the commission in Holland in 1948 and in England in 1949. He is the editor of *The Biblical Archeologist*, and he has written several books in that field and in Biblical theology. His *Challenge of Israel's Faith* was published in America in 1944 and in Great Britain in 1946, where it was a Religious Book Club selection. He is co-author with Floyd V. Filson of the well-known *Westminster Historical Atlas to the Bible*.

II

Modern Biblical scholarship was introduced into this country under the direct influence of German study during the first half of the last century. The two men who were most responsible for this introduction were Moses Stuart of Andover Theological Seminary and Edward Robinson of Union Theological Seminary in New York. Both consciously carried on their work within the framework of a conservative Christian theology and in the service of the Church. Both were primarily professional students of the Old Testament which they approached as Christians completely devoid of any tendency toward Marcionism, that is of conceiving of the God of Israel as somehow very different in character from the God of Jesus Christ. During the second half of the last century, however, a great change occurred, in which the scholarly study of the Old Testament was shaken loose, very largely, from its churchly mooring. Separated from the New Testament, it was carried on as a neutral science closely allied with the fields of oriental research and the history of religions.

The intellectual climate during the second half of the last century has been the subject of frequent treatment and does not call for analysis here. Archaeological work in Bible lands, the decipherment and intensive grammatical and philological study of Accadian and Egyptian, the discovery of the antiquity of man, the theory of evolution, Mesopotamian parallels to the Biblical creation and flood stories, intensive study of comparative religion, Hegelian idealism—these and many other factors, all tied together in the optimism of the Victorian era, contributed heavily to the radical new departure taken by the study of the Old Testament. The oriental language and literature departments, particularly at Harvard, Yale, the University of Pennsylvania and Johns Hopkins University were very active and influential. The last mentioned is particularly important since it was then solely a graduate university, founded on the German model and planned to provide graduate students with a scholarly training equal to that otherwise available only in Germany. In 1883 Paul Haupt, a brilliant young German scholar then only twenty-five years of age, was called to the Hopkins as director of the Oriental Seminary and there continued until his death in 1926. His vivid and forceful personality, his vast learning, his voluminous writings (a list of his publications numbers some 522 titles) had an impact upon American oriental studies, including the Old Testament, exceeded only by his pupil and successor, W. F. Albright.

The American Oriental Society was established in 1842; its *Journal* appeared irregularly until 1896, after which it was published in yearly volumes. Virtually all of the productive Old Testament scholars belonged to the Society, regularly contributing linguistic, philological and comparative religion notes and papers to the proceedings. In 1881 the Society of Biblical Literature and Exegesis was founded. Both Old and New Testament scholars participated, but the two fields of study had become so separated that with occasional exceptions the two groups carried on their work with little reference to one another. A comparison of the contents of both the *JAOS* and the *JBL* in the 1880's and 1890's with that of the 1930's and 1940's reveals little difference in the types of articles printed and in the areas of scholarly interest and concentration. The productive Old Testament scholar had become for the most part an orientalist and a technical philologian; his interest in Israelite faith was largely governed by the current methodologies of comparative religion and by the almost exclusive interest in historical growth and development.

Meanwhile the controversy over the Graf-Kuenen-Wellhausen reconstruction of the history of Israel began. The trial of William Robertson Smith in Scotland between 1877 and 1881 attracted great interest in this country. Various articles on the Wellhausen hypothesis were published; perhaps the most important of them initially were from the pen of Charles A. Briggs, a successor of Edward Robinson at Union Theological Seminary in New York.

He was promptly attacked from several quarters, but the acknowledged leader of the opposition soon became William Henry Green
of Princeton Theological Seminary. Green was a scholar whose
learning was respected; he was, for example, the first and only
chairman of the American committee for the Revised Version of
the Bible. Yet the new views were such a radical departure from
traditional conceptions that the emotions of the conservatives
were aroused as fully as were their intellects. The resulting Presbyterian trials of Briggs and Henry Preserved Smith of Lane
Theological Seminary (now affiliated with McCormick Seminary),
who had come to Briggs' defense, took place between 1892 and
1894 and are the most notorious events of American church history at the end of the last century. Union Seminary in New York
resisted the conservative attack and has remained one of the leading seminaries in the country. Lane Seminary capitulated; the
leader of the opposition to H. P. Smith was made President; and
the institution never recovered from the tragedy. As was the case
in Scotland, the trials did more than anything else could possibly
have done to further the new views in this country, and from that
time on most of the leading scholars of the Church gave willing
heed to the enthusiastic and energetic hunt carried on within the
pages of the Old Testament for J, E, D and P, and for the data
with which the literary, institutional and religious history of Israel
could be rewritten.

II

Such was the atmosphere in which the twentieth century began. The main lines along which the study of the Old Testament
was to proceed were already drawn. The conservative reaction
continued, perhaps culminating in a series of twelve volumes called
The Fundamentals: A Testimony to the Truth, published in
Chicago between 1910 and 1912. These books were composed of
essays by British and American conservatives. They were sent
to "English-speaking Protestant pastors, evangelists, missionaries,
theological professors, theological students, Y.M.C.A. secretaries,

Y.W.C.A. secretaries, Sunday School superintendents, religious lay workers, and editors of religious publications, throughout the earth." The title "fundamentalist," derived from this work, came to be used for the conservative movement. Yet it is to be doubted whether this gigantic project did anything to stem the "modernist" tide. Indeed, one of the chief characteristics of American fundamentalism of the twentieth century has been the steady decline of its scholarly work, and very little of real significance in the field of Old Testament study has been published. The fundamentalist atmosphere of largely negative reaction has evidently not been conducive to the production of brilliant, flexible, highly trained, sensitive and scholarly minds.

Meanwhile, a new enthusiasm and energy had invaded liberal Protestant circles throughout the world. While the Unitarian movement of more than a century before had done much to still an interest in scholarly Biblical study, the newer liberalism accelerated the pace of that study to a degree scarcely attained before or since. Large numbers of able young minds were attracted to the field, and many of the greatest works of Old Testament scholarship were produced. Indeed, the two decades between 1890 and 1910 may perhaps be said to be the golden age of Old Testament study. Certainly no comparable period exists for quantity and quality of work produced.

Let us note, for example, some of the books being reviewed in America during the years 1900 and 1901. The Brown, Driver, and Briggs, *Hebrew and English Lexicon* was appearing in parts; the first edition of the Gesenius-Kautzsch-Cowley, *Hebrew Grammar* was reviewed, together with Mandelkern's *Veteris Testamenti Concordantiae*. These works are still basic tools in continuous use by English-speaking scholars, no matter how antiquated the first two may be. Volumes II and III of James Hastings, *Dictionary of the Bible*, were subjected to detailed examination, as were also the first two volumes of the *Encyclopaedia Biblica* and the conservative *Dictionary of the Bible* by John D. Davis. Among the new commentaries being reviewed and discussed were various volumes in *The Cambridge Bible for Schools and Colleges*, which had been appearing since 1880; in the *International Critical Commentary*, including Henry Preserved Smith's *Samuel* and Crawford H. Toy's *Proverbs*, both works of American scholars; in the *Handkommentar zum Alten Testament*, including the first edition of Gunkel's *Genesis*, one of the greatest works of Old Testament scholarship, Rudolph Kittel's *Die Bücher der Könige* and Kraetzschmar's *Ezekiel*; and in the *Kurzer Handcommentar zum Alten Testament*, including Bertholet's *Deuteronomium*, Duhm's *Die Psalmen* and Marti's *Jesaia*. Among the multitude of other works there may be mentioned especially Carpenter and Harford, *The Hexateuch*, the finest and most detailed analysis in English of the Hexateuchal sources according to orthodox Wellhausenism; R. H. Charles, *A Critical Introduction of the Doctrine of the Future Life;* Karl Budde, *Religion of Israel to the Exile* and *Der Kanon des Alten Testaments;* R. W. Rogers, *A History of Babylonia and Assyria*, the first comprehensive history of those countries in English; and L. W. King, *Babylonian Religion and Mythology*.

The purpose of the above brief sampling is simply to indicate the tremendous importance of the period around 1900, which may perhaps be designated as the first great age of consolidation in which the gains resulting from the new Biblical study were elaborated in comprehensive form. Many of the basic tools, including commentaries, on which we are still dependent were then produced. The scholars of that period are, for the most part, the spiritual fathers of the twentieth century. Through the spectacles which they wore our own eyes have been taught to focus on the light; and, especially since the first World War, their general point of view toward the meaning of the Old Testament has increasingly filtered down through the clergy into the churches. They attacked their work with all the enthusiasm of fresh explorers and their zeal to spread the new truth abroad was akin to that of a young missionary just beginning his work for Christ among the heathen.

The most vivid illustration of the last observation was the phenomenal career of William Rainey Harper. He graduated from Muskingum College at the age of fourteen years; his salutatory oration was given in Hebrew. After receiving his Ph.D. degree from Yale four years later, he spent the next dozen years (1879–1892), most of them at Yale, promoting a wide variety of projects. He was an exceptional teacher, and by means of his inductive method for learning Hebrew he interested people all over the country in the study of the language. As President of the University of Chicago (1892–1906), his Old Testament department became in time one of the leading oriental departments of the country, the greatest of his appointees being the young Egyptologist, James Henry Breasted. In 1882 he began publishing a magazine, *The Hebrew Student*, broadened the following year into *The Old Testament Student*. In 1884 he founded another journal, named *Hebraica*, for more technical aspects of Hebrew linguistics and philology. The fate of these two journals is perhaps illustrative of the fate of Old Testament study during the early twentieth century. In 1889 *The Old Testament Student* properly became *The Old and New Testament Student*; in 1893 it was further broadened into *The Biblical World*. In 1921 this was merged with *The American Journal of Theology* and the result was *The Journal of Religion*. In other words, a journal dealing with the wider aspects of Biblical study was unable to maintain itself. In *The Biblical World* it gradually became so watered that there was nothing to do but to merge it into a general journal of religion. On the other hand, the more technical *Hebraica* was likewise unable to sustain itself on its own merits. In 1895 it became *The American Journal of Semitic Languages and Literatures*, which in 1942 was further broadened to *The Journal of Near Eastern Studies*.

To this writer these journals represent something of the tragedy of Protestant Old Testament study during the past century. As a neutral science, largely separated from any responsible feeling for the on-going life of the churches, its productive work has been attuned and directed toward the general religion field, on the one hand, and toward general oriental research, on the other. Of course, there can be no serious study of the Old Testament without scholarly attention to both these fields. But when the scholars of the Church lose themselves along by-paths, both their subject and the Church is bound to suffer. Most of the professional students of the Old Testament are employees of the churches, either directly or indirectly. Yet the paths which they followed too exclusively so separated them from the work of the churches that in many seminaries during the period between 1920 and 1940 the work of the Old Testament department was looked upon by the students more with amusement than with respect; and the occasional young scholar who majored in the subject was frequently one capable of dealing only with technical details, in all events the butt of considerable derision from his fellows in the practical departments or especially in the departments of philosophy and psychology of religion. Consequently, the first great generation of Biblical scholarship before the first War was actually unable to reproduce itself, and the decline in quality and quantity of worthwhile output since then has been steady and lamentable.

The above remarks, however, should in no way be taken in such a way as to devalue the importance of some of the work done. While America thus far has never produced a large series of Old Testament commentaries of a scholarly nature,[1] we did contribute a majority of the Old Testament volumes in the still incomplete *International Critical Commentary*. Most of the important books were assigned to British scholars, and a number of them have never been finished. Yet the American contributions are by no means inferior products; George Foot Moore's *Judges*

[1] The forthcoming *Interpreter's Bible*, to be published by the Abingdon-Cokesbury Press under the general editorship of George A. Buttrick, will be our first major effort along this line.

(1895) and James A. Montgomery's *Daniel* (1927) rank among the most important in existence on these books.[2] Moore must probably be ranked along with Edward Robinson among the giants of American biblical scholarship. As Professor of Old Testament at Andover from 1883 to 1901 and as Professor of the History of Religions at Harvard from 1902 until his retirement in 1928, he was one of our greatest scholars. His *Judaism in the First Centuries of the Christian Era* (3 vols., 1927–30) is the standard work on the subject, as was also for many years in this country his *History of Religions* (2 vols., 1913–19). He contributed nearly forty articles to the *Encyclopaedia Biblica* (1899–1903), those on "Historical Literature" and "Sacrifice" being considerable treatises. The last mentioned is still one of the best surveys of Israel's sacrificial cultus. His point of view was typical of his time in the circles of left-wing Wellhausenism. Montgomery's best work had a more narrow range, but the intensity of his effort on Daniel, for example, together with his balanced sanity of judgment and appreciation of theological issues, probably isolate this work as among the greatest, if not the greatest, of the critical commentaries produced by Americans. In textual criticism especially he was without peer among Protestants, equaled only by the great Jewish scholar Max L. Margolis.

In the field of Old Testament history America has been singularly weak. No book of outstanding importance, comparable shall we say to Rudolph Kittel's *Geschichte des Volkes Israel*, has ever been published. Some student works have been written: for example, C. F. Kent, *History of the Hebrew People* (2 vols.) and *History of the Jewish People* (2 vols., the second by J. S. Riggs; 1896–1900); H. P. Smith, *Old Testament History* (1903); I. J. Peritz, *Old Testament History* (1915); and E. W. K. Mould, *Essentials of Bible History* (1939). None of these books was ever really adequate, but little else was available except as imported from abroad. Today we are able to use the British work by Oe-

---

[2] The same will be true of Montgomery's forthcoming treatment of *The Book of Kings* in the same series.

sterley and Robinson, *A History of Israel* (2 vols., 1932) and a translation of the French work of A. Lods, *Israel* (1932) and *The Prophets and the Rise of Judaism* (1937). Yet these volumes are unsatisfactory, having been antiquated even before publication.

America has done much better in the field of Old Testament introduction. Among others may be mentioned H. T. Fowler, *A History of the Literature of Ancient Israel* (1912); F. C. Eiselen, *Biblical Introduction Series* (4 vols., 1916–23); C. F. Kent, *The Growth and Contents of the Old Testament* (1925); and J. A. Bewer, *The Literature of the Old Testament* (1922). The last mentioned has been the most popular and widely used. The dominant interest in these works is in literary analysis and dating. They are thus introductions to the Old Testament only in the narrow literary sense; but since the end of the last century, such has been the common conception of what such a work should be. There is little that is fresh or original in these American efforts; by and large they are so orthodox in their following of the Wellhausen position, together with numerous popular modifications of it (e.g., the acceptance of Duhm's "Trito-Isaiah"), that the American student was given the impression that for the most part all major literary problems had been finally solved and was left unaware of the fresh currents of thought on the Continent of Europe. Of especial importance for the American college and theological student during the first part of this century was the work of Charles Foster Kent. This scholar at Yale Divinity School did more perhaps than anyone else in making the results of critical research available in what seemed to be stable, non-technical and fairly final form. His major effort was *The Student's Old Testament*, the first five volumes of which were published between 1904 and 1914; the sixth and last was completed after his death by his student, Millar Burrows, and published in 1927. The standard literary introduction in English used by most scholars until 1941, however, continued to be that of the great British scholar, Samuel R. Driver. His *Introduction to the Literature of the Old Testament* was last revised by the author in 1913, but the demand for it has justly been so great that it has been kept in print.

In 1941 the first truly monumental introduction, from the scholarly point of view, to be produced in America was published by Robert H. Pfeiffer. His *Introduction to the Old Testament* is a work of over 900 pages, and is especially important for its bibliographical survey of the work of other scholars throughout the world. The author's own point of view is by and large fairly traditional Wellhausenism, though with many individual variations (e.g., his separation of an Edomite source, S, from the Yahwist material in the Hexateuch). In importance this book can only be ranked with Otto Eissfeldt's *Einleitung in das Alte Testament* (1934), a literary introduction of comparable range and scope. Yet in the post-war period there is an increasing suspicion, long felt in Europe, that this type of purely literary introduction cannot solve the problems of the historical literature of the Old Testament. The almost exclusive concentration of attention on purely literary dissection leads to an extremely atomized and fragmentary understanding of the literature and to a neglect of other matters. It finds difficulty in comprehending the whole or of understanding either the whole or the part over against the total environment in which the writing was produced. Furthermore, its understanding of religious and theological issues, its ability to deal with matters pertaining to faith, is severely limited and lacking in trained penetration, to say the least.

A different type of approach to these problems may be expected in the future under the inspiration of German form criticism. One of the major difficulties with orthodox Wellhausenism was its assumption that the isolation and dating of the Hexateuchal sources furnished the clue to the reconstruction of the history of Israel. This has been a major reason for the almost exclusive attention to literary analysis in the Old Testament introductions. It was assumed, for example, that the later material in the Deuteronomic and Priestly writings furnishes virtually no dependable information on the institutions of early Israel. The material in a given document must be used for the reconstruction of the period in which the document was composed. This naturally meant the almost complete devaluation of the Mosaic era, with the major emphasis being given the prophetic and priestly periods of dominance after the eighth century B.C. The prophets thus came to be thought of, not primarily as great religious reformers, but as the authors of all that was truly distinctive in Israel, particularly of what was called "ethical monotheism." This position of orthodox liberalism was never completely accepted by all scholars, Rudolph Kittel in Germany and Samuel R. Driver in England being the leading exceptions.

It was the German, Hermann Gunkel, in the introduction to his *Genesis* (1st ed., 1901) who initiated a new method of approach to the historical problems of Israel by means of form criticism and the history of tradition. This new methodology was promptly applied to the Gospels with significant results, but it has been very slow in influencing Old Testament study, so strongly intrenched was the other position. During the past three decades, however, some significant work has been done along this line by German and Scandinavian scholars. In this type of research the Hexateuchal documents are generally accepted without question, though naturally with many individual modifications and variations. But these documents are assumed to be solely the final and crystallized form of traditions which have had a long and complicated history before their final written crystallization. In these last stages we have to do with the work of individual compilers whose greatness lay not so much in their invention of material, not in their ascription of current practices back into Mosaic or other antiquity, but rather in the way they gathered, organized and unified old traditions by various means, chiefly by an overall theme which was the product of intensive theological reflexion. At the heart of the Yahwist's work, for example, is the unifying thread of a confessional recital of God's saving acts (a *Heilsgeschichte*), derived ultimately from old forms of confession used at the Tabernacle (so Gerhard von Rad). Such a point of view involves a closer attention to the nature and peculiarity of

written material as a whole, and particularly to the long history
of the tradition which lies behind the final literary form. It thus
means that the age of a document does not determine the date of
the material employed by it. Each item of tradition has its own
history which must be examined on its own merits. Consequently,
the history of Israel cannot be reconstructed simply by dating
final literary compositions; and the ground is cut from under the
older Wellhausenian assumptions. Thus while there is no reason
for assuming that the documentary hypothesis is set aside (quite
the contrary!), the work of Pfeiffer, important as it is, probably
represents the end of an era in that type of purely literary introduction.[3]

III

We do not have space here to describe the various debates
which have been carried on, some of them by no means ended,
on specific Old Testament problems. The reader is referred to
other surveys for detailed analysis of them.[4] By and large discussion in America has followed issues first raised in Europe.
For example, one of the great concerns today has to do with the
authenticity of the Book of Ezekiel. Before 1920 all was well and
few questions were asked. Since that time, Ezekiel has been
viewed by some as the product of Judaism, rather than the
father of it; and in America all shades of opinion are to be found,
even as in Europe.[5] The same is true with regard to the analysis

[3] Contrast, for example, Artur Weiser, *Einleitung in das Alte Testament*
(2nd ed., 1949), and Aage Bentzen, *Introduction to the Old Testament* (2
vols., 1948), the first a German and the second a Danish work. Cf also for
methodology Gerhard von Rad, *Das erste Buch Mose, Genesis Kapitel 1-12,
9* (1949) and *Deuteronomium-Studien* (1947); Martin Noth, *Überlieferungs-
geschichtliche Studien* I (1943) and *Überlieferungsgeschichte des Pentateuch*
(1948).

[4] See especially Raymond A. Bowman, "Old Testament Research between
the Great Wars," in Harold R. Willoughby, ed., *The Study of the Bible
Today and Tomorrow* (1947), pp. 3-31; and George A. Barton, "The
Present State of Old Testament Studies," in Elihu Grant, ed., *The Haverford
Symposium on Archaeology and the Bible* (1938), pp. 47-78.

[5] One of the most extreme of the American works (besides the book of
Torrey to be mentioned below) is that of W. A. Irwin, *The Problem of
Ezekiel* (1943); more moderate is I. G. Matthews, *Ezekiel* (1939). A scholarly

and date of the Book of Deuteronomy, with the attempt of the German scholars, Volz and Rudolph, to do away with the Elohist document in the Hexateuch,[6] with the Gunkel-Mowinckel view of the cultic origin of the Psalms, including the reconstruction of an elaborate New Year's festival in Israel,[7] with the historical problem of whether Nehemiah preceded Ezra, with the various problems connected with the date of the Exodus and the nature of the Hebrew settlement,[8] etc. One of the greatest of American scholars and at the same time the most controversial has been C. C. Torrey of Yale University. Much of his work has been concentrated on the Exilic and Post-Exilic periods as the titles of three of his works show: *Ezra Studies* (1910), *The Second Isaiah* (1928), and *Pseudo-Ezekiel and the Original Prophecy* (1930). Each work has produced as much study and heated debate as did his subsequent attempt to show that the Gospels were originally written in Aramaic. In each case a majority of scholars, while learning much from him, have rejected most of his central contentions. His book on Second Isaiah is the best American study of the subject, an excellent antidote to the scholarly disintegration of Isa. 40–66; but his attempt to prove that the work

---

defense of the older conservative position from the Albright school, and one that will be difficult to answer except by the critique of marginal matters, is the monograph by Carl Howie, *The Date and Composition of Ezekiel* (1950).

[6] For an independent analysis which arrives at a similar position, see Frederick V. Winnett, *The Mosaic Tradition* (1949).

[7] For an American defense of this viewpoint, see now especially Elmer A. Leslie, *The Psalms* (1949), probably the best American commentary produced on this book, though to the minds of the newer school of Hebrew linguistics and philology it leaves much to be desired. An older and independent study of the liturgical origin of the Psalms was written by the American J. P. Peters, *The Psalms as Liturgies* (1922).

[8] An important study in this area was that of the excellent scholar, L. B. Paton, "Israel's Conquest of Canaan," *Journal of Biblical Literature*, Vol. XXXII (1913), pp. 1–53. Another important American treatment of this and other problems of Hebrew origins is that of T. J. Meek, *Hebrew Origins* (1950). The views of W. F. Albright on the Exodus and the Conquest now dominate the scene. For a brief review with references, see G. Ernest Wright, "The Present State of Biblical Archaeology," in Harold R. Willoughby, ed., *The Study of the Bible Today and Tomorrow* (1947), pp. 83 ff.

was not composed much before 400 B.C. has not been generally accepted. Equally instructive and much more voluminous are the publications of the Jewish scholar, Julian Morgenstern. Here again scholars have read to learn without often accepting all of the central hypotheses.[9]

IV

While form criticism has dealt a body-blow to the older approach to the Old Testament, it has thus far received little attention either in England or America and it has done little to influence the course of scholarly study in these countries. It is in the field of Biblical archaeology, on the other hand, that perhaps America's greatest contribution can be said to have been made. The pioneer work in this field was done by Edward Robinson in his *Biblical Researches* (3 vols. 1841). During the second part of the last century, however, little of any significance emanated from America in this area. Then came our first major excavation of a Palestinian site, one of tremendous significance especially for the scientific methodology of digging. That was the Harvard Expedition to the site of Samaria, directed by G. A. Reisner and C. S. Fisher between 1908 and 1910, the results not being published until 1924. It was after the first World War that rapid progress began to be made. On the one hand, James H. Breasted succeeded in interesting the Rockefeller Foundation in archaeology, with the result that the Oriental Institute of the University of Chicago was established, and expeditions were dispatched to every country of the ancient Near East. The work of Breasted for the cause of oriental studies and for the contemporary importance of what he called the "new past" can scarcely be overestimated.[10] Perhaps because of the humanistic direction of Breasted's viewpoint, however, the Oriental Institute has done

[9] See especially his treatment of the Book of the Covenant, his *Amos Studies*, his work on the calendar, etc., as published in successive issues of the *Hebrew Union College Annual*, beginning with the first volume in 1924.

[10] See especially the evaluation of W. F. Albright, "James Henry Breasted, Humanist," *The American Scholar*, 1936, pp. 287–299.

very little for Biblical archaeology, except in many indirect ways.

On the other hand, the most important work for the Bible has been done by those scholars connected with the American Schools of Oriental Research, an institution carried on as a co-operative effort by a large number of American colleges, universities and theological seminaries. It sent its first Director to Jerusalem, C. C. Torrey, in 1900. Thereafter it sent directors and fellows each year until the first World War suspended activities. The influence of Palestinian study was soon felt in such excellent publications as L. B. Paton's *The Early History of Syria and Palestine* (1901),[11] his *Jerusalem in Bible Times* (and his article "Jerusalem" in the 2nd ed. of *The New Standard Bible Dictionary*, 1926), and C. F. Kent's *Biblical Geography and History* (1911). Paton's *Jerusalem* and Kent's *Geography* never attained the popularity of the larger and more vivid British works on the same subjects by George Adam Smith, but in some respects they were better and more usable. The first edition of George A. Barton's *Archaeology and the Bible* was published in 1916; and the seventh edition (1937), though badly out of date, is still much used since it contains such a convenient collection of material.

It was under the directorship of W. F. Albright, beginning in 1920, however, that the Schools rapidly attained a position of scholarly leadership in the field of Biblical archaeology. Albright came to this work after a careful grounding under Paul Haupt in the whole field of ancient Near Eastern study. Today he has become the leading orientalist of the world, a pioneer in almost every area of study which he has touched. Yet his center of interest has always been the Bible, particularly the Old Testament. Consequently, in the vast range of his archaeological, linguistic, philological and historical work (by 1946 a list of his publications numbered some 613 different entries), he has never lost his way nor failed to see the bearing of the whole upon Bible study. As head of the American School in Jerusalem for

[11] Superceded by the monumental work of A. T. Olmstead, *The History of Palestine and Syria* (1931).

twelve years, he became the acknowledged leader in the field of Palestinian archaeology, and many Biblical students came under his influence, not only through his writings but through his lectures and field work in Palestine. One of his most prominent archaeological pupils, Nelson Glueck, became his successor in Jerusalem. Glueck's archaeological survey of Transjordan is of such importance that he must be ranked among the world's leading archaeological explorers. America's first major Biblical atlas was produced under Albright's direct influence, both the historical text and the topography reflecting his points of view: G. Ernest Wright and Floyd V. Filson, *The Westminster Historical Atlas to the Bible* (1945). And certainly the independent work of Millar Burrows, *What Mean these Stones?* (1941), one of the best surveys of archaeological material bearing upon the Bible, could not have been produced in its present form without Albright's pioneering publications. He has raised the scientific tone of this country's work in Palestine to a higher octave than that prevailing in any other country.

For our purposes here, however, it is Albright's influence on Old Testament study which is of major concern. This is difficult to assess at the moment, since his work is so many-sided. In the importance of Canaanite and Northwest Semitic language and literature for Hebrew linguistics and philology he is an acknowledged leader, and several of the best younger men working in this area are either directly or indirectly his students (e.g., H. L. Ginsberg, Cyrus Gordon and Harry M. Orlinsky among our finest Jewish scholars). More than anyone else, however, he has been attempting to show what a vast difference the archaeological revolution must make in our points of view toward the Old Testament and in our method of approaching it. A vast accumulation of facts from every quarter of the ancient Near East are brought to bear on the understanding of Israel's literature, and to Albright they mean the devastation of the Wellhausenian positions, including a more positive and conservative respect for Israel's historical literature. To the fundamentalists his work has been a source of great encouragement, and a major reason for the return of an increasing number of their younger scholars to serious and technical graduate training in the Old Testament. Liberals have blamed Albright for being misleading and overly reactionary (he has even been labelled "a galloping fundamentalist" himself), but a sympathetic reading of his works would lead one only to a more conservative position and by no means to a fundamentalist one. He believes, for example, that the Pentateuch might be called "substantially Mosaic," but the interpretation he places upon the word "substantially" is certainly not that of a fundamentalist. He believes in the documentary hypothesis, but simply affirms that we must take more seriously the basic reliability of oral tradition. The Old Testament probably contains a maximum of the discrepancies in that tradition; we do not have to do with editors whose major work was the invention of material or the radical revision of it to suit their own interests.

Albright further believes that for an understanding of the Old Testament there must be a more serious attempt to come to grips with the vast array of facts now available from the ancient Near East. Literary criticism cannot solve the historical problems of Israel on the narrow inner-Biblical platform on which it has been standing. The Wellhausen reconstruction was based on Hegelian presuppositions which the facts emphatically do not support today; it was formulated before the archaeological recovery of the ancient world had more than started. Furthermore, the archaeological discoveries mean that the older negativism and skepticism, on which the previous work was largely built, must be discarded.[12] These discoveries do not permit a credulous and uncritical viewpoint; archaeology certainly does not support any theory of verbal inspiration. That it is said to do so is a fundamentalist fiction. Yet a more positive and conservative shift in attitude is certainly called for.

Albright's most elaborate attempts to present these views with

[12] For some pungent remarks on the role this liberal skepticism has played in Biblical scholarship and on its ultimate basis in historical relativism, see Paul Schubert, "Urgent Tasks for New Testament Research," in Harold R. Willoughby, ed., *The Study of the Bible Today and Tomorrow* (1947), pp. 212 ff.

a wealth of supporting detail such as almost no other scholar could handle critically are to be found in his two volumes, *From the Stone Age to Christianity* (1940) and *Archaeology and the Religion of Israel* (1942). One of the central contentions in these books is that of Mosaic monotheism, from the traditional Wellhausenian point of view one of the most radical of heresies. So deeply entrenched is the older position that Albright's views are scarcely understood, let alone accepted, save by an increasing number of younger scholars who thus far have not been vocal since they are at the beginning of their scholarly careers. The present writer's *The Old Testament Against its Environment* (1950) adopts Albright's viewpoint on monotheism as the only one consonant with the known facts and attempts to portray in more detail precisely what is involved in the hope of securing wider acceptance of the position. Old Testament monotheism certainly cannot be interpreted as a philosophical monism or in terms suitable to a unitarian position. Yet the farther one is able to push back into the Mosaic era, the simpler the view of the divine world, whereas the later one goes in the literature, the more complex that world becomes.

Since we are at the threshold of a new era of Biblical study, the true impact of Albright's work can only be gauged after another generation. At the moment his school of thought is looked upon in many quarters with some skepticism, even with impatience. A criticism leveled at the historical part of the *Westminster Historical Atlas*, for example, is that sufficient basic work has not been done on literary analysis. This criticism is, of course, based on the assumption that literary work almost by itself can solve historical problems, and it is difficult for those wedded to this assumption to understand that the same literary endeavor does not necessarily lead to the same historical conclusions.[13]

[13] E.g., cf. W. F. Albright, "The List of Levitic Cities," *Louis Ginzberg Jubilee Volume* (1945), pp. 49–73; "The Oracles of Balaam," *Journal of Biblical Literature*, Vol. LXIII (1944), pp. 207–233; Frank M. Cross, Jr. and David Noel Freedman, "The Blessing of Moses," *ibid.*, Vol. LXVII (1948), pp. 191–210; G. Ernest Wright, "The Literary and Historical Problem of

V

It is in the realm of Biblical theology, however, that the most widespread dissatisfaction with the state of affairs at the turn of the century is now felt. It is obvious to most of the younger scholars of the Church today that something was radically wrong with a generation whose scholarship could scarcely envisage a theological treatment of Israel's faith except in terms of a history of Israel's religion, based upon the Wellhausenian reconstruction of the history. Considering the presuppositions, the generation of 1900 produced some good works in this area. First and foremost stand J. P. Peters, *Religion of the Hebrews* (1914) and H. P. Smith, *Religion of Israel* (1914); among others there may be mentioned also H. T. Fowler, *Origin and Growth of Hebrew Religion* (1917) and G. A. Barton, *Religion of Israel* (1919). The point of view to which they adhere was given the most lucid and influential treatment in H. E. Fosdick's *Guide to the Understanding of the Bible* (1938), a beautifully written book which did much to fix the older developmental views in the minds of a countless number of non-specialists, in particular those of college students. That this approach to Israel's faith survives in many circles is further illustrated by the important, though extreme, work of I. G. Matthews, *The Religious Pilgrimage of Israel* (1947). Yet if one denies in large measure the historical presuppositions lying behind these works and as well their philosophical basis, he finds it very difficult to use them. It is on these grounds that the Swiss scholar, W. Eichrodt, has called Fosdick's work an obituary of last century's scholarship.

Basic to all of the above-mentioned books is the developmental viewpoint first evolved in Germany during the decades preceding 1900. The most important thing to be said about the Old Testa-

---

Joshua 10 and Judges 1," *Journal of Near Eastern Studies*, Vol. V (1946), pp. 105–114; John Bright, "The Age of King David," *Union Seminary Review* (Richmond), Vol. LIII (1942), pp. 87–109; and Carl Howie, *The Date and Composition of Ezekiel* (1950).

ment in this view is that its religion was evolved through the
process of the people's discovery over the centuries from primitive
animism and polydemonism, through polytheism and henotheism
to the heights of "ethical monotheism." It is difficult if not completely impossible, therefore, to speak of a theology of the Old
Testament, because, if the above-assumed growth took place,
there were many theologies in the pages of the Old Testament.
The only unity existing is the unity of historical process. Environment and growth are used as the almost exclusive clues to
historical understanding. If something is "primitive," it must be
early; and if something is early, it must be "primitive." Even in
"objective" scholarly work one must constantly employ his
empirically discovered data within a given evaluational framework. This framework is not derived from the Bible, but from
liberal idealism, which in turn attempts to define it vaguely as
"the mind of Christ," though in truth it is mostly a compound
of conceptions derived from secular idealism. The conception
of growth, borrowed from the biological sciences and employed
in this framework of an ascending scale of values, has been a
useful tool when applied to historical data. The impact which it
has had on Biblical studies is so great that never again can we
revert to the earlier static views. Yet as a tool to historical understanding it has been used so exclusively that the manifest unities
in the Bible have been overlooked. Its one-sided use and the
necessity it has imposed upon the scholar continually to evaluate
the "primitive" and the "advanced" according to a set of values
derived largely from Western secular idealism have done more
than anything else to separate the Old Testament from any constructive role in the life of the Church. The study of the faith of
Israel has been carried on almost solely in the search for values.
Israel has been thought to provide the evolutionary background
for the religion of and about Jesus. Its importance is conceived
largely in antiquarian terms, of interest for the understanding
of the way we have come to the pinnacle on which we stand, but
now that we have arrived it is no longer of vital use to us.

It is to this impasse that the confident, optimistic and exceedingly energetic work of our spiritual fathers of the 1900 era has brought us. Yet the course of the times has dealt such severe blows to the idealistic and evaluational framework in which the former views were fixed that the theologians have been taking another look at the Old Testament. The uplifted eyebrows which they have directed toward the Old Testament scholars have so embarrassed them that they too are engaged in a second look and a flurry of uncertain activity. Their scholarly work has been so largely separated from the Church's life that the clergy throughout the present century has looked to the theologians and not to them for enlightenment. Consequently, at the moment they are experiencing severe difficulty in readjusting their perspectives. When they have something of real theological significance to say, they are listened to with a respect which has not been accorded them for fifty years. They thus have before them an unparalleled opportunity, but at the moment there is among them much uncertainty and confusion.

Neither in England nor in America has there ever been produced a careful, scholarly and comprehensive work on Old Testament theology, except for the posthumously edited volume of the Scottish scholar A. B. Davidson, *The Theology of the Old Testament* (1904). This book is still in continuous use, though quite inadequate from many points of view. In America there have been several less comprehensive attempts, among which we should mention the work of A. C. Knudson, *The Religious Teaching of the Old Testament* (1918), a moderate, positive and useful work, though for some reason never widely used; Millar Burrows, *Outline of Biblical Theology* (1946), in which a welcome feature is the attempt to treat the Old and New Testaments together; and Otto J. Baab, *The Theology of the Old Testament* (1949), an earnest and sincere book which attempts to organize the data under the traditional headings of God, man, sin, salvation, etc., an outline which leaves large blocks of material untreated and which raises the question as to whether Biblical theology can actually be comprehended and surveyed through these static categories of dogmatic theology. Badly needed and impatiently awaited in English today is a work of the caliber and comprehensive nature of W. Eichrodt's *Theologie des Alten Testaments* (Vols. I–III, 1933–39), by all odds the greatest work available on the subject and one which is written with exceptional theological penetration.

Our difficulty, however, is that we scarcely know how to proceed. For one thing, we are uncertain as to what the subject is and whether it really exists, as may be seen, for example, in the discussions conducted in the *Journal of Bible and Religion*, particularly the symposia in Vols. XIV, No. 1 (Feb. 1946), XIV, No. 2 (May 1946), and XV, No. 3 (July 1947). A central problem is the relation between the historical and systematic approaches and the balancing of unity and variety. In fact, the whole problem of the unity of the Old Testament is perhaps the central concern of the scholars at the moment in their effort to come to terms with Israel's faith. Furthermore, the World Council of Churches has been focusing the attention of the few Biblical scholars connected with its work on the problem of the relation between the two Testaments, on the interpretative problem of discovering the social and political message of the whole Bible, and on the searching question as to just what Christ means as the goal of the Old Testament for the interpretative work of the Christian scholar. Is it possible for the Church's scholars to be entirely neutral on this last question, or is their assumed "neutrality" a screen for presuppositions of which they have been unaware? [14]

In spite of the difficulties the renewed interest in theology is certainly the dominant characteristic of the Biblical scene at the present time. Liberal scholars of the older tradition are inclined to look upon this new interest with considerable concern. Their

---

[14] Cf. *From the Bible to the Modern World* (Geneva, World Council of Churches, 1947), and the articles by the present writer in *Interpretation*, Vol. III (1949), pp. 50–61 and 450–456.

reaction is largely negative and born of fear. They are afraid that the new movement may crystallize into a new conservativism which neglects the fruits of the Biblical scholarship of the past in tendentious reaction. This is indeed a real danger because it is so easy to theologize without taking sufficient care to ascertain the data on which one's work must be built. On the other hand, there is an even greater danger in doing nothing. To this writer one of the most serious deficiencies of the new movement is the lack of serious attention to archaeology and to the results of the archaeological revolution. One cannot be a scholar in the Old Testament by training oneself solely in literary criticism on the one hand, and in the work of Barth, Brunner and Niebuhr on the other. One must also become a student of ancient polytheism and of ancient history, and the more he knows about ancient linguistics, particularly of Northwest Semitic, the better he will be equipped to handle the Biblical data in their proper setting.

VI

When we survey the whole course of American Old Testament study, we have no reason to be ashamed of what has been done in many areas. Many excellent scholars have produced important and enduring contributions. Yet some of the criticisms leveled at us by J. A. Montgomery in his Presidential Address to the Society of Biblical Literature in 1918 [15] are still valid. While Germany has been our mistress in scholarship, we have lagged at least a generation behind her. Except for the work of Albright and those influenced by him, "it can hardly be said that we have contributed much to the reconstruction of the Biblical history and life. On the historical side our scholarship has been meager. We have carried on, often parrotwise, our analyses, but when we come to the reconstruction of the original picture, where the criticism should go into the footnotes, we have fallen short." Our serious work in textual criticism has not been large. We have produced no basic and up-to-date Hebrew grammar, though to be

[15] *Journal of Biblical Literature*, Vol. XXXVIII (1919), pp. 1–14.

sure we have done several small ones for introductory students,
perhaps the best of which from a scholarly point of view being
O. R. Sellers, *Biblical Hebrew for Beginners* (1941). We have
done nothing in serious Hebrew lexicography since the publication of the Brown, Driver and Briggs, *Hebrew and English Lexicon* which began to appear in 1891 and was completed in 1906.
Yet the advances in our knowledge have been so tremendous
that this work is woefully out of date. Furthermore, it was never
really adequate. Driver's long articles on the prepositions are
excellent, but if one desires to be taught about those things for
which the Old Testament exists, he is left to his own devices. The
preposition "on, upon" is described in fourteen columns of text,
while "righteousness" is given less than four, "justice, judgment"
receives two, and "love" one and one-half. It is small wonder that
the study of Hebrew by theological students is thought to be a
waste of time by the vast majority of the American clergy. Unless
Old Testament scholars can do better than they have done in
the past in providing basic tools geared both to the subject matter
and to the needs of the Church, they can expect nothing but an
even greater diminution of interest in serious Biblical study.

Our work in commentaries and Bible dictionaries has also
not been strong. We have produced the one-volume *Abingdon
Bible Commentary* (edited by F. C. Eiselen and others, 1929)
and the Lutheran *Old Testament Commentary* (edited by H. C.
Alleman and E. E. Flack, 1948), and as well the several volumes
of the *International Critical Commentary* mentioned above. Yet
the person who would like a complete set of small commentaries
in English on Old Testament books, a work which treats seriously
and in a theologically profound manner the faith of which the
literature is a witness, such a person is left without help, except
as he is enabled to obtain it from secondhand copies of the British
Cambridge Bible for Schools and Colleges (1880 ff.) and *The
New Century Bible* (1904 ff.), all of which are old, badly out-
moded, and scarcely adequate in any case. The best thing for
him is the annotated *Westminster Study Edition of the Holy*

Bible (1948), a one-volume work which is a model of what a larger and more comprehensive commentary series should be. It is to be hoped that the forthcoming *Interpreter's Bible*, edited by George A. Buttrick and others, may partially fill the need. As for Bible dictionaries, we have published *A New Standard Bible Dictionary* (edited by M. W. Jacobus, E. E. Nourse and A. C. Zenos in the 1st and 2nd eds., 1909 and 1925; in the 3rd ed., 1936, Prof. Nourse was replaced by E. C. Lane) and *The Westminster Dictionary of the Bible* (1944), a completely revised and rewritten edition, by Henry S. Gehman, of the earlier *Dictionary* by John D. Davis (1st ed. 1898). But for larger and more detailed treatments of Biblical subjects we are still dependent upon the major British works inspired by the 1900 era, edited by James Hastings and by T. K. Cheyne and J. S. Black (*Dictionary of the Bible*, 1898–1904; *Encyclopedia of Religion and Ethics*, 1908–1926; *Encyclopaedia Biblica*, 1899–1903).

As for Old Testament theology, our work here can scarcely be said to be more than beginning. It will be difficult for us to do much of lasting significance, except on detailed topics, before basic, up-to-date work in theological lexicography has been done and before serious consideration has been given to the history of Israel in the light of the vast new store of information now available. A new attention also has to be directed toward comparative religion. For the first time, an adequate understanding of the theological structure of polytheism has become possible; in its light the vast difference and the radical reaction of Hebrew faith at nearly every stage of its normative expression is becoming clearer. The metaphor of growth and the comparison of details are no longer sufficient in themselves to explain or to expound it.[16] Furthermore, the revision of our evaluational framework which has been proceeding so rapidly has left us less inclined to view the Old Testament primarily as a sourcebook for values and the evolution of ethical ideals. We are instead in-

---

[16] So the present writer in the monograph, *The Old Testament Against Its Environment*.

creasingly inclined to emphasize its nature as *Heilsgeschichte*, as the record of a proclamation of the great saving acts of God, a proclamation which is primary and which prevents the distortion which has occurred when the Bible has been made into a buttress and support for a religion of ethical idealism. Precisely what this means as an organizing principle for Biblical theology, and what its implications are for Christian theology, have yet to be made clear.

It is thus evident that at the middle of the twentieth century we stand at the beginning of a new era of Biblical study. While we cannot foresee what course world events are to take, it would appear that unless a new era of darkness descends the Protestantism of the second half of this century may undergo as radical a change as it did during the second half of the last century. Old Testament study during the next three decades bears promise of being as productive as it was between 1890 and 1910, this time, however, more seriously concerned with its proper role as a vital part of the Church's life. The manifest tendencies toward increasing conservatism in Biblical criticism and theology among "liberal" Protestants, together with the new movement toward scholarly training among fundamentalists, is already giving promise, not of eradicating the differences completely, but at least of moderating the tension between the two groups. A new and deep theological interest among many younger Jewish rabbis, accelerated by the extreme secularism of modern Zionism, may make possible a closer rapport in Biblical study between Jews and Christians on other grounds than the purely linguistic and historical. Encouraging also is the phenomenal growth of Roman Catholic interest in Biblical study, though it is very problematical whether the Catholic hierarchy will allow this interest to result in greater attempts at mutual understanding and stimulation which Catholic, Protestant and Jewish scholars on their own would be glad to have occur.[17]

[17] For surveys of Jewish and Catholic Biblical study, see the papers by Felix A. Levy and James H. Cobb in Harold R. Willoughby, ed., *The Study of the Bible Today and Tomorrow* (1947), pp. 98–128.

Thus, while on the whole one must say that the study of the Old Testament in this country is in a very uncertain position at the moment and suffering severely from a lack of highly trained personnel with a deep theological interest and a broad cultural background, the future is nevertheless filled with considerable promise. At the beginning of the century the direction of study was determined by what had happened during the Victorian era. It is probable that the events of the last two decades, and the radical shifts in perspective which have occurred, have established the direction of study in the next half century, even though at the moment precise prognosis is impossible.

BIBLIOGRAPHY *

I. General

Eiselen, F. C., and others, eds., *Abingdon Bible Commentary* (New York, 1929)

Davis, John D., *The Westminster Dictionary of the Bible* (revised and rewritten by Henry S. Gehman; Philadelphia, 1944)

II. Introductions

Eiselen, F. C., *Biblical Introduction Series: The Pentateuch* (New York, 1916); *The Prophetic Books* (2 vols., 1923); *The Psalms and Other Sacred Writings* (1918)

Pfeiffer, Robert H., *Introduction to the Old Testament* (New York, 1941)

III. History, Archaeology and Geography

Kent, C. F., *History of the Hebrew People* (2 vols.) and *History of the Jewish People* (2 vols., the second by J. S. Riggs; New York, 1896–1900)

* The bibliography for this chapter is primarily concerned with books dealing with the Old Testament, just as the bibliography for the next chapter is concerned with books on the New Testament. Perhaps the most useful volumes which illustrate, for the Bible as a whole, the transition from "liberalism" to a "neo-critical" point of view are *The Modern Use of the Bible* by H. E. Fosdick (New York, 1924) and *Rediscovering the Bible* by B. W. Anderson (New York, 1951). See also *The Interpretation of the Bible* edited by C. W. Dugmore (London, 1944). A.S.N.

Olmstead, A. T., *History of Palestine and Syria* (New York, 1931)

Albright, W. F., *From the Stone Age to Christianity* (Baltimore, 1940)

Barton, George A., *Archaeology and the Bible* (1st ed., Philadelphia, 1916; 7th ed. 1937)

Wright, G. Ernest, and Filson, Floyd V., *Westminster Historical Atlas to the Bible* (Philadelphia, 1945)

IV. Religion and Theology

Peters, J. P., *Religion of the Hebrews* (Boston, 1914)

Knudson, A. C., *The Religious Teaching of the Old Testament* (New York, 1918)

Burrows, Millar, *Outline of Biblical Theology* (Philadelphia, 1946)

THE STUDY OF THE
NEW TESTAMENT

Floyd V. Filson

FLOYD V. FILSON was born in Missouri in 1896. After taking his undergraduate studies at Park College, Missouri, and his theological studies at McCormick Theological Seminary, he went to the University of Basel, Switzerland, where he took his doctorate in 1930. His entire teaching career has been at his theological *alma mater*, where he has been Professor of New Testament Literature and History since 1930. He has published several books on New Testament criticism and New Testament theology, his best-known volume being *One Lord, One Faith*. With his colleague, G. Ernest Wright, he produced the *Westminster Historical Atlas to the Bible*, and he is also co-editor of the *Westminster Study Bible*. He has played an important role in interpreting European theological thought to the American mind, in particular having translated from the German Oscar Cullmann's *Christ and Time* and being co-translator of Rudolph Otto's *The Kingdom of God and the Son of Man*.

III

PUBLICATION of the Revised Standard Version of the New Testament in 1946 underlines one prominent feature of Protestant Biblical scholarship in America. There has been a persistent effort to make the results of research widely available. In 1900, for example, *The Biblical World* had been working for many years to combine accurate scholarship with active teaching in the Church. The modern translations of the New Testament, of which those by James Moffatt and E. J. Goodspeed are the best known but by no means the only ones, have aimed at the same combination of the scholarly and the practical.

Broad Horizons of American Scholarship

Not only in relation to the Church, but also in the area of scholarly study, New Testament students have tried to work with wide horizons. While denominationalism is a peculiar characteristic of the American scene, New Testament scholarship has rarely conceived its work as a partisan denominational activity. This is the more surprising in view of the fact that denominational theological schools train most of the ministers and give the basic training to most of the New Testament scholars.

One factor which fosters broad fellowship is the Society of Biblical Literature and Exegesis. Open to qualified scholars of all faiths and views, it was founded in 1880 and is influential through its *Journal of Biblical Literature*. The National Association of Biblical Instructors, not founded until 1909 and publisher since 1933 of the *Journal of Bible and Religion*, aims primarily to promote effective teaching rather than to foster technical research. But it too illustrates the freedom with which scholars and teachers of various denominations work together.

The broad outlook of New Testament study has been helped by friendly co-operation between Protestant and Jewish scholars.

At times this fellowship has failed to face the crucial issues which divide these two groups, but this is by no means the whole truth. Splendid courtesy and mutual helpfulness have marked the relations between scholars of these two faiths.

Not so close have been the relations between Protestant and Roman Catholic scholars. Many cases of personal friendship and helpfulness occur, but the two groups work quite separately. This does not mean that the Roman Catholic Church has discouraged serious Biblical study. Quite the contrary is true. To be sure, the papal Decree *Lamentabili* in 1907 completely crushed any tendencies to "modernism" in that denomination, and its scholarship must operate within the limits of official pronouncements on certain critical issues. For example, it must reject the current Two-Document Theory of the origin of the Synoptic Gospels, and hold that in some way Paul wrote the Epistle to the Hebrews. Yet papal encyclicals and pronouncements have encouraged thorough study of the Bible.

This prompting has yielded fruit in America in two noteworthy respects. One is the organization of the Catholic Biblical Association, which since 1939 has published the *Catholic Biblical Quarterly*. The other is the publication of books intended to promote study of the Bible by priests and laymen; examples are recent translations of the Vulgate and the Greek New Testament,[1] and Steinmueller's three-volume *Companion to Scripture Studies* (1941–1943), which has had several printings. The latter work shows that Roman Catholic writers know and make some use of Protestant scholarship.

Another notable feature of Protestant New Testament study in America has been its constant reflection of European trends. This has always been true and remains true today. It was feared during the Second World War that Europe would be too exhausted by war to continue to fulfill the prominent role it so

---

[1] The Confraternity edition (1941) is a translation of the Latin Vulgate New Testament. F. A. Spencer's translation of the Greek New Testament appeared in 1937 under the editorship of C. J. Callan and J. A. McHugh; Spencer died in 1913.

long had held in this field. Such a judgment was hasty. European scholars are still producing the painstaking, thorough research which has put us in their debt in days past.

Acquaintance with such basic work has always been open to readers of learned journals, monographs, and books. Many of these books have been translated into English to give them a wider field of influence. Lecturers from abroad have brought a personal expression of current trends of European study, and some of Britain's great scholars have settled in America to serve as teachers. The names of Kirsopp Lake, James Moffatt, W. Morgan, and E. F. Scott will suffice to make clear how great is American debt to such scholars. Perhaps American Biblical scholarship has at times needed more originality and independence. But it is a partial compensation that the originality, which has not been lacking, has worked against a background of acquaintance with the best scholarship of other countries.

Archaeological Work Continues

Any report of what American New Testament scholarship has done and should do will inevitably reflect to some extent the personal thinking of the reporter. But certain broad lines of development can be discerned.

Characteristic of the last half century has been the earnest determination to do competent historical study. In dealing with an ancient literature and history, this involves alert attention to geography and archaeology.[2] Such study in the New Testament field is not new. Many of the epoch-making discoveries antedate 1900. But steady progress has continued in spite of two world wars. Notable discoveries of papyri have not only provided new manuscripts of New Testament books but also greatly increased

---

[2] See G. E. Wright and F. V. Filson, *The Westminster Historical Atlas to the Bible* (1945); M. Burrows, *What Mean These Stones?* (1941); C. C. McCown, *The Ladder of Progress in Palestine* (1943); J. Finegan, *Light from the Ancient Past* (1946). Now out of date is C. M. Cobern, *The New Archaeological Discoveries and Their Bearing Upon the New Testament*, published in 1917 and last revised in 1921. G. A. Barton, *Archaeology and the Bible* (1916; seventh ed., 1937), deals mainly with the Old Testament.

the records of the life and culture of the ancient world. Discoveries of ancient synagogues in Palestine and elsewhere, for example, at Dura-Europos on the Euphrates, have thrown light upon the art, architecture, and religious attitudes of Judaism in the early Christian period.[3] In particular, the former theory that the Jews rigidly forbade the artistic portrayal of human beings has been shattered; mosaics and wall paintings depict not only Biblical scenes and characters, but also such pagan features as the signs of the zodiac.

Excavation and exploration has fixed the site of many New Testament cities and towns; Capernaum, for instance, was certainly at Tell Hum. The American Schools of Oriental Research have led the way in exploration of the sites of Palestine, and in particular have mapped all ancient sites in the regions east of the Jordan Valley.[4] The archaeological survey of the city of Jerash, which, like Pompeii, was never fully occupied after ancient times, permits us to see what a city of the Decapolis was like, even if Jerash is mainly a witness to the centuries just after the New Testament period.[5] Various excavations at Athens, Philippi, Ephesus, and other Hellenistic sites have helped to reconstruct the life and history of the days of Paul.[6]

Manuscript Discoveries

Among archaeological finds outstanding importance attaches to discoveries of Biblical manuscripts. Unfortunately, these are usually made by natives who refuse to reveal the place of discovery. At times they even divide a manuscript into parts, in the hope of making a greater profit by selling each part separately.

Fifty years ago little manuscript evidence for the New Testa-

[3] See M. Rostovtzeff, *Dura-Europos and Its Art* (1938).

[4] This exploration has been mainly the work of Nelson Glueck, of the Hebrew Union College. Outstanding in Palestinian archaeology is W. F. Albright. The American Schools publish an *Annual* and a *Bulletin* to provide a permanent record of their work.

[5] The results of the excavations are given in *Gerasa: City of the Decapolis*, edited by C. H. Kraeling (1938).

[6] For non-technical reports, see *The Biblical Archaeologist*, published by the American Schools and edited since its founding in 1938 by G. E. Wright.

ment dated earlier than the fourth century. Further evidence for this later period continues to come to light.[7] American resources and scholarship have brought to publication, among other manuscripts, the notable parchment Washington Manuscript of the Gospels and Acts (W), written in the fourth or fifth century. Perhaps even more significant has been the discovery of papyri from the third and, rarely, from the second century. One such acquisition towers above the rest. The Chester Beatty Biblical Papyri, consisting of eleven manuscripts in all, contains mostly early manuscripts of the Greek Old Testament. But three third-century manuscripts, more nearly complete than any previously discovered New Testament papyri, contain respectively the Gospels and Acts, the letters of Paul, and the Book of Revelation. The manuscript of Paul's letters was sold in three parts, one of which was obtained by the University of Michigan and published by H. A. Sanders (1935).

As a result of these and similar discoveries it has become increasingly clear that no future finds will alter in any essential the text of our Greek New Testament. There are indeed numerous minor variations between manuscripts, and scholars weigh them carefully. But these are relatively unimportant. Even in 1882, as Hort then said, we had a substantially reliable text, and the discoveries of third-century and even second-century evidence makes it doubly certain that we know in all essentials what the first century writers said.

The discovery of thousands of non-Biblical papyri and the more intensive study of Hellenistic writers have thrown much light on New Testament Greek. A century ago, Luke and Paul were compared mainly with the classical authors. Little more than a half century ago, however, Deissmann observed that the Greek of the papyri was much like that of the New Testament.[8] Since

[7] For "an account of manuscripts, texts, and versions of the Bible" see I. M. Price, *The Ancestry of our English Bible*. First published in 1907, its thirteenth printing in 1949 was a thorough revision by W. A. Irwin and A. P. Wikgren.

[8] The best popular presentation of Deissmann's work is his *Light from the Ancient East* (revised Eng. Trans., 1927).

then it has been solidly established that the Greek of these early Christian writers was essentially the good current Greek of that time. That is why Goodspeed and others have insisted that a modern translation should likewise be in the current speech of the translator's time.

For a time the papyri may have been overstressed. The center of interest for students of New Testament Greek should be not in the papyri but in the Septuagint. It was the Bible of all New Testament writers; they frequently quote it and even more often reflect it; it is of primary importance for the study of New Testament thought.

The name of A. T. Robertson, and the grammars and other works from his pen, focus attention upon the genuine contribution of Americans to the study of Biblical Greek.[9]

Studies in First Century Background

In keeping with the recent high development of sociological studies, and the resulting great interest in environmental factors of religious life, American Biblical scholars have investigated extensively the background of emerging Christianity.[10]

The result has been a better understanding of ancient Judaism. In this study Jewish scholars have naturally played a major role, but Protestants have made important contributions. Archaeological work has been a joint interest, and so has study of the "intertestamental" period. The two-volume work by George Foot Moore on *Judaism in the First Centuries of the Christian Era: The Age of the Tannaim* (1927) is the classic on this subject.

Noteworthy among the gains of such studies is the better understanding of the positive strength of the Pharisaic position and its commanding place in the history of Judaism. The chief

---

[9] Robertson's chief scholarly contribution was his *Grammar of the Greek New Testament in the Light of Historical Research* (second ed., 1915), a volume of 1367 pages.

[10] See G. H. C. Macgregor and A. C. Purdy, *Jew and Greek: Tutors Unto Christ* (1936); R. H. Pfeiffer, *History of New Testament Times with an Introduction to the Apocrypha* (1949).

question is whether the Judaism of the first century, before the destruction of the Temple, was not really more varied, and less under the "normative" control of the Pharisees, than Moore and others would lead us to think. The recently discovered Dead Sea Scrolls include a "Manual of Discipline," which promises to throw welcome light on a non-Pharisaic Jewish sect of late pre-Christian or very early Christian times.

Because Philo of Alexandria has often been considered one source of New Testament thought, the vigorous recent study of his life and writings deserves mention. It has examined his kinship with Palestinian Judaism, with Hellenistic thought, and with the attitudes of the mystery religions. E. R. Goodenough has even claimed that Philo thought of his Jewish faith in terms of a mystery religion.[11] The argument, even if unconvincing, serves to call attention to the reverent worship and mystical spirit found in Philo; his basic interest was not philosophical but religious.

Philo and Hellenistic Judaism constitute a bridge from the Jewish to the Hellenistic world, which offers an inexhaustible field of study. In this area H. R. Willoughby's capable book on *Pagan Regeneration* (1929) is in two respects characteristic of much American scholarship. It interprets in a winsome way the strength and attraction of the pagan cults of New Testament times; but it fails to give an adequate critique of the weaknesses of those cults.

The attempt some have made to derive important elements of the New Testament message from pagan cults and philosophies has been widely and rightly rejected. Study of the Gentile world throws light on the background and setting and details of the New Testament. But as Cadbury says,[12] there is a noticeable "absence of traceable Gentile religious influence on the New Testament."

[11] See his *By Light, Light* (1935). A valuable general study is his *Introduction to Philo Judaeus* (1940).

[12] See p. 90 in his essay on "The Present State of New Testament Studies," in *The Haverford Symposium on Archaeology and the Bible*, edited by E. Grant (1938).

The Study of Gospel Origins

Chief attention should center on the origin and meaning of the New Testament documents themselves. The literary problems continue to deserve attention. At the turn of the century the two-document theory was widely regarded as the solution of the Synoptic problem: the writers of Matthew and Luke used as written sources Mark and a collection of Jesus' sayings (Q). Except for Roman Catholics, who now must reject the theory, it still holds its ground.[13] But it is often expanded. Largely under the influence of B. H. Streeter, special written sources for both Matthew (M) and Luke (L) have been proposed, and some have thought our Luke the result of a complicated development, in which Luke's original compilation of teaching (L) was first combined with Q to form Proto-Luke, and only later was this Proto-Luke combined with Mark to give our present Gospel of Luke.[14] These newer source theories are much disputed. Many are content to stand by the two-document theory, and turn to oral tradition for the further light needed to explain the origins of the Gospels.

Akin to the sociological interest which animated environmental studies is Form Criticism, which emerged as a prominent phase of Gospel study after the First World War and has exercised considerable influence in America.[15] It fastens attention upon the oral tradition, in the early period, and seeks the *Sitz im Leben* or actual life situation in which the gospel tradition was used.

[13] A dissenter is M. S. Enslin, who doubts that Q ever existed and suggests that the author of Luke borrowed from our Gospel of Matthew. See *Christian Beginnings* (1938), p. 433.

[14] On special written sources for Matthew and Luke see E. D. Burton, *Some Principles of Literary Criticism and Their Application to the Synoptic Problem* (1904); B. S. Easton, *The Gospel According to St. Luke* (1926) and *Christ in the Gospels* (1930); B. W. Bacon, *Studies in Matthew* (1930); F. C. Grant, *The Growth of the Gospels* (1933).

[15] See F. C. Grant, *Form Criticism* (1934), a brief introduction and translation of works by Bultmann and Kundsin. An early and incisive study of Form Criticism was made by B. S. Easton in *The Gospel Before the Gospels* (1928). For a later description and critique see E. F. Scott, *The Validity of the Gospel Record* (1938); also my *Origins of the Gospels* (1938), ch. 4.

While it directs initial attention to the form in which the tradition was used and shaped, its real purpose is to reconstruct the development of early Christian life and thought. Ostensibly a purely historical discipline, it often operates with philosophical and theological presuppositions which derive tradition from process rather than a great creative figure. Hence Form Criticism has occasionally led to a practical agnosticism as to what Jesus said and did. To be sure, it is a valuable corrective to the purely literary study which divorced the writing of the Gospels from the life of the Church. It has shown how the tradition was used in the worship, teaching, and controversy of the first Christians. But at times it has almost reduced Jesus to an unknown x.

In our own country, the social-historical school, of which S. J. Case was so prominent a member, made a similar attempt to relate the growth and fixing of the tradition to the social setting of the disciples. The tradition was to be tested to see whether it fitted the Palestinian milieu; only if it did could it be considered as genuine. Case's *Jesus* is typical and classic in this field of study.[16] The problem in all test by environment is how to allow for the originality of the central figure of the story. This problem the social-historical method cannot solve; at best it can rule out obviously extraneous features of a tradition.

C. C. Torrey represents a radical rejection of concentration upon oral tradition.[17] He seeks the setting of the tradition in the earliest Aramaic-speaking Christianity, which almost at once became an Aramaic-writing Christianity. In fact, he inclines to think that even in Jesus' lifetime notes were made of what Jesus said, and perhaps of what he did. Beginning with Mark, in A.D. 40, all four Gospels were written in Aramaic within little more than twenty years. Our Greek Gospels, the first half of Acts (to ch. 15:35), and the Book of Revelation are all translations from Aramaic originals. A. T. Olmstead stoutly championed the theory

---

[16] See also D. W. Riddle, *The Gospels: Their Origin and Growth* (1939).

[17] *The Four Gospels* (1933); *Our Translated Gospels* (1936); *Documents of the Primitive Church* (1941). I pointed out weaknesses in Torrey's arguments and assumptions in ch. 3 of my *Origins of the Gospels*.

of an Aramaic Gospel back of our present Gospels,[18] but did not develop so complicated a theory as that of Torrey.

These and other men have at least called attention to the strongly Semitic flavor of the New Testament. Even if our Gospels were written in Greek, as I am convinced they were, they nevertheless were in faithful touch with the early Aramaic tradition from which the oral Greek tradition almost immediately derived.

The Debate Over Ephesians

That the origin of the New Testament writings must be sought in the Hellenistic world has been most vigorously asserted by E. J. Goodspeed. He contends, and rightly, that our Gospels were written in Greek. But his chief claim to present recognition is not in this point, nor in his half century of activity in American manuscript study, but in his view of the origin of Ephesians.[19] His theory is that the writing of Acts, about A.D. 90, stimulated an admirer of Paul, who already knew Colossians well, to gather together and master all the letters of Paul he could find. This disciple then wrote "Ephesians" as a summary of Pauline teaching, and published the collection with this summary at its head.

Goodspeed goes on to argue that the presence of groups of letters in the New Testament—the Pastoral Epistles, the three Epistles of John, the collected Catholic Epistles, the seven letters in Revelation—reflects the influence of this publication of the Pauline collection. Therefore, when he writes his *Introduction to the New Testament*, he makes this collection of Paul's letters the key to the entire process. The collector, who also wrote Ephesians, set the pattern of Christian writing for some decades; letters, in groups, became the leading way of presenting the Christian message.[20]

[18] "Could an Aramaic Gospel Be Written?" was his key article, in *Journal of Near Eastern Studies*, 1942, pp. 41–75.

[19] His chief works of this subject are *New Solutions of New Testament Problems* (1927); *The Meaning of Ephesians* (1933); *An Introduction to the New Testament* (1937); *Christianity Goes to Press* (1940).

[20] A. E. Barnett, in *The New Testament: Its Making and Meaning* (1946),

This brilliant theory, by assuming that the collector knew Colossians almost as well as if it were his own writing, does much to silence the objection that the vocabulary of Ephesians is on the whole Pauline. But what if the letters of Paul were collected as a result of Paul's death,[21] or as a gradual process (cf. Col. 4:16)? Goodspeed's theory holds good only if the collection burst upon the world as a new and striking innovation. Publication and not simply writing is for him the clue to the development.

This theory calls to attention the fact that Ephesians is a general letter. Paul can have written it only if he for once decided to set down a general meditation on the Gospel and its meaning for Christian life in the one world Church. To me this latter view answers more questions with fewer unsupported assumptions than does any other possibility.[22]

Is New Testament Eschatology Valid?

As we move from questions of background and literary origin to consider the interpretation of New Testament content, we find eschatology a focal center of interest. For decades, largely through the influence of militant Bible Schools and the wide use of the Scofield *Reference Bible* (1909), of which I am told two million copies have been sold, pre-millenialism has been a prominent factor in American religious life. This school of thought takes the Biblical references to the future quite literally and welds them into a system in which the end of the world is expected in the very near future. It claims that New Testament references to the imminent end of this age refer not to the first century but to the time of the modern speaker or writer.

Quite opposed to this is the "consistent eschatology" which

---

follows Goodspeed's theory. J. Knox, in *Philemon Among the Letters of Paul* (1935), conjectures that Onesimus collected the letters and wrote Ephesians.

[21] This is the suggestion of H. E. Dana in *A Neglected Predicate in New Testament Criticism* (1934), pp. 14-21.

[22] So argues E. F. Scott in his commentary on Ephesians (1930) in the *Moffatt New Testament Commentary* series.

American scholars learned from Johannes Weiss and Albert Schweitzer.[23] On this view, Jesus expected the end of the world at once, but since the expectation was not realized, that entire way of thinking should be abandoned, and the ethical teaching which Jesus and the early Christians based on this expectation should be discounted as an "interim ethic," given for use only in stop-gap living until the imminent crisis should come. Some modern scholars (E. D. Burton [24] is but one of many) absolve Jesus of any share in this apocalyptic view; they hold that the early Church ascribed to him their outlook, which in reality they derived from Jewish apocalyptic. In either case, there results a suspicion of the eschatological features in the Gospels. It is a view sharply at variance with the New Testament's vivid hope.

The Church has moved towards a position in which the urgent eschatological note of the New Testament is generally recognized. It is widely conceded that Jesus and the Apostles expected the end in the not too distant future, although usually it has been realized that the Schweitzer school overstated the extent to which Jesus' thought focused on the imminent future. There is good evidence that Jesus thought of the Kingdom as already beginning in his own ministry and movement; there is also evidence that he anticipated some interval, even if not extensive, between his death and the coming of the end. With his work a new age began. The situation of man henceforth was new. The New Testament sees that the decisive action of all God's work in time was the historical career of Christ, the crucified and risen Lord. In his earthly career was established a new order which will find complete fulfilment in God's perfect final Kingdom. The necessarily pictorial expression and the uncertainty as to the time of the end do not discredit this faith. New Testament eschatology is an essential part of the early Christian message.[25]

[23] See ch. 13 in C. C. McCown's historical survey of *The Search for the Real Jesus* (1940).

[24] *New Testament Word Studies* (1927), pp. 97 f.

[25] See P. E. Davies on "The Relevance of Apocalyptic for Ancient and Modern Situations," in *The Study of the Bible Today and Tomorrow*, H. R. Willoughby, editor (1947), pp. 279–297.

Is the Gospel a Social Program?

To the "consistent eschatologist" the teaching of Jesus is of little direct use today; it was only a temporary way of living for people who were sure that the world was to end almost at once. This is part of a wider question: What is the relevance of the teaching of Jesus? Some sects would say that it is not a social guide by which to remake the society of our time. Jesus did not intend to transform this world; it is doomed. He simply told men how to live until he comes to establish by his divine power a quite new and different order.

In radical opposition to this view is a school of thought which has had tremendous influence in America during the last half century. It found in the social teaching of Jesus the directions by which Christians can remake the world and build the Kingdom of God, the perfect society. This point of view reflected the characteristic American optimism and activism which so often have been condemned by European Christians. It reached back to the prophets of the Old Testament for powerful support, and often looked with unappreciative eye at the high Christology of the Fourth Gospel and the "labored theology" of Paul. In its extreme form it took the heart of the Bible to be the prophets and the social teaching of Jesus.[26]

The Church so often had been quiescent, while its members shared in and frequently profited by the evils of society, that the new emphasis had a partial justification. But it was one-sided. It had no adequate conception of the tenacity of evil, nor of the central New Testament message of the redeeming grace of God

[26] Among the notable advocates of the social relevance of the New Testament were S. Mathews, *The Social Teaching of Jesus* (1897; completely rewritten, with recognition of the eschatological aspect, in *Jesus on Social Institutions*, published in 1928); W. Rauschenbusch, *Christianity and the Social Crisis* (1907) and *A Theology for the Social Gospel* (1917). In S. Dickey, *The Constructive Revolution of Jesus* (1923); C. C. McCown, *The Genesis of the Social Gospel* (1929); and J. C. Bennett, *Social Salvation* (1935), there is a frank facing of the eschatological accent in Jesus' teaching. What is said above applies more to the average advocate of the social gospel than to the scholars cited in this note.

active in the life, death, and living Lordship of the risen Christ. It too often represented a failure to hold fast to the basic Christian message in points of Christology and Atonement.[27] Certain of its champions felt able, with some help, to work out their own salvation, with very little fear and trembling, and without the Apostle Paul's accompanying feeling that "all things are of God, who reconciled us to himself through Christ."

In the first part of the last half century this strong emphasis on the social gospel moved into a place of prominence. Two world wars and an ominous depression changed the theological climate. It is now widely recognized that the social gospel brought a neces- sary corrective; Christians personally redeemed by Christ are under urgent obligation to give in their social living a positive expression of the mind of Christ. But the strength and permanent truth of the classic Christian message, set forth in the full outline of the Gospels, in the speeches of Acts, and in the letters of Paul, is the real hope of sinful man living in a deeply corrupt society.[28]

Hence in retrospect it is clear that something essential was represented by such militant conservatives as J. G. Machen. He was not infallible in critical questions, he had no proper sense of the social problems of our time, and he was not winsome in theological debate. But his book, *The Origin of Paul's Religion* (1921), and his contention that classic Christian theology is the necessary outcome of faithfulness to the New Testament, were far truer to fact than much shallow theology which often marked the social gospel. Much criticism of such men, as of "Neo- orthodoxy" today, was in reality directed against the common New Testament Gospel. It was only by ignoring the Fourth Gos- pel, the Acts, the Epistles, the Book of Revelation, and much of the Synoptic Gospels themselves that the Gospel could be repre-

---

[27] See J. W. Bowman, *The Intention of Jesus* (1943), on Jesus' own thought of himself and his work, and Elias Andrews, *The Meaning of Christ for Paul* (1949), for the full scope of Paul's thinking on these themes.

[28] The earnest attempt of Rauschenbusch (see note 26), though it was honest and constructive in spirit, did not issue in a balanced and adequate theology.

sented as a non-Christological social message with no central word of atonement.

The pendulum may now be swinging too far in the other direction. There may be such a reaction against shallow aspects of the social gospel that a quiescent Church will fail in its social responsibility. This would be damaging first of all to the Church and its members; genuine new life in Christ cannot fail to express itself in social relations.[29]

Is There a New Testament Theology?

The insight that the Gospel is more than the teaching of Jesus leads to the consideration of New Testament theology.[30] Typical of the best work in this field a half century ago was G. B. Stevens' *The Theology of the New Testament*, first published in 1899.[31] The rights of literary and historical study were fully conceded, but the scholarly treatment was accompanied by the solid conviction of the uniqueness, unity, and permanent authority of the New Testament message. This positive conviction recognized but confined to a secondary role the diversity of thought the New Testament contains.

On various grounds this favorable view has been attacked.[32] The very possibility of a New Testament theology has been de-

[29] Stress on the ethical teaching of the New Testament is found in E. F. Scott, *The Ethical Teaching of Jesus* (1924); H. Branscomb, *The Teachings of Jesus* (1931); M. S. Enslin, *The Ethics of Paul* (1930). See also A. N. Wilder, *Eschatology and Ethics in the Teaching of Jesus* (1934; revised ed., 1950).

[30] Surveys and analysis of developments on this subject are offered by C. T. Craig, "Biblical Theology and the Rise of Historicism," in *Journal of Biblical Literature*, 1943, pp. 281–294, and A. N. Wilder, "New Testament Theology in Transition," in *The Study of the Bible Today and Tomorrow*, pp. 419–436.

[31] Similar in position was A. C. Zenos, *The Plastic Age of the Gospel* (1927).

[32] R. E. Wolfe, for example, opposes the new interest in Biblical theology. He stands for objective study based on the history-of-religions approach, demands the rigid exclusion of the idea of revelation, and would center attention on the prophets and the Synoptic teaching of Jesus. See his article, "The Terminology of Biblical Theology," in *The Journal of Bible and Religion*, 1947, pp. 143–147.

nied. It has been insisted that the treatment of the New Testament writings as a separate collection is artificial; historical study must ignore the canon, and treat all ancient Christian writings as on the same level.

It has further been asserted that sound historical study outlaws New Testament theology. Such study can only describe the history and religious life of the New Testament movement. No thought of relevance or normative character, no personal faith or thought of divine revelation, can be allowed to influence this purely objective presentation. Sympathy and imagination the scholar must have, but his personal faith and his final evaluation of the results of study must be rigidly excluded from his work. Therefore the word theology should not be used; what we can expect is a treatment of the religion of the New Testament.[33]

Some have heightened this last statement. They deny that there is any basic unity in the New Testament, and so they speak rather of the "religions" of the New Testament.

Further objection to the term, New Testament theology, has come from the claim that the writers of the New Testament books are dependent on non-Christian sources for essentials of their message. The early decades of the twentieth century were marked by diligent study and comparison of the various ancient religions. As the contemporary Jewish and Gentile backgrounds became better known, some scholars were deeply impressed by the parallels between the New Testament and other religious literatures. Perhaps it was natural that at first the similarities drew more attention than the differences. Moreover, chronology was often neglected. Evidence from the second, third, and even much later centuries was freely used to show that the New Testament was dependent upon these other religions, whose data were

[33] E. W. Parsons, whose book on *The Religion of the New Testament* (1939) is the best American liberal presentation of New Testament thought in print, insists also that the lack of reflection and system makes the word theology inapplicable. The same point animates E. F. Scott in *Varieties of New Testament Religion* (1943), but Scott sees the deep unity in the New Testament message.

actually too late to warrant such a conclusion. Lack of balance appeared also in the striking readiness to explain as Gentile in origin features of the New Testament message which had a much closer and more natural setting in Judaism, and more specifically in the Old Testament. Furthermore, the stubborn unwillingness to recognize adequately the fresh, creative factor in the emerging Christian movement vitiated much of the earnest study in this field.

Independence, therefore, and not servile dependence, marks the New Testament. The common centering of faith and thought in Jesus Christ, the unvarying interpretation of his career as the redemptive work of God, who has now brought to fulfillment his promises to Israel and through his Spirit is offering the benefit of Christ's work to Jew and Gentile alike—this one basic message, shared by all writers and binding them to the Old Testament, sweeps aside all talk of many competing "religions" in the New Testament. Here is one unique and crucial message which warrants the Church in setting these writings apart in a special group. Diversity there is; the bond with non-canonical writers need not be ignored; living touch with environment certainly exists, particularly with Judaism and the Old Testament; but these writings possess a vital unity, relevance, and originality.[34]

It is not surprising, therefore, that recent publications have recognized the rightful role of New Testament theology. Paul S. Minear's *Eyes of Faith* (1946) brings out the theocentric character and the common mind and outlook of the entire Bible. Millar Burrows' *Outline of Biblical Theology* (1946) moves in the direction of a full Biblical theology. Frederick C. Grant, in *An Introduction to New Testament Thought* (1950), while anxious to stress the diversity of the thought, is nevertheless concerned to do justice to the underlying unity within the New Testament and also between the Testaments.

[34] I have argued for this position in *One Lord, One Faith* (1943). The point leaves full room for dependence upon the Old Testament, kinship with Judaism, and contact with Hellenistic life. Cf. also my argument in *The New Testament Against Its Environment* (1950).

Still disputed is the question whether historical study must be rigidly objective. The necessity to be honest, to avoid wishful thinking and partisan bias, is the essential point in the demand for objective scholarship. But life is not the neutral area which this position assumes; it is impossible to study, correlate, and present truly the origin and classic history of a religious movement without the element of evaluation entering into the process.

This is not all. By the Christian scholar, committed as he is in mind and life to Christ, the demand that he do his historical study without personal response and evaluation must be rejected. Honesty, integrity, fairness, patience, and a sense of his limitations as a man and scholar may be demanded, but neutrality is out of the question. New Testament theology, broadened to become Biblical theology, and frankly combining with its diligent historical research the grasp of the meaning of history in the light of the Gospel, is a Christian necessity as well as a scholarly activity. It is time to be done with the deceptive myth of neutrality.

The Tasks That Lie Ahead

In what directions may we expect New Testament study to move in the next few years? No one can give a complete answer to this question.[35] In textual criticism we may expect solid work but no sensational results, unless unforeseen manuscript discoveries open up new possibilities. An international project to provide a much needed up-to-date textual apparatus of the Greek New Testament is just moving out of the planning stage into the actual detailed work, in which scores of American scholars are participating and the University of Chicago is providing the American center (the other center is at Oxford in England).[36]

[35] The best and most detailed attempt to forecast future trends is *The Study of the Bible Today and Tomorrow* (1947), a symposium of twenty-four essays sponsored by the Chicago Society of Biblical Research and edited by H. R. Willoughby.

[36] The Society of Biblical Literature and Exegesis is sponsoring this project, which the Rockefeller Foundation has aided in its initial stages.

This project concerns church history as well as the New Testament. The essential reliability of the Greek text is now beyond question, and two things remain to be done: we must reconstruct as closely as possible the original text, and write the history—of the text in the various periods of the ancient and mediæval Church.

The study of background will never end, for the material and questions are inexhaustible. Three lines of study should prove important and fruitful. In the Gentile area, the origin and development of Gnosticism will receive increased attention. Extensive new manuscript materials, recently discovered in Egypt, will soon make possible more careful study of this elusive aspect of ancient life.[37] In the Jewish field, further study of Hellenistic Judaism is needed, to determine as clearly as possible the situation in which the Gospel reached out into Gentile lands. More specifically, the Septuagint, which for long was neglected by New Testament scholars because it was the Old Testament and by Old Testament scholars because it was in Greek, calls for even more intensive study; here is the most rewarding single field of study for an understanding of New Testament background.[38]

The study of the canon, which was of considerable interest fifty years ago, has seemed much less important in recent years. But the necessity of a new study of the canon is beginning to be realized. In the last twenty years there has been much objection to the very idea of a canon. I expect to hear less in the next twenty. But the renewed study will not seek merely to determine when and where the New Testament books were first known and

---

Eighteen American scholars are on the Editorial Committee, whose Executive Committee consists of E. C. Colwell, Chairman; M. M. Parvis, Executive Secretary; K. W. Clark; B. M. Metzger; P. Schubert; and A. P. Wikgren.

[37] Thus far I know these discoveries only from a report in the *Theologische Literaturzeitung* for December, 1949, columns 760 f. They are like other evidence for Gnosticism, however, in that they are of post-New Testament date (third and fourth century; in Coptic).

[38] A lexicon of the Greek Old Testament, and a new lexicon of the Greek New Testament, are urgent needs. They should give major attention to the theological usage of the words.

when and how they were declared authoritative; it will center attention rather upon the reasons, including the theological reasons, for the establishment and final definition of the canon.

Since the date and origin of so many New Testament books is still in dispute, there will inevitably be much further study in these areas. Most troublesome is the wide disagreement concerning the Book of Acts [39] and the Gospel of John.[40] Crucial as they are in building a picture of New Testament history, they still offer many unsolved problems. While I hold that Acts is by Luke and gives a basically dependable account of Apostolic Christianity, and that the Gospel of John is built upon eyewitness and blends with that a devout interpretation which is convincing to faith, later datings and less favorable attitudes towards the historical and theological value of these books make urgent their further study.

It may be that the chief cause of difficulty, our immense ignorance of the last third of the first century, can never be overcome. Once the story of Acts ceases, we catch but glimpses of the next few decades. While scholars debate learnedly whether to put a book in the seventies or eighties or nineties, the truth is that we know little about events and developments in the Church during those years. This not only weakens the case for any system of dating of the documents, but also makes it hard to refute conclusively a confident scholar who unhesitatingly dates documents here or there in this ecclesiastical wilderness. It

[39] Basic for thorough study of the Book of Acts are H. J. Cadbury, *The Making of Luke-Acts* (1927), and *The Beginnings of Christianity, Part I, The Acts of the Apostles,* 5 volumes (1920–1933), edited by F. J. Foakes Jackson and K. Lake. No later book has completely superseded A. C. McGiffert, *A History of Christianity in the Apostolic Age* (1897). There is need for an up-to-date one-volume commentary on Acts and for a new comprehensive history of the Apostolic Age.

[40] American scholars have not done much outstanding work on this Gospel. It was a major interest of B. W. Bacon; see *The Fourth Gospel in Research and Debate* (1910) and *The Gospel of the Hellenists* (1933). Among conservative treatments are A. T. Robertson, *Epochs in the Life of the Apostle John* (1925), and H. E. Dana, *The Ephesian Tradition* (1940). Noteworthy critical studies are B. W. Robinson, *The Gospel of John* (1925), and E. C. Colwell, *John Defends the Gospel* (1936).

may not sound either exciting or promising, but there must be continued study to see whether a reasonably strong case can be made for some system of dating the New Testament books.

The central problem of all has to do with the relation between history and theology. Now that the possibility and even the desirability of a strictly neutral and objective presentation of the New Testament message is being denied, and the historian's own interpretative activity is seen to be an integral part of all historical writing, there must be careful study of the proper way to use historical material in Biblical theology as well as in systematic theology.

Biblical theology is essentially an interpreted account of the Biblical history, seen as the advancing work of God Himself. Therefore the real purpose of New Testament study in the days to come must be to get a clear grasp and give a clear statement of the gospel story of the saving work of God in Jesus Christ, the living Lord of the Church. In doing this task it must use every help which geography, archaeology, linguistic and literary study, general historical research, and psychological analysis [41] can give. But it will know that none of these supporting studies yields or controls the Gospel. The climax of all this labor is given by Biblical theology.

Systematic theology, if based on purely philosophical rather than historical foundations, must be asked whether it deserves any longer a place in the life of the Church. The Christian Church gets from the Bible the story of what God has done for men, and its message is that story thus interpreted. It is not the task of theology to surrender that basis of faith and seek a new one. Theology must deal with that Biblical history more directly and seriously than many theologians have done in the last half century.

Future New Testament study will recognize clearly the community-building nature of the New Testament message.[42]

[41] E. M. Ligon, in *The Psychology of Christian Personality* (1935), aims "to interpret the teachings of Jesus in terms of modern psychology" (p. vii).

[42] F. C. Grant stresses this point in his *Introduction to New Testament Thought*, Ch. 11.

Overemphasis on eschatology made the Church look like a lame afterthought. Extreme individualism made it an optional feature of Christian life. A social message bent on political and economic reform often slighted the role of the Church. In the New Testament, however, the Church is essential. Thorough study of the New Testament Church must be an important phase of New Testament history and theology.

BIBLIOGRAPHY

Enslin, Morton Scott, *Christian Beginnings* (New York, 1938). A comprehensive liberal survey of background, history, literary questions, text, and canon.

Filson, Floyd V., *One Lord, One Faith* (Philadelphia, 1943). An evaluation of recent critical theories and an argument for the essential unity of the New Testament message.

Finegan, Jack, *Light from the Ancient Past* (Princeton, 1946). A good popular presentation of "the archeological background of the Hebrew-Christian religion."

Grant, Frederick C., *An Introduction to New Testament Thought* (New York and Nashville, 1950). An excellent up-to-date study in the field of New Testament theology.

McGiffert, Arthur Cushman, *A History of Christianity in the Apostolic Age* (New York, 1897; rev. ed., 1899). An excellent presentation at the turn of the century.

Mathews, Shailer, *Jesus on Social Institutions* (New York, 1928). An outstanding expression of American interest in the social gospel.

Moore, George Foot, *Judaism in the First Centuries of the Christian Era: The Age of the Tannaim* (2 vols. Cambridge, 1927). A third volume, of notes, was issued in 1930. Indispensable.

Parsons, Ernest William, *The Religion of the New Testament* (New York, 1939). An outstanding liberal presentation.

Price, Ira Maurice, *The Ancestry of Our English Bible* (New York, 1907). Thirteenth printing, revised by William A. Irwin and Allen P. Wikgren, 1949. "An account of the manuscripts, texts, and versions of the Bible."

Stevens, George Barker, *The Theology of the New Testament* (New

York, 1899; second ed., 1906). A classic treatment at the turn of the century.

Wilder, Amos Niven, *Eschatology and Ethics in the Teaching of Jesus* (New York, 1939; rev. ed., 1950). The revised edition serves to show what vital problems are under discussion at the present time.

Willoughby, Harold R., Editor, *The Study of the Bible Today and Tomorrow* (Chicago, 1947). Twenty-four essays which survey recent research and discuss the unfinished tasks.

THE PHILOSOPHY OF RELIGION

George F. Thomas

GEORGE F. THOMAS was born in Texas in 1899, and he received his undergraduate training at Southern Methodist University, Dallas. He then spent three years studying theology as Rhodes scholar from Texas at the University of Oxford. On his return to America, he taught at Southern Methodist University, proceeding to Harvard in 1926, where he did graduate work for his doctorate in philosophy. Since 1927 he has taught philosophy at Swarthmore College, at Dartmouth College, and at the University of North Carolina. From 1940 he has been Professor of Religious Thought and since 1946 Chairman of the Department of Religion at Princeton University. He is the author of *Spirit and Its Freedom*, editor of *The Vitality of the Christian Tradition*, and contributor to various symposia. He is an Episcopalian layman, being a member of the Joint Commission of the Episcopal Church on Approaches to Unity, and he is a past president of the American Theological Society.

IV

THE FIRST half of the twentieth century has witnessed a vigorous effort on the part of some of our leading philosophers and philosophical theologians to investigate the nature and validity of religion. This effort has been made, for the most part, by men who have combined a strong personal interest in religion with a firm determination to maintain the independence of their thinking against the claims of every kind of religious authority, whether of Church or Scripture or Creed. Only in the United States, perhaps, could such a combination of religious concern and complete independence have been possible. In the United States the powerful religious impulses set in motion by the Reformation had given rise in the nineteenth century to a number of religious communities, no one of which could dominate the common life as an established church. All of these communities had to make their appeal to the mind and heart of the individual American, without the aid of any external authority. Moreover, the leading universities which were the centers of critical thought had achieved by the end of the century a remarkable degree of academic freedom. Above all, the spirit of American life was very individualistic in the late nineteenth and early twentieth centuries. The frontier had bred a habit of self-reliance and independence. Economic and political life encouraged individual initiative. The liberal spirit favored experimentation and change. As a result, the religious thinking of Americans was almost inevitably individualistic and heterodox, and no one type of religious thought was accepted by all or even most American thinkers. Therefore, it will be necessary to consider several different types as represented by outstanding personal examples. Because of the limitations of space, we shall not be able to deal with all of the various types and combinations of types and we shall have to confine ourselves to one or two personal examples of each type.[1]

Until the first World War, "Absolute Idealism" was the dominant philosophy in America, though for some time it had been challenged vigorously by Empiricism. Josiah Royce had offered a classic defense of Absolute Idealism at the end of the nineteenth century in *The World and the Individual*. In the first decade of this century his thinking underwent a substantial change. *The Philosophy of Loyalty* (published in 1908) and *The Problem of Christianity* (published in 1913) indicated that his thinking differed from that of Hegel in significant ways. It is worth while to examine *The Problem of Christianity* with the question in mind: How far had Royce freed himself from the Hegelian way of thinking about religion?

The essence of Christianity is best discovered, Royce thinks, by a study of St. Paul. Pauline Christianity developed the teaching of Jesus about the Kingdom of God into a doctrine of the Church. The three fundamental ideas of this type of Christianity are: (1) the salvation of the individual man is determined by membership in a religious, indeed, a divine, community in whose life the spirit of Christ attains earthly fulfilment;[2] (2) the individual "is by nature subject to some overwhelming moral burden from which, if unaided, he cannot escape";[3] and (3) the only escape for the individual is provided by an atonement for his sin and guilt which "makes possible the entrance of the individual into a saving union with the divine spiritual community."[4] No one can read Royce's interpretation of these three ideas without being impressed by his insight into certain aspects of the Christian doctrine of sin and atonement. But one cannot read far without discovering not only

---

[1] For example, we have selected E. S. Brightman rather than B. P. Bowne as representative of Personalism, largely because of his influence during the last generation, and we have not considered thinkers as significant as J. B. Pratt, E. Boodin, E. Lyman, and R. L. Calhoun. Paul Tillich also is not included because he is to be dealt with thoroughly in a forthcoming volume.

[2] *The Problem of Christianity*, I, 39.

[3] *Ibid.*, I, 4.   [4] *Ibid.*, I, 43.

that Royce has greatly oversimplified the meaning of Christianity by reducing it to these three assertions but also that he has radically reconstructed Christianity until it has become nothing more than "the most typical, and so far in human history, the most highly developed religion of loyalty." [5]

The most striking example of this is his subordination of Christ to the Church. "Not through imitating nor yet through loving any mere individual human being can we be saved," says he, "but only through loyalty to the 'Beloved Community.'" [6] He concedes that Jesus had taught a doctrine and lived a life that made the Christian community possible, but his doctrine of the Christian life was incomplete and the founding of Christianity was primarily due to "the united spirit of the early Christian community." [7] The name of Christ has always been for Christians simply "the symbol for the Spirit in whom the faithful—that is to say the loyal—always are and have been one." [8] Consequently, Jesus' teaching about love needs to be reinterpreted. Above all, love means loyalty to the "beloved community," one person loving another not merely with "amiable sympathy" but as a potential member of the "beloved community." The eschatological element in early Christianity is dropped and man becomes the builder of the "beloved community" as an earthly Kingdom of God. The "moral burden" or sin of the individual is interpreted as treason to the community rather than rebellion against God. The atonement of Christ becomes a symbol of the "loyal love" of many "suffering servants" for those who have betrayed the "beloved community." It is not so much an act of divine love for sinners as a purely human act of suffering to restore the unity of the community.

In the light of this thoroughly human and social interpretation of Christianity, we are prepared for Royce's virtual identification of the divine with the "beloved community." "Man the

---

[5] *Ibid.*, I, xviii.   [6] *Ibid.*, I, xxv.
[7] *Ibid.*, I, 418.   [8] *Ibid.*, II, 426.

community," he says, "without ceasing to be thoroughly human, may also prove to be divine." [9] That this may be only an extreme expression of the typically Idealistic doctrine of the immanence of God in man is suggested by the later statement that "the divine spirit dwelling in the living Church redeems mankind." [10] But it comes perilously close to a deification of the "beloved community."

It is obvious from all of this that Royce has not really overcome the tendency of Hegelian Idealism to transform an historical religion by distinguishing between its "accidental" historical elements and its "essential" meaning. Following this tendency, he regards Christian doctrines such as the Incarnation and Atonement merely as "myths" which express universal human experiences and needs. This results from his rationalistic approach which does not take seriously the claim of the Christian faith to be a revelation from God and regards as valid only those Christian affirmations that can be demonstrated by an appeal to universal human needs and experiences. In this view, Christianity becomes merely a symbolic expression of the truths of Absolute Idealism, and it will endure not because its basic religious beliefs are true but because "love and loyalty will not lose but grow in human value, as long as man remains alive." [11] Despite his attempt to do justice to Christianity, therefore, Royce does not really see the most distinctive thing about it: that it springs from the conviction that in Christ God has revealed Himself and has reconciled the world to Himself. Without that conviction, the Christian Church as the "beloved community" would never have come into existence and could no longer maintain itself. For the Christian faith is centered in Christ, not in the Church; and it depends for salvation upon God's grace and not upon any human "beloved community."

W. E. Hocking's *The Meaning of God in Human Experience* (published in 1912) is the most important book on religion in

[9] *Ibid.,* I, 418.   [10] *Ibid.,* II, 426.   [11] *Ibid.,* I, 422.

general which has been produced by an Absolute Idealist in the last half century. He attacks the subjectivistic view that religion is feeling and that the metaphysical element in it is unimportant. As "anticipated attainment," religion certainly includes feeling. But feeling is unstable and incommunicable; and it cannot be understood except in terms of its cognitive intention, its "destiny" being knowledge of its object. Though we can never comprehend the infinite, it is the object of all our ideas, since knowledge begins with the whole. Moreover, our "whole idea" is the source of our values and their growth.

Hocking's world view as an Idealist is that of monism and absolutism. Monism, which asserts that evil is less real than good, is a necessary condition of optimism. Absolutism is essential because there is a necessary and changeless Reality. However, Hocking seeks to define his monism and absolutism in such a way as to avoid the criticisms of James and others. It is true that monism sometimes averts its eyes from evil instead of combatting it, but the "true use" of the monistic principle of ignoring evil is that "the evil is not merely forgotten, but genuinely disposed of by that to which the attention is turned." In other words, evil is known as "an alterable aspect of a reality which is good." [12] Similarly, Hocking denies that absolutism necessarily swallows up the individual self. "Besides the Absolute," he says, "my Self is necessary to account for my motion." [13] Thus, in his defense of Absolute Idealism Hocking transforms it in the direction of personalism.

Perhaps the highest achievement of Hocking's philosophy of religion is his penetrating study of worship and mysticism. He points out the worth of worship in deepening knowledge of the self and reality, in detaching the self from its immediate environment, and, above all, in renewing its devotion to the Absolute or the Whole as the ultimate Source of all our values. As to mys-

[12] *Ibid.*, 178.   [13] *Ibid.*, 190.

ticism, he describes the "alternation" between work and worship, between the active pursuit of relative values and the enjoyment of the whole which includes them. Only through such an "alternation" can spiritual staleness and fatigue be overcome and the sense of the worth of living be recovered. Moreover, mysticism at its best does not lead to a withdrawal from action on the stage of history. Like Bergson, Hocking insists upon the connection between mysticism and action, going so far as to say that "mystic experience must complete itself in the prophetic consciousness" which seeks to control the forces of history.[14]

Though William James began to write about religion before the end of the nineteenth century, three of his most important books on the subject appeared in the present century: *The Varieties of Religious Experience* (1902), *Pragmatism* (1907), and *A Pluralistic Universe* (1909). Also, he has had his greatest influence in our time, affecting deeply the thinking not only of Pragmatists but also of Realists. Indeed, his Empiricism gave rise to several different types of empirical theology, and during the generation following the first World War it was probably the most powerful force in American religious thought.

James was the sworn foe of scientific, philosophical, and religious dogmatism. He vigorously opposed the Materialism and Agnosticism of scientists, the Absolute Idealism of philosophers, and the rigid orthodoxy of theologians. To all of these ways of thinking James opposed his "empirical theism." He did not claim that he could demonstrate the existence of God by logical argument, but sought to show that belief in Him was more satisfactory than disbelief when all the demands of man's nature are taken into account. Any philosophy must be not only internally consistent and adequate to the facts of nature but also satisfactory to the emotional and volitional side of man's nature. When both of these requirements are taken into account, Theism is more adequate than Materialism or Agnosticism. Moreover, when we are presented with a decision between two hypotheses which is

14 *Ibid.,* 511.

"forced, living, and momentous," we have the "right to adopt a believing attitude in religious matters, in spite of the fact that our logical intellect may not have been coerced." [15]

But James does not think that belief in God is arbitrary, and in *The Varieties of Religious Experience* he marshals the positive evidence. Feeling is primary, philosophy secondary, in religion, he argues. Natural theology fails to convince by its arguments those who do not already believe; dogmatic theology sets forth "metaphysical attributes" of God such as "simplicity" which make no practical difference to us and "moral attributes" which are important but not proved; and philosophical Idealism is equally unconvincing in its dialectical arguments. James concludes from this that the role of philosophy in religion must be a modest one and that she must "abandon metaphysics and deduction for criticism and induction." [16] When he attempts at the end of his description of religious experiences to draw some general conclusions about the truth of religion, however, the results seem rather meagre, though they are important as far as they go. For example, the religious man is conscious that the "higher part" of him "is conterminous and continuous with a *more* of the same quality, which is operative in the universe outside of him." This "more," James suggests, "is on its *hither* side the subconscious side of our conscious life." Moreover, we are "continuous with a wider self," through our communion with which "work is actually done upon our finite personality, for we are turned into new men." [17] In short, "God is real since he produces real effects." [18]

Thus, religious experience gives us an awareness not only of the divine "presence" but also of the divine "action." It produces "fruits" not only in elevated feeling but also in enthusiasm and incentive for heroic moral effort. One of the most characteristic things about James' Theism is his subordination of contemplation

[15] "The Will to Believe," 1, 2.
[16] *Varieties of Religious Experience*, 445.
[17] *Ibid.*, 505, 6.
[18] *Ibid.*, 507.

and enjoyment of God to active moral effort in co-operation with Him, of security and peace in union with Him to adventurous and ceaseless struggle by His side. This is the key to James' "meliorism." While optimism asserts that the world's salvation is inevitable and pessimism that it is impossible, "meliorism" holds that it is a possibility. Moreover, it is a possibility that depends for its attainment not only upon God but also upon each of us. While the "tender-minded" seek peace and security, the "tough-minded" can find zest and incentive in the knowledge that there is real risk of loss. Moreover, though there is no assurance that evil can be wholly overcome, men do not stand alone in their struggle against it but shoulder to shoulder with their fellows and with God.[19]

The further implications of this "meliorism" were developed in *A Pluralistic Universe*. James attacked traditional Theism as too "dualistic" and "monarchical" in its conception of God as wholly transcendent and remote from man. In contrast, Absolute Idealism restores the intimacy of God with man by virtually identifying them, but its logical argument for an absolute monism is unconvincing and it cannot do justice to the reality of error and evil. In opposition to both, James argues for the pluralistic view of God as a "superhuman consciousness" which has an external environment and consequently is finite. As such, He is not foreign to us, like the God of traditional Theism or "the static timeless perfect Absolute" of Idealism. He is in time and is working out a history like ourselves.[20]

In his anti-intellectualism, moralism, meliorism, and temporalism James is perhaps the best representative of America's moral robustness and optimism in the generation before the Age of Disillusionment dawned.

After James' death, his plea that religion break its alliance with Rationalism and follow the method of Empiricism was heeded beyond his expectations. Absolute Idealism seemed to disintegrate

[19] *Pragmatism*, ch. 8.
[20] *Ibid.*, 318.

after the first World War and by 1925 there were few outstanding Idealists left. Various types of Realism took its place. The new
"Empiricism" affected deeply the philosophy of religion of the
twenties and thirties. However, it took strikingly different forms,
since it was used by advocates of both Theism and Naturalism.
In several seminaries, theology came to be regarded as, in its basis,
an "empirical science"; and in more than one department of philosophy the empirical method was used to defend religious humanism. We shall consider each of these tendencies in turn.

The most outstanding champion of an empirical theology was
D. C. Macintosh of the Yale Divinity School. In 1919 Macintosh
published his *Theology as an Empirical Science* and in 1931 he
edited and contributed a long essay to a volume entitled *Religious
Realism*. The empirical method, he argued, must become "scientific" if it is to be effective. What is to be the nature of this
"theology as an empirical science"?

First, we must start with certain "presuppositions." The most
important of these is that God, the object of this science, exists.
Macintosh insists that this is not a dogmatic procedure, because
"on the basis of knowledge of God through religious experience,
one can scientifically assume *that* God is, although he may have
as yet very little knowledge as to *what* God is." Second, we must
analyze the "empirical data" of theology in order to distinguish
the "divine elements within human experience, the qualities or
events which are to be regarded as more immediate products of
the divine activity" and hence as "revelations" of God to us. Third,
we must seek to discover "theological laws" or "generalizations
as to what the divine Being does on the fulfilment of certain dis-
coverable conditions." [21] The method of attaining these "laws,"
which are based upon the postulate of the "dependableness" of
divine activity, is to start with hypotheses about God and His
activity and then to verify these experimentally by acting upon
them and attaining an "immediate awareness" of the reality of what
was supposed in the hypothesis. To the obvious objection that the

[21] *Theology as an Empirical Science*, 26.

following of certain religious experiences upon certain conditions merely provides the content of psychological laws rather than theological laws, Macintosh replies that according to his realistic theory of knowledge the antecedent cause of the experienced effects can be surely known to be an objective divine Reality.[22]

What is the nature of a "theological law"? It is a law describing the dependable working of God under suitable conditions. The practical importance of "theological laws" is that they give us the power to predict the results of right religious adjustments and thus provide a basis for evangelism and religious education. The religious reader is likely to find little that is new or startling in the examples of "theological laws" offered by Macintosh. For example, one of the "laws of the answer to prayer" is: "On condition of the right religious adjustment with reference to desired truly moral states of the will—God the Holy Spirit produces the specific moral results desired." [23] In view of the nature of these generalizations, one wonders whether they should be called "laws" in the strict scientific sense. Are they formulated exactly enough and can they be verified by every competent observer in such a way as to satisfy the requirements of the scientific method? Are they anything more than simple descriptions of the beginning and development of the Christian life? What assurance is there that, even if the satisfactory results occur, they are caused by "God the Holy Spirit"?

Finally, Macintosh holds that, on the basis of "theological laws" like these, "theological theory" can be developed. On the principle that the Object of religious experience must be such as to account for what It (or He) does, we can infer conclusions about God's attributes and His relation to the world. For example, God is "absolute" in the pragmatic sense of "absolute satisfactoriness as Object of religious dependence, absolute sufficiency for man's religious need." It should be noticed that "theological

[22] In *The Problem of Knowledge*, Macintosh had developed his theory of knowledge, which he termed *Critical Monism*.
[23] *Theology as an Empirical Science*, 48.

theory" consists of rational inferences from religious experiences and theological laws, so that it is not exclusively empirical. As such, it can hardly be regarded as part of "theology as an empirical science," which is thus seen to be very restricted in scope. Moreover, since the basic problems of "theological theory" must be solved by rational argument, the certainty which would end conflicting opinions in theology seems as far away as ever. In view of this, Macintosh's sanguine hope that his empirical method would "separate the gold of genuine religious truth from the dross of untenable dogma" seems unfounded. Actually, his own attempt to apply the scientific method in theology resulted only in a restatement and rationalization of the essentials of evangelical Liberal Protestantism.

The empirical method has also been used to defend the "Personalistic Idealism" which was first developed in America by Borden P. Bowne. Under the influence of Lotze and others, the Personalists broke with Absolute Idealism because it seemed to deny the reality and freedom of finite persons and to conceive of God in impersonal terms. During the last generation Edgar S. Brightman of Boston University has been the most influential advocate of this point of view.

Brightman writes as a philosopher of religion rather than a theologian. Philosophy of religion, he points out, makes use of the conclusions reached by the science of religion, but its own aim is to determine the validity of religious beliefs and to investigate the relation of religion to other aspects of experience. Its method must be empirical rather than rationalistic. This means that it must make a broad survey of religious experiences, develop hypotheses to explain them, and verify these hypotheses by an appeal to experience as a whole. It is at this last point particularly that his empiricism differs from that of Macintosh, for he does not believe that any hypothesis in philosophy can be verified by the experimental method of science. Rather, the test of the truth of any hypothesis is its coherence with all other propositions and with experience as a whole. The claims of religious knowledge that come from every source must, therefore, be arbitrated by reason according to the principle of coherence. Religious experience, intuition, and revelation may all be sources of religious knowledge, but reason is "the supreme source of religious insight." [24] Brightman insists that this appeal to reason and coherence is not a "defection from the empirical method," since "to demand coherence is to demand full attention to all the facts of experience, to neglect none." [25] An important implication of this is that no religious knowledge can be absolutely certain. New experiences will constantly be emerging; and other hypotheses for the interpretation of the facts will always be possible. But, though we must be content with probability rather than certainty, we can accept a "practical absolutism" since our most coherent hypotheses at least enable us to move towards further truth.

Brightman's conception of religion is value-centered. Religion is concern about experiences of value and devotion towards the power that originates, increases, and conserves these values. [26] The primary problem of the philosophy of religion, in view of the precariousness of values, is whether the relation of the universe to man's highest values is indifferent, hostile, or friendly. Brightman's answer to this question is that of Theism: man's values have their origin in the will of God whose purpose is to realize these values and who can be trusted to conserve them. For God is a Person in the sense of a rational will which is creative and purposeful. The evidences for such a personal God include the law and order of nature, the adaptation of means to ends and the presence of a directive force in evolution, the fact that value as a personal experience must have a personal source, and the trend towards monotheism in the history of religion.

The most interesting contribution of Brightman, however, is his argument for a finite God. God, he holds, is "genuinely limited within his own nature by 'Given' experiences eternally present,

[24] *A Philosophy of Religion*, 192.
[25] *Ibid.*, 192.
[26] *Ibid.*, 17.

which his will does not create, but which his will can control, no matter how refractory they may be." [27] He was led to this theory by reflection on the problem of evil. Much, if not all, moral evil can be explained in the traditional way as due to man's freedom of will. But the fact that man was not created so as to avoid moral evil while retaining his freedom cannot be explained that way. Moreover, natural evil is due, not to man, but to God the Creator. Now, the pervasiveness of evil, if it is avoidable, is not consistent with the goodness of God. Since the goodness of God must be maintained by the Theist above all else, we must assert that nature is "the work of a power which aims at ends and achieves them, and also that this power is working under great difficulties." [28]

Brightman shrinks from the theory of Plato that the limiting factor is outside of God, on the ground that this implies a complete dualism. Rather, the limiting factor is inside God; it is "The Given," the passive element, in His nature, which He did not create and which He is ever struggling to control and overcome. This theory, he argues, is not only more in accord with the facts than the traditional one, it is also in harmony with the religious experience of co-operation with God in the struggle against evil. Since it asserts the "perfectibility" rather than the "perfection" of God, it is similar to James' "melioristic" view. But it is dubious whether "The Given" inside God is not open to the same objection of dualism as Plato's "matter" outside Him and whether it does not imply that God is only potentially rather than actually perfect goodness.[29] The appeal of the doctrine, however, is shown by the fact that similar views have been offered in W. P. Montague's *Belief Unbound* and R. A. Tsanoff's *The Nature of Evil*.

The left-wing position in the philosophy of religion is "Naturalistic Humanism," i.e., religious Humanism based upon the philosophy of Naturalism. Religious Humanists, as E. A. Burtt

[27] *The Problem of God*, 10.
[28] *Ibid.*, 331.
[29] W. H. Werkmeister, *A History of Philosophical Ideas in America*, 339-341.

has pointed out,[30] felt that Protestant Modernists had not gone far enough in meeting the demands of modern science. The development of biology, psychology, and anthropology in the nineteenth century made it appear to them that there was no evidence for a cosmic mind and purpose supporting human values and that the universe was an impersonal system ruled by natural laws. The order of nature must be taken to include all reality, since there is no scientific verification of a supernatural or transcendental Reality. Thus, the only philosophy compatible with modern science, they thought, is Naturalism. Some of these philosophers, however, recognized that religion had been a powerful factor in human life, giving meaning to the lives of individuals and directing their energies to the service of social ends. Was it possible, therefore, to reinterpret religion in such a way that it would be compatible with Naturalism and thus enable it to continue serving useful ends? The history of religion suggested the way in which this could be done, by pointing out that religion had always involved a quest for fuller life.[31] Might it not be possible to drop beliefs and rites that rested upon supernaturalism so that religion could serve the same end of fuller life more directly and efficiently?

This way of thinking affected certain theological circles rather strongly in the twenties,[32] but it did not attain an adequate philosophical expression until John Dewey published *A Common Faith* in 1934. Dewey makes a distinction between "a religion," which includes definite beliefs, practices, and institutions, and the "religious attitude," which is simply an aspect of the experience of individuals. In effect, he argues that the latter can and should be separated from the former. The "religious attitude" is devotion to ideal ends that have been constructed by the imagination out of experienced values. Devotion to these ideal ends serves to integrate the self and to direct its energies to worthy social goals.

[30] *Types of Religious Philosophy*, ch. IX.
[31] See A. E. Haydon, *The Quest of the Ages*.
[32] E.g. E. S. Ames, *Religion*.

Unlike most naturalistic Humanists, Dewey makes a place for the term "God," using it to designate "all the natural forces and conditions—including man and human association—that promote the growth of the ideal and that further its realization." [33] This idea of an "active relation between ideal and actual," says Dewey, helps to overcome the lack of "natural piety" in militant atheism. For the religious attitude "needs the sense of a connection of man, in the way of both dependence and support, with the enveloping world that the imagination feels is a universe." [34]

Perhaps it is not unfair to say that Dewey is more interested in harnessing men's religious impulses to the service of ethical and social ideals than he is in religion itself. This is suggested by his insistence that devotion to a transcendental and eternal Reality drains away men's energies from the realization of ideal ends here and now. He believes that Humanism makes it possible to avoid dualism between the "secular" and the "sacred" and to see religious significance in such "secular" activities as science and politics. His chief contribution is not his positive conception of religion, which bears little relation to the facts of religion, but his sharp criticism of otherworldly religion and its reactionary attitude towards social change.

There is no doubt that A. N. Whitehead has been one of the most important philosophers during the last half century. He has probably had a greater influence on philosophy of religion than any other philosopher except William James. Several of his most important works bearing upon religion were published after coming to Harvard from England: *Science and the Modern World* (1925), *Religion in the Making* (1926), and *Process and Reality* (1929). Part of his influence upon the philosophy of religion has been due to his classic study of the implications of modern science in the first of these books, part to his development of a metaphysical system in the grand style in the last of them. His inter-

[33] *A Common Faith*, p. 50.
[34] *Ibid.*, p. 53.

pretation of the nature of religion and of Christianity in the second
of these works, though suggestive, is probably less significant.

Perhaps Whitehead's philosophy can be regarded most fruit-
fully as a modified and modernized form of Platonism. Plato ac-
counts for the actual world by postulating three primary factors:
an indeterminate "matter" capable of receiving forms; determinate
"forms" which are eternal and universal; and a divine "soul" or
"demiurge" who imposes "forms" upon "matter" and thus creates
an orderly and good cosmos. Similarly, in *Religion in the Making* Whitehead asserts that the "formative elements" that constitute the character of the actual world are three: "creativity"
or pure indeterminate activity; "ideal entities," "forms," or
"eternal objects" which are not actual but are exemplified in
everything actual; and the actual but nontemporal entity men call
"God" which transmutes the indeterminate creativity into "determinate freedom." [35] The similarity to Plato's analysis is obvious,
except that a dynamic factor "creativity" has taken the place of
"matter." This change radically alters Plato's point of view,
emphasizing the creative "process" by which novelty emerges in
the actual world.

Why is it necessary to postulate God as well as creativity and
ideal forms? In *Science and the Modern World* Whitehead tells
us that "every actual occasion is a limitation imposed on possibility" and that "every occasion is a synthesis of all eternal objects" and of "all occasions" in a particular gradation.[36] This is
made possible, on the one hand, by an "antecedent selection" of
an "actual course of events which might be otherwise so far as
concerns eternal possibility," [37] and, on the other hand, by an
"antecedent limitation among values." [38] "God" is the name of
this "principle of concretion" which determines the particular
actual occasions that shall grow together (con-crescere) out of the
boundless range of possibilities and the way each of them shall

[35] *Religion in the Making*, 90.
[36] *Ibid.*, 244, 5.
[37] *Ibid.*, 248.
[38] *Ibid.*, 249.

"prehend" or be related to all other actual occasions and ideal forms. It will be noted that this is essentially a form of the cosmological and teleological arguments for God. Though Whitehead does not rule out the possibility of further knowledge about God derived from "the region of particular experiences," i.e., religious experiences,[39] he seems to regard it as definitely secondary.

An interesting distinction is made between the "primordial nature" and the "consequent nature" of God. The "primordial nature" is His nature considered as the primordial limitation upon creativity which is the first condition for the definite character of the actual world. It is described as the "conceptual realization" or "envisagement" of the ideal "eternal objects" which orders or evaluates them. It is not only "evaluation," however, it is also "appetition" and this "involves the becoming of *some* temporal course of events." [40] There is an ambiguity here, since Whitehead speaks of God's "primordial nature" as an "accident" or "creature" of creativity. The distinction between creativity and God seems to be "merely a logical one," both being "complementary sides of the same thing," like the Father and the Logos in early Christian doctrine.[41]

The "consequent nature" of God, on the other hand, is the incoming of the order of "eternal objects" into the temporal course of events; it is God as immanent in the actual world. On Whitehead's view, God and the world need each other. God needs the world because His conceptual feelings become conscious in his "consequent nature"; the world needs God because He "holds the actual entities of the past as objectively immortal in the immediacy of His own nature" [42] and thus conserves the values realized in them. Thus, there is a mutual involvement of God and the world. But his view is not the pantheistic one which identifies God with the world as a whole. For there is evil in the world, and it is not grounded in God but in a lack of conformity of things with

[39] *Ibid.*, 250.
[40] Dorothy Emmet, *Whitehead's Philosophy of Organism*, 258.
[41] *Ibid.*, 258.
[42] *Ibid.*, 263.

His creative order. Evil is positive, since actual entities are not consistent but thwart one another. Hence, Whitehead rejects the optimistic view of Hegelian Idealism. At the same time, he holds that evil is unstable and ultimately self-destructive. There is an overcoming of evil through the development of an order that turns even evil facts to good account.

Religion is "world-loyalty." The purpose of the creative order is the attainment of value, especially aesthetic value. The process of becoming is characterized by a "subjective aim" towards satisfaction. The "subjective aim" of each individual seeks satisfaction, but when he realizes his place in the whole scheme of things and his responsibility towards it he seeks satisfaction in harmony with other individuals and the whole. Though in its primitive form religion is social, in its more developed and rational form it is primarily individual.[43] Dogmas are necessary as "clarifying modes of external expression" but "a dogma which fails to evoke any response in immediate apprehension stifles the religious life." [44] They are at best "bits of truth" which are "in effect untrue when carried over beyond the proper scope of their utility." [45]

It is difficult to determine the precise relation of Whitehead's philosophy of religion to Christian beliefs. It is clear, as we have said, that it is based upon the general character of the universe rather than upon an historical revelation. As such, it is silent with respect to Christian doctrines based upon faith in particular historical events, e.g., the Incarnation. The question, then, is whether his metaphysical conception of God and His relation to man is compatible with and can be supplemented by the Christian conception. The answer to this question will be determined partly by one's decision as to whether Whitehead's God is personal. Charles Hartshorne insists that it is. For Whitehead God is both conscious and individual, he says; He is the "personal order" of the universe, which is His body.[46] It would certainly seem that

[43] *Religion in the Making*, 47.
[44] *Ibid.*, 137.
[45] *Ibid.*, 145.
[46] P. A. Schilpp (ed.), *The Philosophy of Alfred North Whitehead*, 549.

an eternal actual entity that conceptually envisages and evaluates all possibilities would have to be analogous to human personality. But Whitehead does not say unambiguously that it is personal and his use of terms is so peculiar to himself that it is difficult to decide his full meaning. Certainly, his discussion of the matter in *Religion in the Making* suggests that he rejects the Christian conception of a personal and transcendent God. He argues that "religious experience does not include any direct intuition of a definite person or individual" and that reflective Indian and Chinese religious thought "disclaims the intuition of any ultimate personality substantial to the universe." [47] He adds that the "Semitic concept" of a personal God accepted by Christianity includes His absolute transcendence, whereas any proof of God that starts from the actual world leads to an immanent God.[48] Yet he approves of the stress upon the love of God in the Gospel of John and complains that the Church transformed the Gospel of love into a Gospel of fear. Does not love imply personality? Also, is not the view of God as ordering the world and transmuting its evil more compatible with a personal than an impersonal God? Yet he does not explicitly attribute personal character to God, perhaps because he wrongly assumes that it implies the complete transcendence of God and leads to a dualistic world view.

Whatever may be said about his conception of God, Whitehead's view of religion is inadequate from the Christian point of view. In his view, religion is largely individual and the indispensableness of the religious community is completely neglected. Moreover, it is based upon a conception of the meaning of the world that is more aesthetic than moral. As Kant "saw the necessity for God in the moral order," he says, his own metaphysics "finds the foundations of the world in the aesthetic experience." [49] Though "aesthetic experience" is a far broader term with him than it usually is, it stresses *feeling* rather than purposive *activity* as pri-

[47] *Religion in the Making,* 61, 62.
[48] *Ibid.,* 71.
[49] *Ibid.,* 104, 5.

mary, and religion as moral obedience to the will of a righteous God falls into the background or out of the picture altogether.

The great influence of Whitehead during the last twenty-five years is illustrated by the "Theistic Naturalism" of H. N. Wieman of the University of Chicago Divinity School. Wieman rejected the Naturalistic Humanism of Dewey and others because it minimized or overlooked the dependence of man for his values upon a cosmic principle and not merely upon his own efforts. At the same time, he was convinced that in the interest of truth a more radical reconstruction of traditional Theism was necessary than philosophical Idealists and theological Liberals had been willing to make. Therefore, he attempted to make a synthesis of Theism with the "higher" Naturalism which had been emerging in Whitehead and other thinkers.

In *The Wrestle of Religion with Truth*, published in 1927, he argued that true religion must be based upon a knowledge of and adaptation to reality, upon which man depends for his values. But most religion has been indifferent to truth and has even blinded itself with illusions in order to provide man with "a fairy realm where all is beautiful and happy." [50] Therefore, it is necessary to distinguish between the beliefs and practices of ordinary religion and the basic religious concepts implied in them. The popular *belief* about God in the churches is that He is "someone who will take care of you" i.e., it is an illusion due to wishful thinking. But the *concept* of God is quite different. "God is that character of events to which man must adjust himself in order to attain the highest goods and avoid the greatest evils." [51] Though we do not know fully the nature of this "behavior of the universe," we can discover more about it by living experimentally and observing carefully the results.

In his latest book, *The Source of Human Good*, published in 1946, Wieman develops further his "Theistic Naturalism" and

[50] *The Wrestle of Religion with Truth*, 2.
[51] *Ibid.*, 14.

shows its implications for the theory of value and for Christian doctrine. The "newer naturalism" differs from the older "reductive materialism," he asserts, in holding that "there is nothing in reality accessible to the human mind more basic than events and their qualities and relations." [52] This view is in accord with the Jewish-Christian tradition which "declares that the sovereign good works creatively in history" but it ignores "the transcendental affirmation in the Jewish-Christian tradition of a creative God who not only works in history but resides beyond history." [53] "The only creative God we recognize," says Wieman, "is the creative event itself." [54] As if to emphasize the naturalistic meaning of this assertion he adds that "the form of the creative event itself at our higher levels of existence is determined by the creative process at more elementary levels." [55] Thus, he denies completely every "transcendental reality." Significantly, he now rejects Whitehead's "identification" of God with "an inactive primordial order" and asserts that "the order or structure of the creative event is not imposed upon it but is intrinsic to the very nature of such an event." [56]

Wieman makes a sharp distinction between "created good," which is defined as "qualitative meaning," and "creative good," which is the source of qualitative meaning and which yields the best possible by transforming the mind and the world. God is this "source of human good." Man can do much to provide the conditions that release the full power of the "creative event," giving himself to its service above all "created goods," but he cannot do its work. He is always being tempted to make some "created good" an object of the absolute loyalty that should be given to its source, "creative good," as in modern nationalism or industrialism. "Creative good" is absolute in the sense that its goodness is not relative to human desire, its demands are unlimited, its

[52] *The Source of Human Good,* 6.
[53] *Ibid.,* 7.
[54] *Ibid.,* 7.
[55] *Ibid.,* 7, 8.
[56] *Ibid.,* 193.

worth is incommensurable with created good, and it is entirely trustworthy.[57] The religious life, on this view, consists in yielding to the process of creativity at work in each situation so that one's awareness of meanings is enlarged and unified and one's sense of community with other persons is deepened in a never-ending process.

In *The Source of Human Good* Wieman attempts to do justice to Christian doctrines, but he radically transforms them in the process. He attacks as "religious obstructionists" Christian thinkers who hold that God "transcends reason and cannot be observed" and that He transcends time. He rejects the Christian belief in the personal nature of God. He holds that the Christian faith began not with Jesus as such but with the domination of the "creative event" over the lives of his disciples under his influence. Since men need salvation in the sense of emancipation from idolatry of "created good" or human purpose, there is truth in the Christian idea that faith arises from despair of human effort. The "grace of God" is the "creative transformation become dominant in the life of man." [58] It is only in history, not eternity, that man's fulfillment must come. "History is the supreme achievement of the creative event," says Wieman.[59] "Whoever in despair appeals beyond history betrays the holy cause for which we fight, for here in time it must be lost or won." [60]

It seems obvious that, whatever may be said about the "religious availability" of Whitehead's God, Wieman's conception of God as the wholly immanent, impersonal, "creative event" that is the "source of human good" is not, from the Christian point of view, religiously adequate. However, it is greatly superior to the purely humanistic conception of Dewey and other Naturalists, because it springs from an understanding of the fact that man cannot save himself but must be saved by a cosmic creative principle. In addition, there is much insight in *The Source of*

[57] *Ibid.*, 79–81.
[58] *Ibid.*, 49.
[59] *Ibid.*, 307.
[60] *Ibid.*, 309.

Human Good about the spiritual life and the conditions of its growth. However, it is impossible to reconcile Christian Theism with philosophical Naturalism without doing violence to both, and it is significant that his attempt to synthesize them has satisfied comparatively few supporters of either point of view.

Whitehead's influence upon Charles Hartshorne of the Department of Philosophy at the University of Chicago has also been strong. But the results have been quite different. Hartshorne thinks that the new philosophy represented by Whitehead provides a better philosophical framework for theology than the Aristotelianism of St. Thomas Aquinas. In three books, *Beyond Humanism*, published in 1937, *Man's Vision of God*, published in 1941, and *The Divine Relativity*, published in 1948, he seeks to develop a theistic conception of God and His relation to the world which will be adequate to express the fundamental religious insight that God is love. Thus, while he does not appeal to revelation, he regards his conception as in harmony with Christianity and reserves his attacks for what he regards as the Aristotelian perversion of it by Aquinas.

The method he employs differs from the empiricism that has been so popular in recent American thinking about religion. The inductive method alone, he thinks, is not adequate in metaphysics. How, for example, could necessary being be dealt with by observation of and generalization from contingent beings? What is needed is a synthesis of the empirical and the rational or a priori methods. Therefore, much of Hartshorne's work consists of analysis of theological concepts such as "absolute," "perfection," and "power," undertaken in the hope of contributing to the philosophy of religion "logical rigor." On the other hand, he is not a rationalist in the traditional sense, because he holds that we must never deny any fundamental aspect of experience.

One of the main problems dealt with by Hartshorne is that of the perfection of God. In *Man's Vision of God* he points out that Anselm's definition of a "perfect being" as "that than which none greater can be conceived" has usually been taken to imply "absolute perfection in all respects." But there are other possible interpretations, the most important being that which attributes to God "absolute perfection in some respects, relative perfection in others." Hartshorne holds that this is a more adequate interpretation than the traditional one of Anselm. The traditional one regards God as immutable in all respects; but if He cannot change in any respect there can be no time and no possibility of decrease or increase in value for Him in relation to the world. Again, the traditional view implies omniscient or perfect knowledge in all respects; but this is logically hard to reconcile with the contingency of future events such as acts of free will. Further, the traditional view implies that God possesses perfect power or is omnipotent; but "even the greatest possible power (and that by definition is 'perfect' power) over individuals cannot leave them powerless, and hence even perfect power must leave something to others to decide." [61] "In their ultimate individuality," says Hartshorne, "things can only be influenced, they cannot be coerced." [62]

The traditional view of God's perfection as implying immutability, omniscience, and omnipotence is really based upon the Aristotelian conception of Him as transcendent to and unaffected by the world. To this conception Hartshorne opposes Whitehead's view that "all-existence is social" and that God as the highest and all-inclusive being is "social." Far from being "impassible," He feels all the joys and sorrows of all His creatures. In *The Divine Relativity* Hartshorne also attacks the Thomistic doctrine that God's relation to the world is not a "real" relation to Him and that He is "absolute" in the sense of "independent" of His creatures. God says Hartshorne, is "absolute" in one aspect of His being but "relative" in the sense of related to and affected by everything in the world. He is characterized by a "sympathetic dependence" on the world, His sympathy being "exactly colored by every nuance of joy or sorrow anywhere in

[61] *Man's Vision of God*, 14.
[62] *Ibid.*, xvi.

the world." [63] Moreover, God's glory is not so absolute that we cannot contribute to His greatness or value. God is not only the "supreme source" but also the "supreme beneficiary or recipient" of all achievement.

This "social" doctrine of God seems to verge on a pantheistic identification of God with the world, but Hartshorne insists that God is personal and that His essence does not require the actual totality of things. However, since God is relative to all, He has nothing outside Himself. Therefore, Hartshorne asserts the doctrine of "panentheism," "the view that deity is in some real aspect [64] distinguishable from and independent of any and all relative items, and yet, taken as an actual whole, includes all items." [65]

Whatever may be thought of Hartshorne's ideas, they show the fruitfulness of Whitehead's metaphysics when it is used for the purposes of a Theism that is fundamentally Christian.

As one reflects upon these different types of American religious thought, the first thing that strikes him is the tendency to interpret religion as primarily an *individual* rather than a social thing. Lacking a vivid sense of the power of religious institutions to awaken and deepen the religion of individuals and estranged by the rigidity and narrowness of many Protestant churches, many American philosophers have preferred to sit loose to the Church, its corporate worship and its traditional creeds. In his *Varieties of Religious Experience* at the beginning of the century, James admitted his lack of interest in the social forms of religious experience. He was influenced by his interest in extreme rather than ordinary cases of religion but also by his individualistic idea that the religion of average churchgoers is second-hand and conventional. Though Royce stressed the "beloved community," as we saw, it was distinguished by him from all visible, actual churches as an ideal community which was still to be created by the loyalty

[63] *The Divine Relativity*, 48.
[64] That is, in its absolute aspect.
[65] *The Divine Relativity*, 90.

of men. Whitehead gave the most striking expression to the individualistic view of religion when he said that "religion is what a man does with his solitariness," and Wieman's thought has always shown more of a negative than a positive relation to the Church. As a result, many recent American philosophers of religion in their thinking have seemed remote from and irrelevant to the religious life of the Church and have written mainly for a minority of intellectuals on the fringe or outside of it. Among the most outstanding exceptions have been Hocking, Macintosh, Brightman, and Pratt.

In the second place, the philosophy of religion has usually been conceived during the last half-century as *impartial* between the conflicting claims of historical faiths, examining religious phenomena provided by the history and psychology of religion in an objective fashion and maintaining a complete independence of special revelation. This has enabled the philosophy of religion to take account of varieties of religious experience and belief little known to the ordinary churchgoer and in this way to broaden the popular conception of religion. Several philosophers have made substantial contributions of their own to the history and psychology of religion, e.g., James, Hocking, and J. B. Pratt.[66] One of the beneficial effects of this enlargement of the religious horizon is the growing realization of the virtual universality of religion. Many have come to see that the most convincing ground for belief in God is the actual experience of Him, though the diversity of religious beliefs held by men in history may make it more difficult to reach complete agreement as to the right interpretation of the religious experience.

But this "neutrality" of the philosophy of religion has tended to weaken its interest in and contact with Christian theology and philosophy. In the case of many, philosophy of religion has become an enemy rather than an ally of the special revelation and

---

[66] Pratt's *The Religious Consciousness* is still one of the best books on psychology of religion and *The Pilgrimage of Buddhism* is perhaps the most interesting book in English on the development of Buddhism.

doctrines of Christianity. Consequently, it has weakened Christian theology and philosophy by depriving them of the sympathetic but critical thinking of some of the ablest minds of the last generation. It is significant that Royce's *The Problem of Christianity* in 1913 was the last careful attempt of an outstanding philosopher in America to make a philosophical examination of Christianity as a whole. Also, by detaching itself from the Christian revelation and theology, American philosophy has more and more impoverished itself. Attracting the interest of almost all outstanding American philosophers until the first World War, religion has lost its appeal to most philosophers of our generation. Some of the most distinguished philosophers of today, especially Naturalists and Logical Positivists, have paid no attention whatever to it. Moreover, as interest in the problems of religion has declined, concern for the closely related problems of metaphysics has languished and the problems of logic, epistemology, semantics, and social philosophy have taken their place.

In the third place, the philosophy of religion of the last half century has been fundamentally *anthropocentric* rather than theocentric. J. B. Pratt has pointed out in his posthumous book, *Eternal Values in Religion*, that Protestant worship tends to be primarily "subjective" rather than "objective," aiming at beneficial results in the life of the worshipper rather than the glory of God. Similarly, Protestant philosophers of religion have been concerned above all with "the meaning of God in human experience," "religious values," and "the source of human good." Their thinking has been value-centered rather than God-centered. In an essay in the volume *Religious Realism*, Richard Niebuhr pointed out that the religious Realism which had followed the collapse of Idealism, though it stressed the knowledge of God as an objective reality, was itself infected with the spirit of subjectivism and humanism. "Hence it tends," he said, "to define religion in terms of adjustment to divine reality for the sake of gaining power rather than in terms of revelation which subjects the recipient to the criticism of that which is revealed," with the result that "man remains the center of religion and God is his aid rather than his judge and redeemer." [67] Doubtless, this has been due partly to preoccupation with the new philosophy of value but it has also resulted from the complete substitution of general religious experience for the special revelation of historical religion as the source of religious knowledge. It has encouraged the idea that religion is oriented towards God primarily because He is the source and conserver of human good. The Naturalistic Humanism of Dewey simply carried anthropocentric religion to the extreme when it insisted that religion should substitute devotion to ideal human ends for faith in God.

Because of these weaknesses of individualism, neutrality, and anthropocentrism, the theological seminaries have tended to neglect philosophy of religion during the last fifteen years. Absorbed with the theological struggle between Liberalism and Neo-Orthodoxy, the keenest minds in the seminaries have depreciated the philosophical approach to religion. The fact that the indifference of most philosophers to religion has been met by the hostility of many theologians to philosophy is one of the most striking signs of the cleavage between reason and faith in our day.

In this situation two things are needed. One is a recognition by *philosophers* that the neutral, objective approach of *philosophy of religion* to the problems of religion, though useful, is limited in its sphere and function. It can broaden men's knowledge of religion and help them to see its place in experience as a whole, but it cannot take the place of commitment to a definite faith without impoverishing the religious life. Therefore, philosophers who have a strong Christian faith cannot and should not pretend that they are neutral, starting their investigation of religion without presuppositions. They should start with their faith and seek to develop its implications in a *Christian philosophy*. They have every right to do so because God has given them faith to illuminate their reason and reason to understand their faith and to interpret the

[67] *Religious Realism*, D. C. Macintosh (ed.), 425, 6.

world in the light of it. In the process of doing this, they should be ready to use philosophical insights from any source whatever but with a clear realization that any philosophy such as Absolute Idealism or Naturalism whose presuppositions and categories are unchristian must be used only in a very guarded way.

The other thing that is needed is that *theologians* should become more rather than less philosophical in order that they may perform the task of *Christian apologetics* more effectively, especially among philosophers who are contemptuous of religion in general and Christianity in particular. The philosophy of religion of the last fifty years has been living off religious capital accumulated by Christians in the past. As that capital has become exhausted, philosophy of religion has become impoverished and has almost lost its influence. Philosophy of religion will flourish again in America only as a revitalized Christian community produces more Christians and encourages them to become Christian philosophers or Christian philosophical theologians. For deep interest in religion in *general* springs from a religious experience which is *particular*.

BIBLIOGRAPHY

Boodin, J. E., *God* (New York, 1934)

Bowne, Borden P., *Personalism* (Boston, 1908)

Brightman, E. S., *The Problem of God* (New York, 1930)

Dewey, John, *A Common Faith* (New Haven, 1934)

Hartshorne, Charles, *Man's Vision of God* (Chicago, 1941)

Hocking, W. E., *The Meaning of God in Religious Experience* (New Haven, 1912)

James, William, *The Varieties of Religious Experience* (New York, 1902)

Lyman, E. W., *The Meaning and Truth of Religion* (New York, 1933)

Macintosh, D. C. (editor), *Religious Realism* (New York, 1931)

Royce, J., *The Problem of Christianity*, Vols. I, II (New York, 1913)

Whitehead, A. N., *Religion in the Making* (New York, 1926)

Wieman, H. N., *The Source of Human Good* (Chicago, 1947)

SYSTEMATIC THEOLOGY

Walter M. Horton

WALTER MARSHALL HORTON was born in 1895 in Massachusetts. After taking his A.B. at Harvard in 1917 and his theological work at Union Theological Seminary, he studied in Paris, Strasbourg and Marburg, taking his doctorate at Columbia University in 1926. After serving as instructor in Philosophy of Religion and Systematic Theology at Union for three years, he became *Fairchild* Professor of Theology in Oberlin Graduate School of Theology in 1925. He has been actively engaged both in travel and study for the ecumenical movement, serving as consultant at the Oxford, Madras, and Amsterdam World Conferences. He was also attached to the Study Department of the World Council of Churches at its central office in Geneva, Switzerland, during the year 1947. He has traveled extensively in India, China, Japan, Australasia, South America, and Europe, and he is the author of many important books both in systematic theology and the relevance of Christianity to contemporary culture. His latest volume is *Toward a Reborn Church*.

V

Systematic Theology in America has gone through three main periods in the last half-century: (1) a period of growing *liberalism*, roughly from 1900 to 1920; (2) a period of sharp controversy and revolutionary realignment, between 1920 and 1935; (3) a period of constructive restatement, since 1935.

1. Liberalism, 1900–1920

To understand the American theological situation in the early years of the twentieth century, it is necessary to remember that *Calvinism modified by the influence of revivalism* was the leading tradition in American Protestantism; that the New England Theology, uniting Calvinism and revivalism in a rationally coherent and defensible system, had lingered on in many theological schools until late in the nineteenth century, when it suddenly and completely went to pieces; that the idealistic liberalism of Horace Bushnell and his successors, dating from the middle of the nineteenth century, had proved able to cope with the new problems posed by natural science, Biblical criticism and the new social conscience, as the New England Theology was unable to do; finally, that while conservative Calvinism survived in a pretty vigorous form at Princeton Theological Seminary and elsewhere, it was consciously on the defensive. The prevailing trend in theology continued to get more and more liberal until shortly after the close of the First World War. Conservative theologians felt themselves to be in a state of siege, with insurgent bands of liberals rising up and marching against them from every quarter. Let us examine this situation more in detail.

Of the historic types of Protestantism, there can be no doubt which has done most to shape theological thought in America: *Calvinism*. Anglicanism and Lutheranism have been relatively small minority movements, the one long associated with the

British Crown—hardly a recommendation after the Revolution!—
while the other was largely confined to German and Scandinavian
immigrant groups, isolated from other Protestants by barriers
of language and culture.[1] The American tradition is thus mainly
conditioned by the two remaining forms of original Protestantism:
the Calvinist and the Anabaptist or sectarian. No other country
has been so deeply affected by radical sectarianism; but *Calvinism
is the traditional theology of many sectarian bodies.* The *Westminster Confession* was formally accepted by Congregationalists
as well as by Presbyterians, while the Calvinistic Baptists have generally outnumbered their theological rivals in that most numerous
of all American denominations. Wherever American theology remains conservative, the outlines of the Calvinistic system can
clearly be descried. This is true of the two conservative textbooks of systematic theology which were most influential in the
opening years of this century, and are still widely used: *Outlines
of Theology* by A. A. Hodge of Princeton (Presbyterian) and
Systematic Theology [2] by A. H. Strong of Rochester (Baptist).

By 1900, the Calvinistic tradition in American theology was
already seriously impaired. The New England Theology of
Jonathan Edwards and his school had given Calvinism new vigor
and new relevance by infusing into it the spirit of the Great
Awakening and making it the favorite vehicle of revivalistic
preaching. If in the hands of the later Edwardians the position
tended to gravitate from Calvinism toward Arminianism, that
made possible a friendly alliance between these "New School"
Calvinists and the Methodist Arminians who were their principal
partners in the evangelization of the western frontier. So long
as the winning of the West was Protestantism's main concern, this
Calvinist-Arminian alliance held firm. But with the passing of the

[1] *The Resurgence of the Gospel,* by T. A. Kantonen (Philadelphia, 1948),
may be taken as evidence that Lutheran thought is now entering the main
stream of American theology, and will make important contributions henceforth. The immense influence of Archbishop Temple's theology in recent
years is the best proof that the same can now be said of Anglican thought.

[2] Conveniently streamlined in his *Outlines of Systematic Theology,* New
York, 1908.

frontier and the rise of grave intellectual problems concerning the authority of the Bible and the implications of Darwinian evolution, it became evident that New England evangelical Calvinism was played out. F. H. Foster remarks that in 1880 the chairs of theology at all the Congregational and some of the Presbyterian seminaries were occupied by adherents of the New England school, and fifteen years later every one had been filled by some one of an entirely different temper. "As it were, in a night," he says, the New England Theology "perished from off the face of the earth" [3]—a most serious break in our one strong link with the Protestant Reformation. If Calvinism survived this break, as it did at Princeton and other conservative schools, it was no longer the aggressive, forward-looking Calvinism of Edwards and Finney, but a defensive, armor-clad system, beset with "fightings and fears, within, without."

What replaced Calvinism in the early twentieth century as the leading American theological tradition was a liberal theology derived from German philosophical idealism—Kant, Schleiermacher, Hegel, Ritschl, Lotze, Troeltsch. In Germany, the idealistic movement was strongly polarized into opposite trends: a mystical, metaphysical trend leaning toward pantheism (Schleiermacher, Hegel, Lotze) and an ethical, social trend leaning toward positivism or humanism (Kant, Ritschl, Troeltsch). In America, as in England, both of these extreme antithetical trends were strongly resisted, by philosophers and theologians alike. At the very beginning of the liberal movement, there were philosophers like Emerson and theologians like Parker, who followed the mystical-metaphysical trend to the verge of pantheism. At the very end, there were philosophers like Dewey and theologians like G. B. Smith and Shailer Mathews who followed the ethical-social trend to the verge of humanism. But far more typical were evangelical liberals such as Bushnell, Bowne, George A. Gordon, Henry Churchill King, William Newton Clarke, William Adams

[3] F. H. Foster, *History of the New England Theology*, p. 543 (Chicago, 1907).

Brown, and Walter Rauschenbusch, who felt the influence of both opposing trends in German thought, and held a fair balance between them. Of all the German idealists, the most generally influential in the early twentieth century were Schleiermacher (his appeal to Christian experience, not his pantheism), Lotze (interpreted as a personal theist by Bowne, King and many others), and Ritschl (whose ethical theism became a principal source of the Social Gospel Movement).

It would be a mistake to suppose that American liberal theology was simply German idealistic philosophy in an American dress. William DeWitt Hyde did, it is true, remark that "metaphysics must be the Alpha, and ethics the Omega, of any theology which is rooted in reason and fruitful in life"; [4] and there was a marked tendency throughout the liberal period for philosophy of religion to get more attention and enjoy more prestige than systematic theology. Yet the two most influential textbooks of liberal theology, Clarke's *Outline* (1898) and Brown's (1906) were Biblical in substance and evangelical in spirit. Clarke went through a long personal struggle to overcome verbal literalism in his use of the Bible,[5] and at length came to the conclusion that systematic theology had a right to seek its sources "anywhere"; [6] but *the Bible centered in Christ* actually remained his principal source, with *evangelical Christian experience* as an almost equally important source. Brown, who at first used Clarke's *Outline* in his teaching, finally decided it needed rewriting because it "included almost no historical material" and "omitted the Church altogether." [7] In Brown's revised version, the Clarke-Brown system contained many of the original definitions slightly modified (as Ritschl often quotes and alters Schleiermacher's definitions) but

---

[4] *Outlines of Social Theology* (New York, 1895), Preface. Examination of the book reveals that all its contents can be deduced from the Hegelian-Lotzean conception of an Absolute Mind or Supreme Person manifested in the world, the self, and the social order.

[5] See his *Sixty Years with the Bible* (New York, 1909); cf. *The Use of the Scriptures in Theology* (1905).

[6] *Outline of Christian Theology*, p. 10.

[7] Brown, *A Teacher and His Times*, p. 109 (New York, 1940).

the whole effect was much more traditional and churchly, expressing Brown's life-long conviction that "underneath all differences of theological expression, there is a common gospel which makes the Church, in fact, one." [8] Brown was a "critical idealist" in philosophy, but his systematic theology was no mere deduction from idealism; it sprang from a conception of the "common Gospel" which had deep historical roots and wide ecumenical sympathies.

Clarke and Brown have had no real successors as systematic liberal theologians. Dr. A. C. Knudson's two volumes on *The Doctrine of God* (1930) and *The Doctrine of Redemption* (1933) together constitute a system, unmistakably liberal, based on Bowne's personalistic philosophy fused with Biblical concepts and evangelical convictions. But these two volumes have never achieved anything like the wide currency of Clarke and Brown; and they came too late, when liberalism was already on the defensive against neo-orthodoxy. During the period of liberal ascendency, theological books were mostly "programmistic" rather than systematic, developing special points of view and proposing specific theological reforms. The most comprehensive of these programs of theological reform was that proposed in Henry Churchill King's *Reconstruction in Theology* (1901). King summarized the new influences shaping theology at the turn of the century in a way that won wide assent: evolutionary natural science, Biblical criticism, and the new ethical-social conscience, with its dual emphasis on the sacredness of the person and his social responsibility. The battle over the first two of these influences had already been fought and won, as is evident from the calmness and maturity of King's treatment of these topics; in the third, he knew he was pioneering. Throughout the first two decades of this century, the new social conscience expressed in the Social Gospel Movement was the most active formative force in liberal theology. Landmarks in this development were King's *Theology and the Social Consciousness* (1902), Gerald Birney

[8] *Ibid.*

Smith's *Social Idealism and the Changing Theology* (Taylor Lectures for 1912) and finally Rauschenbusch's *Theology for the Social Gospel* (1918).

The Social Gospel, with its hope of Christianizing the social order and building the Kingdom of God on earth, was the main positive message of American liberalism at its height, before and during the First World War. In Rauschenbusch himself, and in many others, it was combined with a message of personal redemption [9] derived from evangelical Protestantism; in some of the more radical members of the school, particularly those influenced by Chicago pragmatism, it tended to displace both evangelical religion and idealistic metaphysics, preparing a purely humanistic interpretation of Christianity. Between the continuing Calvinists, the idealistic liberals, and these radical humanitarians, there were deep theological chasms. How matters stood between theological conservatives, liberals and radicals at this period may fairly be judged from a symposium on "The Task and Method of Systematic Theology" in the *American Journal of Theology*, Vol. XIV (1910), in which Warfield of Princeton, Brown of Union and G. B. Smith of Chicago represented the three parties.

Warfield defines the task of systematic theology as the systematic formulation of the results of exegetical theology, which gives us perfect knowledge of God (*i.e.,* God's own verbally documented self-revelation) in its *disjecta membra*, needing only to be logically ordered. Brown distinguishes three main tasks: to define and expound the Christian religion, to establish its supreme value, and to rise through the appreciation of its value to belief and trust in the divine Cause and Source of that value—the third being a task which Ritschl and the pragmatists seek to avoid, but which Brown thinks inescapable. G. B. Smith, in terms reminiscent of Troeltsch, defines theology's task as the confrontation of our historic religious heritage with present religious needs, in such a way as to suggest convictions that are pragmatically efficient

---

[9] See *Theology for the Social Gospel*, Chap. X, "The Social Gospel and Personal Salvation."

and apologetically defensible. Such convictions are frankly relativistic, can claim no divine authority, and are not guaranteed to be Christian; but if Christianity can continue to meet modern needs out of its historic traditions, it will survive. It is evident that Warfield's and Smith's conceptions of theology were poles apart, and controversy between them was bound to break out; but between Brown's constructive idealism and Smith's relativistic pragmatism there was also deep tension. Liberalism was not inwardly self-consistent, and might easily become disunited—as in fact it did, between 1920 and 1935.

II. Controversy and Realignment, 1920–1935

We have set 1920, not 1914, as the end of the supremacy of idealistic liberalism, and the opening of a new period of theological controversy and theological realignment. The spirit of idealism, of liberalism, of social optimism, was very marked in America during the fighting of the First World War. It was afterward, when the liberal aims for which the war was allegedly fought were rudely frustrated, that reaction set in, and a series of controversies began which eventually proved fatal to liberal theology in its earlier form.

The first of these was the *fundamentalist* controversy (1920–1925). Fundamentalism as a widespread movement dates back to 1910, when interdenominational conferences began to be held and booklets on *The Fundamentals* began to be issued. But it was soon after the First World War that the fundamentalists took the offensive, and began to challenge "modernists" as wolves in sheep's clothing, who must not be allowed to get into the Christian fold. Candidates for ordination in the Presbyterian, Baptist, and other denominations were certain in those years to be asked whether they believed in the verbal inerrancy of the Scriptures, the Virgin Birth and bodily resurrection of Christ, the blood atonement, and all other distinctly supernatural elements in Christian teaching. Attempts were made to get whole denominations to subscribe to the new list of Fundamentals, and anti-evolution bills were passed and enforced in several states. Many candidates were refused ordination, and many liberal preachers (notably Dr. Harry Emerson Fosdick) were made the objects of violent "smear" attacks; but no major denomination accepted the fundamentalist creed, and the Bryan-Darrow debate over evolution at Dayton, Tennessee (1925), tended to discredit fundamentalism and put an end to its aggressive influence.

There were discerning critiques of liberalism in some of the fundamentalist writings, which ought to have been taken to heart by the liberals. Machen in his *Christianity and Liberalism* (1923) vigorously protested against the defective sense of sin and the excessive optimism of most liberal theology. E. Y. Mullins in his *Christianity at the Crossroads* (1924) pointed out the tendency of liberal theology to "reduce" the unique, supernatural elements in Christianity—the divinely revealed Scriptures, the unique and heaven-sent Savior—by including them in a rational scheme with other sacred books and other religious leaders. The *reductio ad absurdum* of this reductive trend would be materialism, which reduces the spiritual to the biological, and the biological to the physico-chemical.[10] To all these warnings, the liberals turned a deaf ear, because these true contentions were mixed with exaggerated charges, plainly untrue, and because the attack upon evolution seemed to prove that the whole fundamentalist movement was "pre-scientific" and "obscurantist" in its outlook. It was only when the humanists attacked the liberals from the opposite quarter, charging them with timidity and half-heartedness in carrying out their own logic, that the liberals were able to feel the force of some objections already made by the fundamentalists.

To understand the *humanist* controversy (1925–1930), consider its economic and social background. Until the Wall Street crash started the depression in 1929, Americans enjoyed a period of unparalleled prosperity and social optimism. It seemed to many

---

[10] It is a question whether Mullins should be called a fundamentalist. His theological system, *The Christian Religion in Its Doctrinal Expression* (New York, 1917), might be described as "modern-positive," like the writings of P. T. Forsyth.

that science, technology and industrialism had at last solved the problem of human welfare, without the aid of any supernatural force whatsoever. If religion was to survive in this new age of ever-expanding prosperity, it was argued that it should drop all supernaturalistic terms, all words like "salvation," redolent of a "pain economy" now happily superseded by a "pleasure economy," and redefine its function positively, humanistically, as "the shared quest of the good life." [11] Instead of trying to reconcile ancient scriptures with modern knowledge in some illogical liberal compromise, religion should boldly and unreservedly put its trust in modern science and modern social idealism, as all-sufficient guides to faith and morals. All this was said with sublime confidence, just when our ephemeral prosperity began to crack beneath our feet, and the abyss of cosmic tragedy began to open up, just two steps ahead! [12] Faced by this startling contradiction between the claims of humanism and the actual course of events, liberals as a group stoutly refused to exchange God for man as their final object of trust, or to abandon the Bible for science as their final source of guidance. In attacking the pretensions of humanism, they recoiled from scientism to the very verge of accepting Biblical revelation; and rejected man-worship so decisively that God's sovereignty loomed up commandingly in their theology. Whatever led toward humanism in their previous thinking, they now heartily repudiated.[13]

In the early years of the great economic depression (1930–1935), many books sharply critical of liberalism and newly appreciative of European neo-orthodoxy began to appear: Walter Lowrie's *Our Concern with the Theology of Crisis* (1932), Edwin

[11] Cf. A. E. Haydon, *The Quest of the Ages* (New York, 1929); cf. C. F. Potter, *Humanism: a New Religion* (New York, 1930).

[12] Cf. Beard's Symposium, *Whither Mankind?* (New York, 1928) with its amazing confidence that our civilization, at last, had found the formula for everlasting expansion.

[13] The reasons for this shift are best stated in Harry Emerson Fosdick's sermon, "Beyond Modernism" (*Christian Century*, 1935). "The watchword will not be, Accommodate yourself to the prevailing culture! but, Stand out from it and challenge it!—we cannot harmonize Christ himself with modern culture."

Lewis's *Christian Manifesto* (1934) and G. W. Richard's *Beyond Fundamentalism and Modernism* (1934). The names of Barth and Brunner, regarded with indifference heretofore, became names to conjure with. Few indeed became their full followers; but their criticisms of liberal theology were widely acknowledged to be sound, and their renewed emphasis upon scriptural revelation and divine sovereignty found favor in many minds. Some preferred the moderate British way of going orthodox (Forsyth, Oman, Temple) to the violent Continental way. Some were influenced by the neo-Thomism of Maritain or the revised Eastern Orthodoxy of Bulgakov and Berdyaev. Piper of Princeton and Tillich of Union, exiled allies and critics of Barth and Brunner, won a considerable following through their continued residence and teaching in this country. But most important of all the influences that turned us about during these five crucial years was no voice from overseas, but a prophetic voice in our midst: that of Reinhold Niebuhr. His *Moral Man and Immoral Society* (New York, 1932) played the same part in America which Barth's *Römerbrief* played on the Continent and Dean Inge's criticism of the idea of Progress played in Britain; it showed that the hope of a Kingdom of God on earth was not immediately realizable by human efforts.

The recoil from humanism did not lead at once to a new constructive effort in theology, but only to a realignment of theological forces, and a general willingness to move in new directions, if a promising lead should be given. By "realignment" we mean the formation of a strong central bloc, opposed to humanism on the left and fundamentalism on the right, in which repentant liberals and moderate conservatives were temporarily united. The slogan under which this variegated host began to rally was *"Realism"*— a broad term covering a multitude of differences, some of them irreconcilable, but still indicating a general orientation. Negatively, the term indicated a sharp decline in the prestige of *idealism*, which had formed the philosophical basis of liberal theology since the time of Bushnell. Personal idealism of the Bowne tradition did retain its vigor, but its ablest representative, E. S. Brightman of

Boston University, took the element of evil in the cosmic process with new seriousness, in his doctrine of "The Given." [14] Evil, matter, "irreducible and stubborn facts" of all kinds, tended to be more emphasized than ideas and ideals. Positively, realism pointed out beyond the self and its subjectivity, beyond humanity and its hopes, beyond the changing processes of nature, to some deep objective Ground of faith and hope, too deep to be shaken by the earthquakes that shatter the dreams of idealists.[15]

How to reach this Ground? By faith in Biblical revelation, said the followers of Barth and Brunner. By mystical intuition, rationally tested, said Rufus Jones and Eugene Lyman. By scientific screening of religious experience, said Macintosh of Yale and Wieman of Chicago, so as to isolate the divine "Dependable Factor" from all subjective and relative factors, and learn the objective conditions upon which human good and human redemption really hang. All these varieties of realism, and more, were included in the Macintosh symposium on *Religious Realism* (1931), the best source-book for the realistic movement in its early phases. It was Professor Macintosh's hope, when the book was published, that these various methods of escape from subjectivism and anthropocentrism might be held together in a sort of three-story theology, beginning on the ground floor with strict scientific theism, such as he had outlined in *Theology as an Empirical Science* (1919), and working up to rational faith and speculative surmise on the upper floors. This hope was frustrated shortly afterward, when Wieman, in a three-cornered debate [16] with Macintosh and Max Otto, a humanist, flatly refused to use any method but scientific empiricism; while those who felt the influence of Barth and

[14] *The Problem of God* (New York, 1930); *The Finding of God* (New York, 1931).

[15] *Cf.* the analysis of the various meanings of "realism" in my *Realistic Theology* (New York, 1934). See also *Christian Realism in Contemporary American Theology,* by George Hammar (Uppsala, 1940). The "provisional realism" of A. N. Whitehead was an immensely important factor in the philosophical revolution which underlay this whole theological realignment; but the influence of political events was still more basic. See also *Man as a Sinner in American Realistic Theology* by Mary Frances Thelen (New York, 1946).

[16] Macintosh, Wieman, Otto, *Is There a God?* (Chicago, 1932).

Brunner presently renounced the empirical method altogether. The realistic united front thus tended to break up as a theological reconstruction began; but the common impulse toward objectivism and theocentrism continued in the ensuing period.

Credit should be given to Macintosh and Wieman for first presenting a persuasive alternative to humanism, in terms which appealed widely to former liberals, and opened the way for them to an objective super-human Ground of trust and faith. At Chicago Divinity School, where the pragmatic theology of G. B. Smith and E. S. Ames was unable to cope with the humanism of Haydon,[17] Wieman's empirical theism really overcame humanism and started a new era. Shailer Mathews adopted the new approach in his *Growth of the Idea of God* (1931) and was hailed by Macintosh as a fellow-realist. While Niebuhr led the negative attack on "utopian idealism," it was Macintosh and Wieman who first gave a positive realistic orientation to American Protestant theology. "Wieman was my Barth," said Charles Clayton Morrison, and others could say the same. If many of Wieman's followers (including Morrison) later turned against him, they ought never to forget that he "kept the bridge" for them at a most critical moment—the bridge they all passed over, from idealistic or pragmatic subjectivism to realistic objectivism.

III. Constructive Restatement, 1935–1950

Since the realignment of 1930–1935, American theology has gradually gathered strength for new constructive endeavors. Fifteen years of world chaos, world war, and world leadership have provided plenty of stimulus for such endeavors. A stunned and reeling world has been reaching out desperately for something to cling to, and if an orderly, constructive credo is not available, will clutch blindly at straws. So far, only constructive *trends* have manifested themselves; but a period of constructive *system-building* seems to be at hand.

[17] Cf. the feebly concessive essay in Smith's *Current Christian Thinking*, Chapter IX (Chicago, 1928).

To chart the theological trends of the last fifteen years, we may take our departure from a series of articles published in the *Christian Century* during 1939: "How My Mind Has Changed in the Last Decade." When this series is compared with two other series— its direct sequel in the *Christian Century* ten years later, and a somewhat similar autobiographical collection issued six or seven years earlier [18]—the trend of thought stands out pretty clearly. The first of the three series, though it appeared in the midst of the revolution of 1930–1935, shows little evidence of what was going on, and reflects the checkered variety of American theology at the end of the liberal era. The contrast between fundamentalism (Machen) and modernism (William Adams Brown) still seemed more important than any other. Henry Nelson Wieman was perfectly clear in his conviction that "we are in the midst of an enormous revolution in all our thinking"; and he announced his intention "to promote a theocentric religion as over against the prevalent anthropocentric"; [19] but only a few of his twenty-two collaborators yet saw the necessity and importance of this realistic shift. [20] By 1939, on the eve of World War II, our most representative religious thinkers had almost all made the shift, but were beginning to be divided into two sharply contrasting schools of realism: neo-naturalism led by Wieman and neo-supernaturalism led by Reinhold Niebuhr, who had suddenly stepped forth in *Beyond Tragedy* (1937) as a great constructive theologian. No such dramatic shift occurred between 1939 and 1949, in spite of the terrific events that crowded those years. The second series on "How My Mind Has Changed" turned out to be far less revolutionary than the first. What did occur during the war years, however, was a resurgence of liberalism in a modified form, dividing the neo-supernaturalists into a neo-orthodox and a neo-liberal wing. Three sorts of realism thus emerged.

[18] *Contemporary Theology:* Theological Autobiographies, edited by Vergilius Ferm. First series (New York, 1932). Second series, 1933.

[19] *Op. cit.,* Vol. I, pp. 344, 346.

[20] Eugene W. Lyman (Vol. II, p. 119) does speak of "the reaction against subjectivism which has been taking place in many fields of thought." Niebuhr does not appear in the symposium; no one then thought of him as a theologian.

The contrast between neo-naturalism and neo-supernaturalism was beginning to appear by 1936, when E. E. Aubrey published his valuable analysis of *Present Theological Tendencies*. Aubrey points out that the new naturalism of Wieman, like that of Lloyd Morgan and Alexander, Smuts and Whitehead, makes room in "nature" for a whole realm of values, meanings and purposes excluded by the old mechanistic naturalism, making it easy to find God in nature; but he also points out that the new naturalism denies all "disjunction between God and nature" and conceives of God as "one aspect of the natural world"—that which supports values and makes for increasing mutuality. Against this identification of God with an aspect of nature, Aubrey sees a "striking reaction" beginning to assert itself, represented in Britain by Oman, Inge, and Temple; in America, by Lyman, Rufus Jones, and Macintosh. If Niebuhr is not named as leader of this trend, it is only because he is somewhat misleadingly classified along with Barth and Brunner, as a dialectic theologian. No one has stressed more than Niebuhr the need of a "dimension of depth," transcending nature, transcending history, if ethical action here and now is to be sustained by a faith that touches absolute bottom. Wieman has steadily refused to admit any such transcendent dimension into his thinking, and remained content with what his former follower, C. C. Morrison, calls a "behavioristic theology." [21] Niebuhr considers that theistic naturalism is a particularly flagrant instance of "absolutizing the relative"—his constant formula for the sin of idolatry. On this issue, American realistic theology remains sharply divided.

For a time, it seemed as though American supernaturalists might reassert divine transcendence as emphatically and one-sidedly as Barth and Kierkegaard. The influence of Continental neo-orthodoxy was visibly increasing on the eve of World War

[21] See the important passage, pp. 33–37, in *The Source of Human Good* (Chicago, 1946), Wieman's definitive work, where the idea of divine transcendence is sharply rejected. If there was doubt hitherto as to whether Wieman was a theologian as well as a philosopher, Chap. 10 in this book removed it.

II. Translations of Aulén and Nygren, plus Ferré's able interpretation of their theology,[22] made a strong impact. The completion of the English translation of Kierkegaard during the War, might have been expected to produce results such as the German translation produced in Germany after World War I. If this did not occur, it was because *the war revealed considerable residual strength in the liberal tradition, both in politics and in theology.* Niebuhr spoke less emphatically during the war about the utopian illusions of liberal democracy, and more about the need of defending its sound core against the perils that beset it.[23] Wieman wrote a political book called *Now We Must Choose* (1941), in which he also called for discriminating support of political liberalism in its time of testing. Since there are historical and logical connections between political and theological liberalism, a similar revival of discriminating liberalism was likely to take place in theology. Dean Sperry of Harvard expressed a common attitude when he said that though liberalism must plead guilty to many of the charges brought against it before the war, *the alternatives to liberalism were generally far worse.* A symposium called *Liberal Theology: An Appraisal* (New York, 1942) marked the first concerted expression of a neo-liberal trend. John Bennett in his contribution to this volume defends human nature and human reason against neo-orthodox pessimism, while acknowledging that earlier liberal optimism needed to be corrected by the tragic insights of Augustine, Luther and Calvin.

In summary, the theological center of American Protestantism now consists of three strong parties, neo-orthodox, neo-liberal, and neo-naturalist, all related to the realistic movement of 1930–1935, but differing between themselves at many points. It is important to note that scarcely any of our neo-orthodox would repudiate the use of reason in theology to the extent that Barth or the Swedish Lundensians do; while, on the other hand, even Wieman and the

[22] *Swedish Contributions to Modern Theology,* by Nels Ferré (New York, 1939).

[23] *Christianity and Power Politics* (New York, 1940); *The Children of Light and The Children of Darkness* (New York, 1944).

naturalists now give more weight to Biblical revelation and its paradoxical symbols than many liberals were disposed to do twenty-five years ago. This being the case, there is measurably less tension between our right and left wings than there was then. Fundamentalists still exist, and they denounce neo-orthodoxy as "The New Modernism"; [24] but many of them would now admit that there are "Bible-believing Christians" in the neo-orthodox and neo-liberal ranks, with whom they can argue as friends instead of parting as foes. Humanists still exist—graduated in thousands each year from our secularized universities; but their faith in man has been greatly chastened by tragic events since 1930. Some of them have found in neo-naturalism a stepping-stone to Christian faith in God.

If American theology is to play the important part in ecumenical conversations to which the course of world events seems to call us, it is highly desirable that our theologians should do more *systematic* and *comprehensive* work than they have in the recent past. It is an amazing fact that the systems of Hodge and Strong, Clarke and Brown (essentially nineteenth-century systems) have had no real peers in the twentieth century as yet. There are signs that we may not have to wait much longer. Christology, the central core of every system of Christian theology, is coming to concern many minds. Biblical theology is becoming more and more productive, and exercising a stimulating effect on systematic theology. Short sketches of the Christian faith, for the laity and clergy, are becoming numerous.[25] Reinhold Niebuhr, in *The Nature and Destiny of Man*, has produced a masterpiece covering half the ground of the Christian faith. Nels Ferré has already begun to issue a series of books presenting a theological system half-way between Swedish neo-orthodoxy and American neo-liberalism. Paul Tillich is issuing the first of two volumes on *Systematic Theology* this year, uniting the philosophic and revela-

---

[24] *The New Modernism*, by Van Til (1946).
[25] *E.g.*, Bennett, *Christian Realism;* Horton, *Our Christian Faith;* Rall, *The Christian Faith and Way;* Harkness, *Understanding the Christian Faith.*

tional approaches at every point: Reason and Revelation, Being and God, Existence and the Christ, Life and the Spirit, History and the Kingdom of God. Closely associated with Reinhold Niebuhr for many years, Tillich shares many of his friend's views; but his mind has a generous comprehensiveness peculiarly his own. May he be the new Aquinas who will find a place within his system for the truth in all our contending theological schools.

BIBLIOGRAPHY

Hodge, A. A., *Outlines of Theology* (New York, 1861; rewritten and enlarged, New York, 1900; Grand Rapids, 1928)

King, H. C., *Reconstruction in Theology* (New York, 1901)

Brown, W. A., *Christian Theology in Outline* (New York, 1906)

Rauschenbusch, Walter, *A Theology for the Social Gospel* (New York, 1918)

Machen, J. G., *Christianity and Liberalism* (New York, 1923)

Macintosh, D. C., *Religious Realism* (New York, 1931)

Ferm, Vergilius, editor, *Contemporary American Theology*, Series I and II (New York, 1932–1933)

Aubrey, E. E., *Present Theological Tendencies* (New York, 1936)

Hammar, George, *Christian Realism in Contemporary American Theology* (Uppsala, 1940)

Roberts, D. E. and Van Dusen, H. P., editors, *Liberal Theology: An Appraisal* (New York, 1942)

Niebuhr, Reinhold, *The Nature and Destiny of Man*, Vols. I and II (New York, 1941–1943)

Tillich, Paul, *Systematic Theology*, Vol. I (Chicago, 1951)

Wieman, H. N. and Meland, Bernard, *American Philosophies of Religion* (Chicago, 1936) *

* This particular book is inserted in the bibliography of this chapter because, as Dr. Horton rightly points out, "philosophy of religion" during the heyday of the liberal period, practically speaking, was identified with "systematic theology." A.S.N.

CHRISTIAN ETHICS

Waldo Beach and John C. Bennett *

* In the writing of this chapter, Waldo Beach was responsible for sections I–V and John Bennett for sections VI–VIII but "the contentions of the whole chapter are shared by both contributors." A.S.N.

WALDO BEACH was born in 1915, and he graduated from Wesleyan University in 1937; subsequently he studied at Yale Divinity School, taking the degree of B.D. in 1940, and the Yale Graduate School, where he took his doctorate in 1944. He then served as College Pastor and Professor of Religion at Antioch College, Ohio, before joining the faculty of Duke University, where he is Associate Professor of Christian Ethics in the Divinity School and the Graduate School of Arts and Sciences. He is a member of the Study Commission on the Church and Economic Life of the Federal Council of Churches.

JOHN COLEMAN BENNETT was born in 1902, and he was educated at Williams College, Oxford University, and Union Theological Seminary. After teaching for eight years at Auburn Theological Seminary, he joined the faculty of the Pacific School of Religion in 1938, leaving there in 1943 to become Professor of Christian Theology and Ethics at Union Theological Seminary, New York. He was Secretary of the Section on the Church and the Economic Order at the Oxford Conference in 1937, and he acted in the same capacity for the Section on the Church and the Social Disorder at the Amsterdam Assembly of the World Council of Churches in 1948. He is the author of several books both on the theory and practice of Christian Ethics. His two latest volumes are *Christian Ethics and Social Policy* and *Christianity and Communism.*

VI

The history of the Christian ideal of the "good life" may fairly be treated as variations on the themes sounded in the gospels. Indubitably one main theme of the gospel ethic is the tension between the Christian way and the way of the world, a primal opposition between the requirements of the Kingdom of God and the requirements of the kingdom of the world. The main historical types of Christian ethics can well be understood as attempts to resolve this tension. The monastic version of the Christian way proposed a discipline whereby the Christian could be saved *out* of the world, for the vision of God. Orthodox Protestantism of the sixteenth, seventeenth and eighteenth centuries proclaimed a faith whereby the Christian could be saved *in* the world, for the next life, by living under the Kingship of God. The last part of the nineteenth and the early part of the twentieth century saw the rise and decline of still another attempt to overcome this tension. The "liberal" movement (so-called in this essay for lack of a better name) without being completely "this-worldly" yet construed the Christian life neither as a way whereby one was saved *out* of this world, nor saved *in* this world for the next, but simply as an effort *to save the world*. It proposed that the cause in which the Christian was to lose his life, and thus save it, was in the gradual Christianisation of the social order, to the end of the coming of the Kingdom of God on earth. All of the distinctive features of liberal Protestant ethics are made coherent when viewed in the light of this highest good for man.

The gospel according to liberalism was long in the making. Its theological roots go back to Immanuel Kant, whose philosophy gave impetus to a development in German theology associated with the names of Schleiermacher, Ritschl, Harnack, Hermann, and many others. From nineteenth-century secular thought liberalism also drew heavily: from the environmentalism of the Marxists

and English socialists, a realisation of the conditioning impact of
social institutions upon human personality; from Utilitarianism,
the ideal of social reform to extend the "greatest happiness of the
greatest number"; and from Darwin and his followers the evolutionary theory of the unilinear and upward development of the
course of human affairs. These ideas permeated the nineteenth-
century era of expansion and growth in England and the Continent. When appropriated by the distinctively American temperament of robust optimism, activism, and practicality, the liberal
movement penetrated deeply American Protestantism for almost
half a century.

There were many preachers and teachers who, at the close
of the Civil War period, began speaking the message of a "social"
Christianity. Washington Gladden, a leader in its early develop-
ment, was succeeded by men who led the movement into the
1900's, when the Social Gospel "came of age": Lyman Abbott,
George Herron, Samuel Batten, Francis Peabody, G. B. Smith,
Shailer Mathews, and above all Walter Rauschenbusch, its major
apologist.[1] The more turbulent years following the first World
War saw the continuing influence of this gospel in men like
Francis J. McConnell, Harry F. Ward, Arthur E. Holt, Harry
Emerson Fosdick, G. Bromley Oxnam, and Kirby Page.

There is always a "cultural lag" in religious thought, and the
rank-and-file of Protestants in the hinterlands have remained
largely untouched by the insights of Protestant liberalism. The
virulent reaction against liberalism from the ultra-conservative,
Bible-minded Protestants, now on the increase in the mid-century,
is one indication that the impact of liberalism on the total Protestant mind was much smaller than its leaders supposed. Nonetheless,
the slow percolation of liberal ideas, passing down through semi-

---

[1] The subsequent treatment of liberalism will draw most heavily on
Rauschenbusch's thought. His most important books are *Christianity and the
Social Crisis* (1907), *Christianizing the Social Order* (1912), and especially
A Theology for the Social Gospel (1917). The best historical treatment of
the Social Gospel is Howard Hopkins: *The Rise of the Social Gospel in
American Protestantism, 1865–1915.* See also Henry May: *Protestant Churches
and Industrial America.*

nary education and denominational literature, was the most positive and creative trend in the early years of this century.

II

The task of liberalism was to recall the Protestant church to the prophetic content of the Hebrew-Christian tradition. During the latter part of the nineteenth century, Protestant ethics had fallen, for the most part, into the doldrums of a Victorian, pietistic, socially myopic, and cushioned-pew program for personal purity. The common ideal of the Christian life was to avoid the gross sins of the flesh, to follow the Benjamin Franklin virtues of thrift, honesty, and respectability, to love one's immediate neighbor in good deeds of charity, and thus to prepare oneself for the destination of heaven. The economic structures of life were either regarded as outside the province of ethics or else given a tacit sanction through the Puritan doctrine of vocation, which had been transformed into the "gospel of work" and thence into the "gospel of wealth." The notorious "rugged individualism" of capitalism was blessed as Christian if mitigated by active philanthropy. The Protestant church looked at questions of economic ethics through the eyes of the middle-class bourgeoisie. It passed by on the other side from the masses of immigrant labor, or else offered them other-worldly bromides for their spiritual and economic hungers.

Into this complacent atmosphere blew the fresh winds of the social gospel. Men like Gladden and Rauschenbusch found that the counsels of pietistic Protestantism were woefully inept in speaking to the condition of men crushed under the weight of industrial capitalism. They found it futile for the church to try to "save souls" one by one when society was destroying them *en masse*. For them the task of the church was imperative: to attack the social order, to remake it after the pattern of the Kingdom of God envisaged by the Hebrew prophets and Jesus, an earthly kingdom of justice, brotherhood, and democracy.

There was a clear unanimity among liberals in defining the Kingdom and in asserting its primacy. "By the Kingdom of God

Jesus meant an ideal (though progressively approximated) social order in which the relation of men to God is that of sons, and therefore to each other, that of brothers. . . . This ideal is not beyond human attainment, but is the natural possibility for man's social capacities and powers." [2] "The Kingdom of God is humanity organised according to the will of God. . . . It implies a progressive reign of love in human affairs." [3]

The highest good for the individual is to do battle for this Kingdom. He must contribute to the amelioration of human life by altering the environmental circumstances so as to restore the dignity and worth of persons. Over against orthodox Protestantism, the liberals were environmentalists, in that they discerned both the crippling power and the redemptive possibilities of economic and political institutions. But they avoided the deterministic collectivism of Marxist socialism. They kept the individual and the "personal equation" to the forefront, both in terms of the criteria by which institutions were to be judged and the leverage by which institutions were to be changed.

One of the most radical features of the liberal development was its claim that ethics is prior to theology. Starting with the ethical conviction of the primacy of the Kingdom, the liberal mind judged traditional theology by that faith, and altered it in keeping. The title of Rauschenbusch's most influential book, *A Theology for the Social Gospel* is symbolic. And G. B. Smith's Taylor Lectures of 1912, *Social Idealism and the Changing Theology*, appealed for the transformation of theology to keep pace with the new social consciousness of the church.

The attempted transformation of tradition affected every department of Christian theology. The Christian view of man's nature underwent a considerable revision. The long-established Calvinistic estimate of man as a creature fallen from his original

---

[2] Shailer Mathews: *The Social Teaching of Jesus* (1902), pp. 54, 77.

[3] Walter Rauschenbusch: *A Theology for the Social Gospel* (1917), p. 142.

nature into a state of sin from which, powerless to free himself, he can only be saved by grace—this view was amended to a more favorable estimate of man's condition. Among liberals, man was taken essentially to be a creature of divine worth and dignity, endowed with intelligence and native goodwill, who sins but who is not congenitally a sinner, and who is capable of moral growth in this life by his own initiative and inspiration from God. It must be remembered that the major thinkers of the Social Gospel took the phenomenon of sin with prophetic seriousness. Rauschenbusch made a penetrating analysis of the pervasiveness and tenacity of sin in "the superpersonal forces of evil," socially transmitted from generation to generation.[4] His was a realism not characteristic of the later ebullient enthusiasts for God's dawning day. But even Rauschenbusch shared the dominant liberal conviction in viewing sin in primarily "horizontal" terms, as selfishness in defiance of neighbor-needs, rather than primarily as the rebellion of the will against the sovereignty of God. Moreover, evil must be regarded "as a variable factor in the life of humanity," he wrote, "which it is our duty to diminish for every young life and for every new generation."[5] Else what is the point of education, or of what use free will? Here he betrays an optimism quite alien to the tone of the Westminster Confession.

Of all the rewritings of the Christian tradition attempted by liberalism, the most thoroughgoing was in the area of philosophy of history. Traditional eschatology looked away from the present "fallen" state of man to a final end brought about by God's intervention and discontinuous with the present and future line of time. This concept proved troublesome if not weird to minds nurtured in evolutionary and romantic nineteenth-century thought. In the stead of the traditional *eschaton* was put the earthly Kingdom of justice and brotherhood, approximated progressively through time by gradual continuity on an upward

[4] See *Theology for the Social Gospel*, chs. IV–IX.
[5] *Ibid.*, p. 43.

plane. In short, a Christianised version of the progress philosophy of history, in the name of the Kingdom of God ideal, supplanted orthodox Christian eschatology.

Such a philosophy of history influenced profoundly the ethical temper of liberalism. The bow of moral effort was bent by the tension between the present and the future. What sustained moral energy was the confidence that as the present was superior to the past so the future would realise what was still now unfulfilled. In a real sense, liberalism construed the traditional Protestant dictum of "salvation by faith" in a way quite foreign to the intention of Luther and Calvin. For "faith" came to mean confidence in the future. In effect, then, men are saved by hope, and by works that bring that hope nearer.

The 1910's and 1920's saw the fruition of this new spirit in organisational expression at every level. At the denominational level, various commissions of social service tried to awaken the consciences of their constituency with various "social creeds" and manifestoes. The Federal Council of Churches of Christ in America, established in 1908, provided an agency for the inter-denominational expression of the social convictions of liberalism. Its Social Creed (1912) dealt almost wholly with economic issues. Its support of labor unionisation and of shorter hours and higher wages for labor was viewed (and still is) as "radical socialism" by many of the rank-and-file in the Protestant hinterlands. By 1932 the Federal Council statement of principles extended its scope to include the rural problem, marriage and the home, race relations, and international affairs. Though again the laity remained dubious or inarticulate in their attitude toward war, during the 20's and 30's, Protestant liberalism joined the anti-war crusade with enthusiasm. It was boldly affirmed that "the institutions of religion should never again be used as agencies of warfare." The type of pacifism prevalent in this era among the large denominations was quite different from that of the historic sectarian groups. The Quakers and Mennonites abhorred participation in war for their own adherents as part of their whole perfectionist renunciation of the sinful "world." This new, more positive pacifism sought to convert the nations to the way of Christ by substituting for the way of the sword Christian goodwill and reasonable negotiation among nations to settle their disputes. The "world-renouncing" pacifism and the "world-affirming" pacifism in these decades was a curious compound of sectarian and liberal motifs.

III

It would be difficult to try to discern a date during the last half-century when the reaction against liberalism began to set in. The slow ebb-tide of liberalism came with the devastating and profoundly unnerving events of the 1930's and 40's, which dashed the high hopes of liberalism for the arrival of the Christian century. It found itself with little to speak to the condition of men in conflict, tragedy, and failure. In a dark time, the writings of Barth and Brunner were taken up on the Continent and in England. The school of "Neo-Protestants" (called variously the school of "neo-orthodoxy," "Crisis" or "Dialectical" theology) came to ascendency. In America, the most influential figures in the transition have been Paul Tillich and Richard and Reinhold Niebuhr.[6] The voices of this new school seem to speak much less in chorus than did the liberals. Its themes are more difficult to make out. Moreover, at the point of specific ethical decision, Niebuhr and his followers have joined forces with liberals considerably left of center in matters of economic policy, race relations, and political alignment. With the exception of the issues of pacifism and world government, Niebuhr is found "voting" the same way as the liberals who are his theological opponents. The crucial difference, then, between liberalism and neo-Protestantism is not to be seen

[6] Since Reinhold Niebuhr has been the chief spokesman for neo-Protestantism in America, it is his thought which comes in for consideration in the material which follows in this essay. It is imperative to note, however, that he differs widely from European neo-Protestants at certain crucial points, as too he differs from other neo-Protestants in America.

at the level of the specific measures of social ethics, but at the deeper level of the theological premises, sanctions, and ends which underlie Christian policy in public and private affairs.

The central theological stress of neo-Protestantism is the recovery of the major note of Augustine, Luther, and Calvin: the absolute transcendent sovereignty of God, Whose Will orders the whole universe. God is the continual Creator, Judge, and Redeemer of the world. Neo-Protestantism finds the theology of liberalism lamentably wanting at two crucial points: (1) In construing God as the immanental force for good in society, it loses the sense of the majestic transcendence of God, who is above and beyond any force for good in society. (2) It overlooks the "Fall" of man and the "wrath" of God. In centering thought on God as Creator and Redeemer, making a good order of creation gradually better, it neglects the Judgment of God on man's perpetual corruption of creation.

The transcendence of God is not absolute. In Jesus Christ, the absolute separation of time and eternity is broken through from the side of God. In Christ, He "invades" history from above. The final and unique Word is spoken for man in Him. Neo-Protestantism shares with liberalism a Christo-centric faith. But the Jesus of history who is normative for the liberal is understood more as humanity reaching divinity, while for the neo-Protestant mind the Christ of faith must be understood as the Divine reaching humanity. The "lordship" of Jesus Christ is conceived by liberalism in moral terms; for neo-Protestantism in metaphysical or cosmic terms as well.

These theological affirmations involve important shifts in ethical theory. In the treatment of man's sin and salvation, the transaction is conceived in the "vertical" (man-to-God) dimension, in contrast to its "horizontal" (man-to-society) treatment by liberalism. To be sure, both the condition of sin and the process of salvation have for the neo-Protestant "horizontal" expressions, but these are the fruits of the dislocation and re-creation of man in his primal relation with God.

Neo-Protestantism is well-known for its heavy stress on "original" sin. By its critics this emphasis is dismissed as morbid, pessimistic, and morally enervating. In what sense sin is "original" to man's finite life is not, however, an issue as important in neo-Protestant thought as is its diagnosis of the locus and character of sin itself. Sin is not essentially ignorance, to be exorcised by education and rational enlightenment. Nor does it lie in the body's downward pull upon the upward aspirations of the spirit. Nor again is it to be located in corrupt institutions which defile the naturally innocent intentions of individuals. All these views of sin, more or less current in Protestant circles, are superficial; at the most they are symptoms rather than the causes of man's dilemmas. The real essence of sin is man's wilful (albeit often unconscious) rebellion against the sovereignty of God and the effort to organise his universe of values around himself as the center. It is "pride," presumption, self-will, ego-centrism. "Selfishness" is an appropriate word, if this be defined as self-centeredness in man's encounter with God. In the misdirection of his will toward his own ends in preference to the will of God, man falls perennially into an "eccentric" (off-center) manner of life. His reasoning is corrupted into self-defensive rationalisation, his institutions become the instruments of his will-to-power. He commits all manner of inhumanities to man, often in the name of good. The consequences of this sin are the inner unrest and outer warfares which plague his days—the expressions of God's judgment.[7]

The process of salvation from this sin is somewhat more obscurely and variously described by neo-Protestant theologians. In the main, however, it may be said that salvation is realised by man's appropriation in faith of God's act of forgiveness in Jesus Christ, which effects in the believer the mood of contrition for sin, partial escape from egocentrism, and a predisposition to judge one's own case as severely as another's, as under the judgment of God. Humility and contrition enable one to approach the issues of inter-personal relations with a non-selfdefensive, outgoing

[7] See Niebuhr's *Nature and Destiny of Man*, vol. I, chs. vi–viii.

love, in response to God's love revealed on the Cross. This kind
of salvation does not mean "perfection." It will not "solve" the
moral problems of our day. But it can mitigate the conflicts of
life, secure some reconciliations out of broken community, temper
justice with love, and bestow on the believer a sense of being for-
given, even within the grays of sinful existence.

IV

The theological emphases sketched above provide the basis for
the neo-Protestant critique of liberalism. In the first place, it finds
liberalism's philosophy of history not only inadequate but hereti-
cal. The Kingdom of God, says Niebuhr, should not be described
in the future perfect tense, but in the present indicative. The
phrase means the Kingship of God, the sovereignty of God, a
very present reality. It is God's constant activity of creation, judgment, and redemption. Even in sin, men are not outside the Kingdom. The psychological and social maladjustments which follow
upon sin are the very signs of God's rule, His "left hand" bringing
judgment. It becomes dangerous sentimentalism to claim any as-
sured progressive victory of good over evil within finite time.
History gives no sign of being automatically redemptive in itself,
for the good achievements of history bring new perils and new
corruptions. The realization of this truth leads to despair only if
one's faith is grounded in hope for the future. But the true Christian's faith is grounded in a God transcendent of all time and historical achievement.

This difference becomes highly important for ethics. The moral
dynamic of much of liberalism was derived, as we have noted, from
the disparity between the present possibility and the future hope.
This gives a teleological character to liberal morality. The moral
dynamic of neo-Protestantism stems rather from the tension between God's transcendent command and the present human situation. It does not first ask: What can we hope for? Its first question
is: What does God's sovereignty require of me in this present?

How shall I respond to God's action in faith and integrity? The obedience of the Christian in witnessing to God's command may not be "successful." Indeed, it may fail, when judged by the standards of the world. But the success of the Christian's efforts in terms of the future happiness of man is a quite secondary matter. The first and final sanction of moral action is faithfulness to the will of God.

A second attack of neo-Protestantism is aimed at the liberal view of human nature, in which it finds a curious ambiguity. The social gospel arose as a strenuous prophetic attack against the sinister economic forces of industrial capitalism which were destroying the personality of its subjects. Yet as the social gospel developed in the twentieth century, it was betrayed by its understanding of human nature to what now appears, in hindsight, as a superficial prescription for the "mystery of iniquity." Even Rauschenbusch believed that in America the institutions of the family, education, the church, and political life had become Christianised.[8] It only remained to convert the institutions of capitalism from competition to co-operation. In so far as liberalism located evil externally in institutions, it overlooked the way institutions are sustained from within by corrupted wills. In so far as it regarded some institutions as safely within the fold of the Kingdom, it overlooked the ubiquity of sin to which no institutions are immune.

There is a third point at which the ethics of liberalism is found wanting by neo-Protestantism. The liberal claims that the solution of our social problems lies in the extension of the personal virtues of the Sermon on the Mount to the relatively impersonal areas of man's collective relationships. But the kind of Christian "love" appropriate to the small circle of the family becomes tortuously difficult, if not impossible, to apply to the relations of economic groups and the affairs of state. One cannot "love" one's far-distant neighbor as one can "love" one's close-at-hand neighbor, given the limiting barriers of the political and economic structures

[8] *Christianising the Social Order* (1912), Pt. III, ch. 2.

through which alone moral motives can be expressed. The situation is worse confounded in that one's self-sacrificial love for one's own neighbor, one's kind, may become the instrument of the collective egoism of patriotism or of ecclesiastical imperialism. "Moral man" thus aggravates the sins of "immoral society." So it becomes too facile to speak of Christianising the social order by the establishment of love and justice in the body politic. Such a high-looking hope trips over the moral ambiguities involved in every finite moral choice.

Another illustration of the ineptness of liberal ethics, according to the charge, is its pathetic innocence in dealing with the problem of power. One of the most important fruits of the social gospel was the pacifist movement between World Wars I and II. This pacifism counterposed the "Christian way" to the "way of power," expressed in the use of military force or economic sanctions. The only alternative for the Christian must be the renunciation of power and might. Reinhold Niebuhr, the most influential critic of this pacifism, has maintained that this alternative is too "simple." Unless the Christian retreat from the world entirely and leave it to be run by burly sinners, he is involved inevitably in power relationships at every level of his corporate life—relationships which are always an admixture of relative good and evil. The real question is not, then, shall the Christian employ coercive power? The real question is how can the necessary use of power be made to secure a relatively more just and a relatively less tyrannical social order? These Niebuhrean strictures against liberal pacifism were in part responsible for a sharp shift among Protestant leaders from pacifism to interventionism during the nervous uncertainties prior to Pearl Harbor. After World War II, the problems of Christian ethics in international affairs have continued to be couched in these terms, rather than in terms of the liberal pacifist's alternatives.[9]

[9] See for example, *The Amsterdam Assembly Series*, Vol. IV: *The Church and the International Disorder* (1948).

EDITOR'S NOTE:—Another important contribution to thinking in this area has been John Bennett's book, *Christian Ethics and Social Policy* (1946).

V

At mid-century, neo-Protestantism is certainly the most influential school of thought at the levels of Protestant theological education, in America hardly less than in England and on the Continent. A closer look at the tenets of this school, particularly in its American variety, discloses that while it has attacked liberalism at some points, it is deeply (and often unconsciously) indebted to liberalism at others. It is not a straight return to the beliefs of orthodox Protestantism as it evolved in the sixteenth, seventeenth, and eighteenth centuries. Something new has been added. And the "new" is derived precisely from the whole liberal development in theology, along with its nineteenth century concomitants in scientific and social thought. In its method, for one thing, it shares with liberalism an empirical temper, receptive to truth from all sources, "secular" or "sacred." In its characteristic themes, the neo-Protestant movement in theology and ethics can best be understood as a transitional synthesis of Protestant orthodoxy with Protestant liberalism. It has drawn its cardinal theses from orthodoxy, but it has also been greatly beholden to certain insights of liberalism which arose in antithesis to orthodoxy.

Niebuhr and others like him have returned to the orthodox belief that sin and salvation must first be understood as taking place in the heart of man, as he stands in vertical transaction with God. To turn from Him is to fall, in misdirected love, toward one or another idolatry. To be turned again to Him by grace is to be restored. The real locus of sin, then, is the inner man. But on the other hand, with liberalism, neo-Protestantism has affirmed that the most destructive expressions of sin are to be seen in the *public* rather than the private life of man. The sins of the prideful heart run rampant in nationalistic imperialism, racial pride, and economic misbalances of power. The neo-Protestant, like the liberal, is quite nonchalant about the kinds of private and fleshly sins that preoccupied the Puritan, and still constitute the scope of "ethics" for many orthodox pietists.

The early Reformers inherited a medieval conservatism which regarded the social structures of the family, the state, and economic life as God-given and fixed orders, *within* which the individual was to work out his salvation. One looks in vain in Luther, Calvin, Baxter, Wesley, Edwards, and all the major figures of three centuries of Protestant writing, for any more than incidental treatment of the problems of the economic, political and legal *structures* of life. The realisation of the fluidity of social structures and the capacity of man to alter his political and economic environment is a nineteenth century insight, which became the inheritance of liberalism and neo-Protestantism as well. The Oxford and Amsterdam Conferences of the World Council of Churches, where neo-Protestant thought was central in influence, were deeply concerned with structures of contemporary Western civilisation. By its serious view of sin, neo-Protestantism is kept from the too-easy confidence of liberalism that the social order can be transformed into the divine. But that does not constrain it the less to judge man's disorder by God's design, and to redeem these disorders in so far as possible. Thus the inward and vertical perspective of orthodoxy is conjoined with the outward and institutional reference of liberalism into a bi-focal perspective of high importance.

VI   BENNETT

The theological development of neo-Protestantism, a development that is so fluid that any label can easily mislead, has changed the assumptions on which Christian ethical thinking now goes forward, but it has meant no abandonment of the essential impulse expressed through the Social Gospel. In this tragic period of history Christians may have to act in quite different ways from those which were assumed to be "Christian" in calmer days. But the requirement of responsible Christian action is made no less urgent by the loss of the optimistic hope of the Social Gospel. What may now be said of some of the major ethical problems which must engage the thought of Christians during the next half century?

The most urgent and, perhaps the most baffling problem is to discover Christian guidance for action in society under conditions which preclude the absolute identification of Christian ethics with any of the decisions that are open to us. Protestant Christianity differs from Roman Catholicism in having no clear Christian law interpreted by an absolute authority for the complexities of economic and political life. The Protestant knows the ultimate standard by which all things are judged. He knows many of the goals that he should seek, but there is a twilight zone of methods and next steps in which Christians have to use their best judgment without benefit of absolute guidance of any kind.

If we ask what a Christian should do to prevent a third world war, we find ourselves forced to make decisions which are highly ambiguous and often repellent. For one thing, the prevention of a third world war is not the only end that we must have in view. Another end which is to many Christians more important is the prevention of worldwide tyranny. If this second end is emphasized, the prevention of a third world war must be sought by methods which will not put one group of nations into the position of having to surrender to the overwhelming power of another group of nations. What these methods are is much debated among Christians who seem to be equally sincere in their loyalty to Christ. Judgment about these methods depends in part on interpretations of fact, in this case on interpretations of the intentions of the rulers of the Soviet Union. There are no Christian answers to those questions of fact and yet every decision about preventing war today which a Christian makes will depend upon his judgment concerning such questions of fact.

Another example of the kind of issue which no Christian ethical precept can settle for us is the attempt to secure stability of employment in our economy. It is obvious that a period of mass unemployment in our society would be ruinous, that Christians are obliged to do what is possible to prevent such a catastrophe from occurring. Here decisions depend upon expert knowledge of economic cause and effect. They depend also upon our scale of values, because the prevention of unemployment is not the only end to be sought. It is also important to find methods which will not lead us to totalitarianism. And yet this fear of totalitarianism must not be used as a bogey to prevent all social experiment in which the state has an important part. What methods will work and how we relate such competing values as freedom and security are questions to which Christians as Christians have no absolutely clear answers.

It will be hard to live without "Christian" programs, without absolute laws, without panaceas of any kind; but there is no other way open to us. Such economic stereotypes as Socialism and Capitalism are no longer helpful for Christian thinking about economic institutions. The formation of a Christian mind concerning these ethical issues is a continuous process in which the special knowledge of experts and the concrete experience of Christian laymen who participate in all phases of economic and political life are essential factors. Two new emphases in modern Protestantism are especially important. One is the emphasis upon the Christian vocation of laymen and the other is the emphasis on the need of co-operative Christian thinking within the fellowship of the Church. The judgment about what ought to be done cannot be prescribed by ministers or theologians for Christians in other occupations. This judgment must take account of the knowledge and intuitive understanding that are found chiefly among laymen who are directly responsible for economic and political activities. It may seem that this approach to the formation of Christian judgments implies complete ethical relativism. But this process must be guided by Christian faith and love at every point. These should control motives, they should determine goals and they should be a basis for criticism of all methods even though they cannot, of themselves, solve all problems of method. The warning against idolatry that is implicit in the Christian faith is the warning against the very attitudes which are most destructive in society, for one form of idolatry is to put in the place of God one social group or cause or value.

In this process of forming Christian judgments on ethical issues there will be developed from time to time a broad consensus that will have considerable authority. Probably no formulation of this consensus will long be satisfactory. There will always be a large body of opinion that is only nominally Christian or at least uninstructed that will reject such a consensus, but it may be an important source of ethical guidance and provide its slow ferment of influence. So far the best statements of consensus that we have are those which come from a succession of national and international conferences such as the Oxford Conference in 1937, the Amsterdam Assembly in 1948 and conferences on world order or economic problems called by the Federal Council of Churches.

VII

A second area of Christian thinking which must go forward is the discovery of the basis for co-operation between Christians and non-Christians in a mixed community. Sometimes the problem involved is the difficulty of deciding how far to go in co-operation with a government that is hostile to Christianity. This is the form of the problem that Christians face in countries that are controlled by Communist governments.

The form of the problem that is most important in America arises out of a widespread acceptance of many common ethical standards by Christians and non-Christians in the American community. Indeed, there are often more serious conflicts between economically progressive and conservative Christians than between Christians and non-Christians with common political views. But even when this co-operation on concrete issues is easy there are problems, often below the surface, about which much more thought is required. One danger is the general dilution of Christian ethics both within and outside the Church. A symptom of this is the tendency of public men to assume that the political and economic policies with which they are concerned are based upon the Sermon on the Mount. Another danger is that Christians will identify themselves too unreservedly with the political and economic problems which, on the whole, they support.

The question of the relation between Christian ethics and ethical ideals which have sources which are independent of the Christian faith is one of the major issues in Christian discussion in Europe. It is one phase of the more general question of the relation between revelation and reason. There is always a danger of a kind of Pharasaism in reverse in Christian ethical thinking. While it seeks to emphasize the uniqueness and authority of Christian ethics it may discount unfairly the moral sensitivity and moral achievements of those who acknowledge no Christian influences upon their thought and life. Whatever of common moral judgment exists in the community which is on the side of honesty, social justice, the rights of minorities, a humane spirit is so precious that Christians should avoid any tendency to isolate themselves from it or to set themselves above it even in theory. To recognize fully this common morality does not mean, however, that we should not see that it is precarious without deeper roots than it often has in our society.

VIII

American Christian ethical thinking will need to enlarge its scope. During the early period of the Social Gospel the emphasis was almost exclusively on economic issues. This was quite necessary at the time, and economic issues are still fundamental. More recently the problem of war has been emphasized. We have been delivered from preoccupation with the pacifism-nonpacifism conflict and much attention has been given by both pacifists and nonpacifists to issues connected with world order. Also, there has developed a Christian form of nonpacifism which involves real gains in Christian sensitivity as compared with conventional attitudes toward war in earlier periods. The issue of race has within the past ten years gained attention in a spectacular way.

None of these issues named can be neglected, but a series of events has forced Christians to give great attention to political issues, to problems of government, to the basis of civil rights. Many of these problems are, of course, interlocked with economic issues. The discussion of the welfare state is inseparably political and economic but it raises a dimension of political problems about which there has been very little careful Christian thinking in this country. The relation of the state to education is a phase of the larger problem of the welfare state but it raises great issues of its own. The problem of Church and State is not far away; that quandry which we thought had been solved by a simple formula of "separation" bristles with open questions. The basis and the limits of the rights of minorities is a most persistent question, for which there are no ready answers. The success of Communism in other parts of the world has forced upon American Christians the responsibility to find alternatives to Communism in countries which are desperately poor and which have had little political experience. Democracy as we know it cannot be universalized but it does stand for values which Christians should seek to preserve in every society. What are those values and how can we define them without appearing to absolutize American institutions and ways of life?

All of these political issues stem from one basic dilemma which we encounter on all sides. It is a dilemma at which political and economic problems meet. How can we preserve freedom for persons and for many non-political institutions in the face of the unity and centralization which are implicit in modern technological developments? The Church, not only in its thinking but also in its very existence, can contribute to the solution of this problem because it is one of those non-political institutions which must preserve large areas of freedom for its own life and work.

BIBLIOGRAPHY

The Amsterdam Assembly Series: Man's Disorder and God's Design (New York, 1948)

Bennett, John, *Social Salvation* (New York, 1935)

Bennett, John, *Christian Ethics and Social Policy* (New York, 1946)

Ehrenstrom, Nils, *et al.*, *Christian Faith and the Common Life* (Oxford Conference, vol. IV) (New York, 1938)

Hopkins, C. Howard, *The Rise of the Social Gospel in American Protestantism, 1865–1915* (New Haven, 1940)

May, Henry F., *Protestant Churches and Industrial America* (New York, 1949)

Niebuhr, Reinhold, *Moral Man and Immoral Society* (New York, 1932)

Niebuhr, Reinhold, *An Interpretation of Christian Ethics* (New York, 1935)

Ramsey, Paul, *Basic Christian Ethics* (New York, 1950)

Smith, G. B., *Social Idealism and the Changing Theology* (New York, 1913)

Rauschenbusch, Walter, *Christianity and the Social Crisis* (New York, 1907)

Rauschenbusch, Walter, *A Theology for the Social Gospel* (New York, 1918)

CHURCH HISTORY

George H. Williams

GEORGE HUNTSTON WILLIAMS was born in Ohio in 1914, and after studying as an undergraduate at the University of Munich, he received his B.A. from St. Lawrence University in 1936. Three years later he graduated with the degree of B.D. from the Meadville Theological School and, as Cruft Traveling Fellow, he studied at the Catholic Institute in Paris and the University of Strasbourg. He received the degree of Th.D. from Union Theological Seminary in 1946. He joined the faculty of Harvard Divinity School in 1947, previously having taught Church History at the Starr King School for the Ministry and the Pacific School of Religion in Berkeley, California. His major published contribution to historical scholarship is *Re-thinking the Unitarian Relationship to Protestantism: An Examination of the Thought of Frederic Henry Hedge* (*1805–1890*).

VII

In a paper[1] read before a session of the American Historical Association and reported in its *Review* for 1899–1900, a member of the Church history section discussed the then recent effect of the study of Church history on the life of the Church. Noting that in the first third of the nineteenth century the spirit of union and co-operation had prevailed, the writer went on to show how this era of good feeling was followed by a second phase extending through the middle third of the century when the several competing denominations become conscious of their special missions. Strife and division ensued. In an effort to ground their several claims, denominations resorted, among other things, to Church history as an instrument of denominational policy. But the unexpected consequence of their enterprise was the gradual diminution of prejudice and the development of mutual respect and appreciation, "the recent service," as the reader of the paper concluded, "of Church history to the Church."

From our present vantage point we may say that the clergyman's third era had reached a high point by 1888. For by that year interdenominational goodwill had been sufficiently advanced to make possible the organization of the American Society of Church History. Hitherto there had been only denominational historical societies which had drawn off the interest and commitment necessary to undertake the forming of an interdenominational learned society. Thus from 1888, about which year cluster a number of significant events and publications in the field,[2] we may conveniently date the next era of American Church

[1] The Rev. William Given Andrews, "A Recent Service of Church History to the Church," *American Historical Review*, V (1899–1900), p. 427.
[2] Henry Steele Commager, in speaking of "The watershed of the 'nineties," has quite recently underscored the importance of this general date line for marking a new epoch in all fields. *The American Mind: An Interpretation of American Thought and Character Since the 1880's* (New Haven, 1950).

history, an epoch that extends roughly to 1933. To characterize the epoch from 1888 to 1933 in the writing of Church history and to set it off from the era we are at present traversing, it may be said that in the former, Church history emphasized *history*, rejoiced in it as a method, as an objective approach to the solution of those doctrinal and institutional problems which had vexed and held apart Christians in the nineteenth century, while in the current epoch, with its mounting interest in social criticism and ecumenicity, Church history has been increasingly concerned to re-examine and redefine the *Church* and has also become amenable to practical assignments laid upon it by the Church.

And there is another important difference setting off the spirit of the two eras from each other. From 1888 on, Church historians were conspicuously eager to assimilate their field and methodology to that of their secular or academic colleagues, but in the epoch beginning with the advent of Hitler and Roosevelt, Church historians have become increasingly aware of their strategic location for returning some answer to the widespread query of our time as to the meaning of history. And there are some contemporary Church historians who, while steadfastly refusing to abandon anything of the methodology of the older scientific school of objective research, are willing to entertain the possibility that a very important supplementary understanding of Church history is vouchsafed to those standing committedly within the historic community of faith. Of this tendency, more in the second half of our survey.

1. The Teaching and Writing of Church History in the Era from 1888 to 1933 [3]

If the formation of the American Society of Church History in 1888 marked the onset of a new epoch, the publication (1893–1895) under the auspices of this Society of a thirteen-volume set of

[3] There are three natural subdivisions within this epoch, 1888–1900, 1900–1918, and 1918–1933, to which I shall occasionally allude as "phases" without allowing this further chronological structuring of the treatment to obtrude.

denominational histories (in which the volume on the Unitarians stands next to that on the Roman Catholics), provided the visible symbol of the recent achievement. Of comparable significance is the proliferation of general Church histories written within the denominational context but informed with the interdenominational spirit and committed to the newer historical methodology. Up to the publication of Schaff's seven-volume *History of the Christian Church* (1882–1894), Americans had depended upon European, particularly German, Church histories, but between 1882 and 1904 substantial American histories and compendia made their appearance.

Philip Schaff (1819–1895) himself belonged actually to an earlier school of ecclesiastical historiography than that of Americans writing Church histories at the time of his revised publication. A pupil of August Neander, Schaff was of the mediatory or Romantic school. It had been in 1851, the year following the death of Neander, that his distinguished Mercersburg pupil first published in German the *History of the Apostolic Church.*[4] Unlike his master Philip Schaff did not feel at all hampered by his Reformation convictions in an understanding and appreciation of the Middle Ages. Indeed, Schaff's conviction that Protestant and Catholic principles or emphases were alike essential to a full Christianity, along with his profound feeling for the liturgical and the institutional (though it called forth a party of opposition to him within his own German Reformed denomination) constituted the basis of his distinctive contribution to the ecclesiastical historiography of the land of the Puritans, as he liked to say; namely, an appreciation and an understanding of the Patristic and Medieval Church. His masterful editing in the English translation of the two series of *Nicene and Post-Nicene Fathers* (1886–1889 and 1890–1900) and of *The Creeds of Christendom* (1890) were the products of his ecumenical and historical convictions.

[4] This was followed by an English translation in 1853–1854. Then under the influence of fresh developments in German historiography, he revised his first study and published his *History of the Christian Church 1—600* in two volumes in 1858 and 1867.

Medieval Church history and, in effect, well-proportioned general Church history could not be adequately taught and written about in American seminaries until the bias against what seemed to be nothing but decline, deviltry, and disaster between the perfection of the Primitive Church and the renewal in this or that sect had been worn away in the numerous academic centers of American Christianity of both Reformed and sectarian antecedents. Within evangelical Christianity Schaff had been a pioneer in the recognition of the achievement of the medieval Church.

Of comparable significance in the academic line was the work of the layman and secular historian, Ephraim Emerton (1851–1935), professor of ecclesiastical history at Harvard Divinity School from 1882 to 1918. Emerton's *Introduction to the Study of the Middle Ages* (1888) was epoch-making in that it aroused widespread interest in medieval history. Emerton thus greatly reinforced a trend suggested by Schaff. One of the founders of the American Historical Association, Emerton was a most articulate spokesman of what may be called "secular" Church history. On several occasions, first in 1883 and subsequently,[5] Emerton insisted that all theological presuppositions must be strenuously eliminated from the study of Church history and rejoiced that for the most part Church historians had indeed acquiesced in the fusion of ecclesiastical and secular history, the former being but a chapter of the whole.

Peers or would-be peers of the academic historians, many American chroniclers of Christianity were, like Emerton, utterly committed to this "scientific" approach to their materials. The decision of the newly formed Society of Church History, to reorganize in 1896,[6] as a section of the American Historical So-

[5] "The Study of Church History," *Unitarian Review and Religious Magazine*, XIX (1883), p. 1; "History in Theological Education," *Theological Study Today, Addresses Delivered at the Seventy-Fifth Anniversary of the Meadville Theological School, 1920* (Chicago, 1921), ch. 5; "A Definition of Church History," *Papers of the A.S.C.H.*, 2nd series, VII (1921), p. 55.

[6] In 1906, the Society of Church History was reconstituted and has remained independent of the American Historical Association ever since.

ciety, heartily favored by Emerton, may be taken as an indication of the victory of the proponents of purely objective science, but there was opposition.

An example of the opposition was the reception of Presbyterian-Congregationalist Arthur Cushman McGiffert's *History of Christianity in the Apostolic Age* (1897), launched in the stormy waters of the Briggs controversy. A long and thorough critique, entitled "Dr. McGiffert's Historical Method," in *The Presbyterian and Reformed Review* for 1900 may be taken as representative of the resistance still offered in some well-informed but conservative quarters to the German methodology. McGiffert was charged with being "subjective." Indeed, he may well have opened himself indirectly to the charge when, in his inaugural address in 1893, "The Study of Church History," [7] he endeavored to distinguish a spiritual and *invisible* behind an *empirical* Church history, the latter being the primary concern of the scientific historian. Yet McGiffert, Harnack's first American pupil, was destined to give the tone and direction to the writing and teaching of Church history in the era spanned by his academic career.[8]

A good representative of the mediatory group between, on the one hand, the "scientific" Church historians like Emerton and McGiffert unqualifiedly committed to the new methodology and distrustful of theology and, on the other, the intransigent conservatives, was the Southern Baptist, Albert Henry Newman. Indeed, the publication in 1900 of the first volume of his *Manual of Church History* provides us with a quite convenient date and production with which to characterize the passage from the nineteenth to the twentieth century. In his Introduction,[9] Newman gives six reasons for studying Church history, pointing out not only that it is a vast commentary on Scripture which shows us

[7] *Bibliotheca Sacra*, L (1893), p. 150.

[8] Harnack, regnant in Germany during the same period, died in 1930.

[9] "Preliminary Observations on the Study of Church History." Newman was head of the Church History Department of the New Schaff-Herzog Encyclopedia, successively professor at Rochester Theological Seminary, McMaster University in Toronto, Baylor University, professor and dean Southwestern Baptist Theological Seminary, and Mercer University.

how the slightest departure from New Testament principles has resulted in error—here the older sectarian concern is operative—but also that the study of Church history nevertheless increases charity and mutual understanding, thus promoting Church unity—here the newer interdenominational interest is to the fore. Newman's references to the sources and to foreign and secondary literature are uncommonly rich.[10] In keeping with its denominational origin and sponsorship, the *Manual* gives prominence—still one of its merits—to the dissenting tradition down through the centuries, a survival of an older denominational objective within the framework of German ecclesiastical historiography.

From the date line 1900, marked in American Church historiography by Newman's *Manual*, we may glance backwards and forwards to take note of other representative mediatory publications in the field. In the extensive Introduction of the two-volume *History of the Christian Church* (1897–1900) [11] by the Methodist John Fletcher Hurst (1834–1903), we are particularly fortunate in having the whole perspective of the history of Church history opened before us as seen by one standing at the threshold of the twentieth century. Student at Halle and Heidelberg, administrator of mission institutes in Bremen and then Frankfort, professor and then president of Drew Theological Seminary, bishop and historian of rationalism and Methodism,[12] Hurst represented the new historiography, situated within the denominational context but keenly conscious of the universal Church and thoroughly committed to, and informed by, the newer German methodology. He thus spoke with authority when, after surveying the comparative poverty of American ecclesiastical historiography thus far and its dependence until recently upon Europe, he declared:

[10] To be regretted, however, are Newman's adherence to a largely political periodization.

[11] "The Science and Literature of Church History," I, 15–57. Hurst also published a *Short History of the Christian Church* in 1893, which had the merit of being translated into Spanish and German.

[12] *History of Rationalism* (New York, 1901); *History of Methodism*, 7 vols. (New York, 1902–1904).

The conditions which have limited our development . . . in the past are rapidly disappearing. The American Church has been compelled to address itself to grave social and evangelistic questions, and has confronted them with courage and vigor. At its distance from the great fields of persecution and protracted controversy it will in time acquire that needful equipoise of mind for inquiring carefully and pronouncing judiciously concerning the great matters of the general life of the Church. Concerning that past we can well expect the American Church will be a wise inquirer and an apt disciple at its feet.

It will be seen that Hurst could write quite easily of *the* Church, in the history of which "we observe the constant presence of the divine and human factors."

Methodist Henry Clay Sheldon (1845–1928) of Boston University wrote his *History of the Christian Church* in 1894 for both students and laymen as a contribution to general culture, reducing the doctrinal portion of his narrative, since he had elsewhere written on the history of theology (1886). Significantly, Sheldon devoted three of his five volumes to the modern Church, feeling that within such proportions he could best explain Methodists and American Christians generally to themselves.

Another representative of the mediatory school was the Congregationalist, George Park Fisher (1837–1909) who in 1901 ended his career as professor of ecclesiastical history at Yale. By disposition and achievement more a theologian than a historian in the new objective sense, Fisher in his *History of the Christian Church* (1887) betrays, or shall we say, preserves something of the older denomination-based theological and apologetic interest in the subject.

Williston Walker (1860–1922) succeeded Fisher at Yale in 1901, affording us thus a convenient basis for comparison and a final opportunity for characterizing the earlier phases of the epoch in terms of representative historians. Fisher had written from within the Church: he had been sustained by its ministrations and he had been committed to its theology, an adaptation of the New England theology in the tradition of Nathaniel Taylor. Walker, a Leipzig Ph.D. and, in his first post, a successor to Woodrow Wilson at Bryn Mawr,[13] was more interested in the biographical than the theological dimension in Church history and never felt prompted, by way of theological and historiographical prolegomena, to define the Church and delimit the scope of Church history. He had a disciplined historian's grasp of the development of his own denomination and that of the larger Calvinist tradition. Yet one detects in his works and particularly in his *History of the Christian Church* (1918) the absence of any sense of his writing from the interior of the Church. In effect, by 1918 the denominational vantage point from which Fisher, Hurst, and Newman once wrote their general Church histories had been pretty much eroded. To say that the universal Church histories of these older men had been disguised expansions of denominational histories reaching for larger perspectives would be inexact, but the anchorage of their authors had been the denominational fellowship more than the academic community. Walker, in contrast, was like Emerton a thoroughly academic historian. The University and the nation were for him the primary communities. Thus in his textbook on Church history, published just as the dominance of Germany in all fields was being brought to a close, Walker curiously reproduces, more than any of the historians mentioned, the perspectives and proportions of the German compendia.[14] It is as if he were seeing Church history from the standpoint of his Leipzig days. England, America, and the sects are assigned the limited space more appropriate in the manual of a German state-churchman than of an American free-churchman. By the time Walker completed his textbook the old denominational basis was no longer adequate for writing a warm, committed history with some sense of "I was there" and "This concerns us." The World War had temporarily shattered the international Christian community. And a consciousness of the Christian whole, in the world but not entirely of it, from the interior of which a vital reconception of

[13] Afterwards he went to Hartford Theological Seminary (1892–1901) as Church historian.

[14] Though for the most part up to date on the monographic literature and skillful in summation, Walker's textbook is chronologically maddening.

universal Church history might have been undertaken,[15] had in effect passed when Walker tried his hand at it in 1918, a belated production.

Yet, despite the inadequacy of their definition of the Church or often indeed their want of any such definition of the primary object of their researches, Church historians from 1900 to 1918 seem to have forced a general acceptance of their own evaluation of the importance of their field. For example, that genre of essay or address, defending and clarifying the function of Church history in the seminary curriculum—common just before and at the beginning of our epoch around 1888 and destined to flourish once again around 1933 and thereafter—falls off markedly in the period of consolidation from 1900 to 1918. Confident of themselves as the peers of their counterparts in college and university and, like these, thoroughly committed now to the monographic approach and the other principles and skills of scientific historiography, the early twentieth-century Church historians are keenly conscious of their advantage over their colleagues in systematic theology. Often in that posture which suggests overbearing deference and sometimes with supercilious expressions of esteem for the theological approach, which they nevertheless eschew, they insist upon their right to explore the same body of tradition by the historical approach. Something of the confident, indeed magisterial, pride which possessed the Church historians (and their allies in biblical studies) of their regnant period in the divinity school curriculum comes out, for example, in the presidential address of Williston Walker before the newly reconstituted American Society of Church History in 1907 and in that of the Unitarian Francis Christie in 1909.[16] Both presidents proudly survey the field like generals from a hilltop, noting the deployment of the

---

[15] But significantly, Walker took part in 1919 in a commission looking toward Congregational and Episcopal unity. He published in that year *Approaches Toward Christian Unity*.

[16] "The Current Outlook in Church History," *Papers of the A.S.C.H.,* 2nd series, I (1907), p. 17; "The Year 1909 in Church History," *ibid.,* II (1910), p. 53.

army of Church historians the world over in the struggle against
ignorance and bigotry. As reports of victories on the various national fronts are communicated from the presidential vantage
point, and the announcement of achievements of American Church
historians follow dispatches from afar, one no longer detects anything of that earlier American uneasiness in the face of foreign
scholarship. To be sure, Walker notes the want of any long-
range, systematic, and collective historical projects such as Europe
knew, but this is intended as exhortation to further effort and not
as depreciation of American achievement to date.

These monographic studies, be it noted, could be undertaken
quite successfully without reference to general concepts of, and
convictions about, Church history as a whole.[17] Significantly, no
important *general* Church histories were written during this period
and, as we have already noted, a comprehensive American Church
history remained for the future, when a new national and churchly
self-consciousness would provide the needed motivation and perspective. But some sense of having passed into a distinctly new
season of American culture informs all these writers as they look
back. Thus far we have considered their view of Church history
as a whole. We turn to their understanding of the historic role of
American Christianity.

The twentieth century had opened with the Church historians
absorbed and reconstituted (1896) as a section of the American
Historical Association, conscious of certain general obligations in
respect to American civilization at large and the history thereof.
Shortly before the absorption, Henry Mitchell MacCracken of
New York University had expressed the conviction that the study
of Church history in colleges would strengthen and encourage
the study of history in general.[18] After an extensive survey of the
place of biblical and ecclesiastical history (subsumed for him together under Church history) in American colleges, Continental

[17] Cf. the characterization of H. S. Commager for the two generations
after 1890: "from seeming order to ostentatious disorder." *Op. cit.*, p. 407.
[18] *Papers of the A.S.C.H.*, 1st series, III (1891), p. 217. Newman in the
Preface of his *Manual* saw in Church history a similar value.

gymnasien, and English public schools, MacCracken with a certain eloquence and with the exhilaration of one sustained by a sense of mission, outlined a program of "Church history" for each of the four college years.[19] In support of his program, the then president of the Society of Church History declared that Church history unifies the study of history and philosophy generally and that Church history is indispensable to a proper understanding of America. It is MacCracken's recognition of the importance of religion as a factor in the rise of American civilization as a whole that we may emphasize, a point of view freshly appreciated by his colleagues as Church historians of the early twentieth century looked back upon the century traversed.

Revivalism had been a characteristic and controversial feature of the surging vitality of Christian expansion in the century gone by. But as early as 1902 sufficient perspective and objectivity had been gained for William James to write his *Varieties of Religious Experience* and therewith to lay the foundation of a new and distinctively American contribution to the understanding of religion and its history. Frederick Morgan Davenport presented the *Primitive Traits in Religious Revival* in 1905, Frank G. Beardsley having recounted *A History of American Revivals* in 1904. Henry M. MacCracken had pushed beyond Jonathan Edwards, the fiery preacher and careful observer of the Revival, to Edwards the American philosophical Idealist in *Jonathan Edwards Idealismus* (Halle, 1899), while Frank Hugh Foster of Finney's Oberlin changed his theological convictions in the course of writing *A Genetic History of New England Theology* (1907).

Three other major elements in the shaping of nineteenth-century American Christianity, conflict between science and religion, the problem of slavery, and the impact of successive waves of Continental immigration, had been so farreaching and complicated that a comprehensive chronicling and evaluation thereof was

[19] Old Testament in the freshman, New Testament in the sophomore, ecclesiastical history proper to the Reformation in the junior, and its continuation to the present in the senior year.

not yet generally essayed, although mention may be made of Rationalist Andrew D. White's spirited *History of the Warfare of Science with Theology* in 1896 and W. E. Burghart Du Bois' report of a social study made under the direction of Atlanta University in 1903, *The Negro Church*.

Tremendous missionary activity had characterized the foregoing century. Delavan L. Leonard traced *A Hundred Years of Missions* (1895), William E. Strong told *The Story of the American Board: An Account of the First Hundred Years* (1910). In the person of missionary and prophet-reformer Josiah Strong, the mission of the Church was radically reconceived by the end of the nineteenth century. His epoch-making *Our Country* (1885) and climactic *Expansion under New World Conditions* (1900) gave expression to two new emphases in the Church's missionary outreach; namely, internally social betterment and externally the spread of American democratic righteousness.

With the same dynamism and much the same concern but with greater resources and with more disposition for self-criticism, the Church historian of Rochester Theological Seminary, Walter Rauschenbusch, published *Christianity and the Social Crisis* in 1907. Scarcely remembered as a professor of Church history, though that he was from 1902 until his death in 1918,[20] Rauschenbusch gives a very good idea of his conception of and indebtedness to Church history in the very year of his epoch-making book in an article, "The Influence of Historical Studies on Theology."[21] With his assertions that "Sectarianism is part of original sin" and that "History broadens the sympathies and counteracts sectarian narrowness" we may make the connection between the more academic Church historians thus far considered and the proclaimer of the Social Gospel who, in reinterpreting the divine mandate of the Church, himself made history, and in

[20] Previously he was professor of New Testament in the German department of the Seminary (1897–1902), succeeding therein his father.

[21] *The American Journal of Theology*, XI (1907), p. 111.

thus enlarging the social outreach of the Church, incidentally, called attention to that social dimension destined to become so prominent in subsequent American Church historiography. "History and prophecy are organically related," he declares, and prophetic churchmen must study history and learn "to prolong the curve of the past," for "prophecy is an essential function of the Christian Church."

Rauschenbusch begins his article on the role of Church history by taking note of the recent overturn in the seminary curriculum to the advantage of "historical theology" (Church history) and at the expense of "systematic theology" so long the ranking discipline. He compares this with the curricular revolution of the sixteenth century occasioned by the Reformation elevation of "exegetical theology" (biblical study) over systematic theology, which had long reigned supreme in the Middle Ages and which recovered the throne only after Protestantism had itself entered a scholastic or credal period, now belatedly, as he remarks, drawing to a close in America.

Rauschenbusch, the prophet-historian, insists on a scientifically realistic examination of history, holding it to be the first duty of the professor to rob students and they in their turn their parishioners of all the facile history they know, in order to clear the way for "Church history to furnish the mind with illustrations of immense force, . . . to proclaim in tones of thunder that sin will wreck both men and nations; that light is sown to the righteous, but that when men or churches say to the Lord 'Depart from us,' not even the Almighty can do anything for them." After enlarging on two examples of realistic historiography (giving a primarily social explanation for the Reformation and revising the story of the Roman persecution to the moral advantage of the Roman Empire over the later Roman Church during the Inquisition and over both Protestant and Catholic states during the Wars of Religion), Rauschenbusch concludes in reference to such "illustrations of immense force" that "No sermon could speak to me with such abiding and compulsory power, bidding me to be up and doing before our country [likewise] is beyond the point of recovery."

Rauschenbusch was not himself the author of a Church history but as a valid interpreter of signs and portents, a maker of it, pointing out also a neglected aspect of Church history that the next generation of Church historians were invited to explore. The whole Chicago school—in whose organ his article had appeared— with its emphasis upon social Christianity and environmental factors exemplifies the later effects of the fresh vitalities released by Rauschenbusch for the study of Church history. The effect of Rauschenbusch specifically on Church historiography in America may be set down as comparable to that of James Harvey Robinson in general history whose several essays and articles brought together in *The New History* (1912) gave definition to an analogous trend in American historiography at large. Just as here Freemanesque history as "past politics" was greatly enlarged by the new emphasis on social and cultural factors, so Church history, alerted by the Social Gospel, became dissatisfied with the role of Church history as past dogmatics.

So much for some of the achievements in the widening and deepening of Christian America's understanding of its own past. The monographic and archival basis had been made for a comprehensive, denomination-crossing history of American Christianity in terms of common trends and factors, but as David Schaff wrote quite simply as late as 1912: "The church history of the United States has yet to be written." [22] To be sure, Friedrich Nippold had published his *Amerikanische Kirchengeschichte* [23] and in the very year of the founding of the Society of Church History, Daniel Dorchester with the intention of distinguishing trends and

---

[22] "The Movement and Mission of American Christianity," *The American Journal of Theology* XVI (1912), p. 51. Schaff's six characterizations of American Christianity and his four directives to American Christianity are still helpful pointers.

[23] As Vol. IV of his *Handbuch der neuesten Kirchengeschichte* (1880–1906).

cutting across denominational lines, published his richly factual
Christianity in the United States (1888). But a more inclusive
churchly self-consciousness and a profounder national self-
consciousness were alike prerequisites for a more comprehensive
history. These, the War and the new conditions and temper that
followed it supplied. As it fell out, the national-democratic-social
emphasis preceded the churchly-theological stress, the latter being
the motif of our second epoch (beginning about 1933).

It was the national-social emphasis that sustained the heightened
interest in American Christian history characteristic of the last
phase (1918–1933) of our first epoch, a quite natural consequence
of the new American self-consciousness resulting from involvement in the War. But it is also related to the general decline of
interest in the Old World during the 'twenties. As such it is the
church historical analogue of isolationism! Peter Mode, for example, despite his Canadian background, in assembling his massive
*Source Book and Bibliographical Guide for American Church
History* (1921) neglected to mention foreign works on American
Christianity and failed incidentally to provide any new categories
or a fresh periodization and principle of organization. Subsequently, however, Mode, following the lead of Frederick J. Tur-
ner, introduced in *The Frontier Spirit in American Christianity*
(1923) a new category into the interpretation of American Church
history. Another production in the field suggested by the times
was that of E. F. Humphrey who in *Nationalism and Religion in
America* (1924) discovered the potency of religion during the
Revolution not unlike that of the churches during the War for
democracy. One of the features of post-war American historiography was the way in which secular (academic) and ecclesiastical
historians turned to the same materials, the former rejoicing in the
freshly discovered resources and dimension of their field,[24] the lat-

---

[24] As representative of the academic historians who have greatly strengthened our grasp on American Church history we may mention Arthur
Schlesinger, Vernon Louis Parrington, Ralph Gabriel, Herbert Schneider,
and more recently Henry Steele Commager, Perry Miller, and Arthur

ter greatly stimulated by the new directions, skills, and categories suggested by the cultural historians.

A good example of the direct impact of academic history on American Church history is the career of William Warren Sweet, himself an academic historian before he came to the Divinity School of the University of Chicago in 1927 to occupy the first chair of American Church history in the United States.[25] After filling a widely felt need in preparing a general *Story of Religions in America* (1930), Sweet energetically expanded his field introducing from secular history the new skills, among them co-operative research. A series of massive volumes on the accommodation of the several denominations to the frontier issued from his hands and those of his students. The exhilaration of the fresh approach had still not spent itself as the theme was applied to ever smaller groups and local situations. All these studies have been rich in sources but perhaps more scanty in theological and interpretive elements than even the poverty of such in the period and area considered would have warranted.

II. The Teaching and Writing of Church History in the Current Epoch, 1933–

Symptomatic of the oncoming interest in the compulsion of ideas, theological and otherwise, and the mounting quest of a regnant principle in the shaping of American Church history was the attempt of Thomas C. Hall (who left Union Theological Seminary to become professor of philosophy at Göttingen) to identify Wycliffite dissent as a dominant though socially obscured factor in America in *The Religious Background of American Culture* (1930). Of much greater significance was the bold pre-empting of the theological and ideational interpretation of New England culture—too long neglected on the part of Church

Schlesinger, Jr., whose contributions to the field fall largely in the period following 1933.

[25] It was Roman Catholicism that first became institutionally conscious of American Church history in instituting in 1922 the Catholic University Studies in American Church History.

historians—by Perry Miller in his brilliant *Orthodoxy in Massachusetts* (1933).

Likewise marking the shift of interest and therewith the onset of a new epoch are two contrasting books by H. Richard Niebuhr. His *Social Sources of Denominationalism* (1929) was a valuable analysis of the history of American Christianity in terms of the social and economic factors to which Rauschenbusch and the whole Chicago school of religious history influenced by him had drawn attention. *The Kingdom of God in America* (1937), written, as Niebuhr says, to correct and supplement the socio-economic interpretation of his earlier work, happily embodies or suggests five of the most distinctive characteristics of the Church historiography of the current epoch: (1) a concern for the ultimate meaning of history, (2) a recovery of interest in doctrines as successive transcripts of divine realities traced for the community of faith out of faith and as such charged with a potency of their own in shaping events, (3) a fresh appreciation of the Church as a divine community, reflecting and pointing to the ultimate Kingdom or Rule of God, and in this connection (4) a renewed interest in the historical dynamic and the achievement of community among the voluntarist "sects" as distinguished from the "churches," and (5) a vigorous re-examination of the historic relation between the Church, democracy, and the state.

For this reconception of the scope and office of Church history as indeed of so many other fields, the advent of Hitler and Roosevelt more clearly mark the beginning of a new epoch than did the termination of the War in 1918. The widespread disavowal of the more than half-secular faith in the inevitability of progress (which had managed to survive the World War in America though shattered in Europe) as the specter of Hitler darkened, could not fail to have profound effects upon American conceptions of history and consequently the task of tracing it. The conjunction of Roosevelt and Hitler pointed to a cosmic opposition of good and evil in history, while at the same time the rapid deterioration of German universities brought emphatically to a close a long epoch of American dependence upon German historical scholarship, and this coincided with the intensification of debate as to the proper role of the American people in world history.

The importance of 1933 specifically for Church historiography is confirmed by the clustering of significant events around this date. The year before saw the publication, for instance, of the first volume of *Church History*, the new organ of the reorganized and revitalized American Society of Church History. This Society had heard a stimulating address by John R. Mott in 1931 and in response to his suggestion organized a Church History Deputation to the Orient to ascertain (1) what had been done and what could be done about preserving the original sources for the history of the younger churches and (2) what place Church history then occupied and should occupy in the training of leaders for these churches.[26] In the same year the Church historians of or affiliated with the University of Chicago, published *A Bibliographical Guide to the History of Christianity*, which, with its nine co-ordinate divisions, including (VII) History of Eastern Christianity [27] and (IX) Christianity in Newer Fields, marked the consolidation of the new ground gained in the course of the foregoing period, from which to view, as from a vantage point at once American and ecumenical, the unfolding of Christian history as a whole.

Kenneth Scott Latourette's multi-volume history of Christianity in terms of expansion is written from this new vantage point.[28] Of significance also is the publication in 1933 of the Augustana

[26] See Shirley Jackson Case, "The Church History Deputation to the Orient," *Church History* I (1932), p. 107.

[27] Matthew Spinka, first of Chicago Theological Seminary and then of Hartford, had already appraised the available Western works on the subject and called attention to the general neglect of Slavic Church history in America in "The Present Status of Slavic Studies in Church History" (1925), *Papers of the A.S.C.H.*, 2nd series, VIII (1928). Since then he himself has, along with Slavic and Byzantine academic historians, greatly enriched the field.

[28] *A History of the Expansion of Christianity*, 7 Vols. (1937–1945); restated in *Anno Domini: Jesus, History and God* (1940).

Lutheran Lars P. Qualbens' *A History of the Christian Church*, one of the first [29] general Church histories to come from among the foreign language churches, a compendium which significantly assigns almost a third of its space to North and Latin American Christianity.[30] In such a textbook, which corresponds in type to the histories produced by the older denominations at the end of the nineteenth century, denominational interest determines selection and emphasis. But also beginning about this time, a new type of interpretive Church history or textbook makes its appearance from the pens of historians standing within the older denominations or at least formed by them. Immediately after the First World War, the few new Church histories had been prepared for young people, an effect of the new religious education emphasis. Then in 1931 the textbook of Henry Kalloch Rowe of Andover-Newton appeared with its fresh periodization and its new conception of the Church as implied in the title, *A History of the Christian People*, an example of what might be called Christian cultural history with a new interest in the full dimension of history and in the compulsion of ideas. This development represents in part the penetration and fructification of American Church historiography by impulses stemming from James Harvey Robinson's *The New History*. Another development, making 1933 stand out in American Church historiography is the collecting and editing of fresh ecclesiastical sources under the Work Projects Administration. And of an entirely different order is the death also in 1933 of Arthur Cushman McGiffert, whose two volume *History of Christian Thought* (1932–1933) constitute a particularly fitting legacy from an epoch of "historical theology" to the new epoch of "theological history."

Such are some of the events which make 1933 the dividing

[29] Save for Schaff's that of Lutheran C. M. Jacobs appears to have been the first such, *The Story of the Church* (1925).

[30] The medieval Church is given less than a tenth of the space. The primitive Church is presented in harmony with a conservative Lutheran view of the New Testament.

line between two eras. By way of corroboration one may remark that 1933 marks also a nodal point in the development of secular historical thinking in America. I refer to the controversial presidential address of Charles A. Beard before the American Historical Association in 1933 "Written History as an Act of Faith" and Theodore Clarke Smith's despairing retort the following year.[31] Significantly it was a German *Church* historian Karl Heussi (*Die Krisis des Historismus*, 1930) along with Benedetto Croce who fortified Beard in his onslaught upon historism (the whole system of supposed objectivity in research and in the delineation of actual history) within the American Historical Association. It should be observed in this connection that academic and ecclesiastical historians in the United States have been in general much more responsive to stimuli from foreign historians, secular or churchly, than either to impulses from their colleagues on the other side of the local "wall of separation." Such has been one of the consequences of scholarly isolation in the land where Church and State, Seminary and Academy are separated on principle.

Since the new epoch in American ecclesiastical historiography, with its renewed interest in the theology of history, is characterized also by its being fully abreast of trends in Europe, phases here being now almost completely synchronized with phases there, and the old cultural lag having been made up, it is appropriate to mention a parallel in Europe precisely in the area of the history of Church history. Walter Nigg, *Die Kirchengeschichtsschreibung* (1934), after distinguishing seven types of Church historiography down through the centuries, looks forward to a new historiography which, while abandoning nothing of scientific methodology so hard fought for in the theological field generally, will reappraise the place of theology in Church history and will be particu-

[31] For Beard, *American Historical Review*, XXXIV (1933–1934); p. 219 and the further attack on presumed objectivity in "That Noble Dream," *ibid.*, XLI (1935–1936), p. 74, and for Smith prepared to go down in the controversy with the flags of studied objectivity flying, "The Writing of American History, 1884–1934," *ibid.*, XL (1934–1935), p. 439.

larly concerned to define the Church and to recover the divine dimension thereof. Walter Köhler had already drawn attention to the problem of historiography in the face of the anti-historical or rather the meta-historical implications represented by Barth.[32] But it has been precisely the American analogue of Barthianism which has insisted upon the importance of history and has in consequence commanded attention for a realistic, Christian, and prophetic analysis of our historical situation. Thanks to Reinhold Niebuhr,[33] Paul Tillich and Wilhelm Pauck among others, the radical reconception of orthodox theology based upon a fresh examination of Reformation and hence Augustinian theology, American Protestants are paradoxically (quite appropriately!) more history-conscious now than during the ascendancy of the historical method.

Perhaps nowhere does the impact on Church historiography of this fresh emphasis become so palpable as in the utterances of Church historians in that special type of literature, already several times alluded to, the essay or address or textbook prolegomena entitled "What Is Church History?" Probably no theological discipline has been more self-conscious, at least in America, than Church history. Again and again, Church historians have felt called upon to defend or define their field. Obviously, behind all these efforts to explain the nature and function of their discipline one can overhear the stresses and strains within the American seminary curriculum, adapting itself to ever new community needs and adjusting itself to all the philosophical and theological blows and counterblows. To catch the full significance of the contemporary articulation of the nature and office of Church history we return

[32] *Historie und Metahistorie in der Kirchengeschichte* (1930).

[33] The Reformation "doctrine of 'justification by faith' contains implications for an adequate interpretation of history which have never been fully appropriated or exploited, probably because most Protestant theologies which are interested in the historical problem, have drawn their inspiration from the Renaissance rather than the Reformation." *Nature and Destiny of Man* (1943), II, p. 155. Cf. his *Faith and History: A Comparison of Christian and Modern Views of History* (1949).

for a moment to the era traversed to take note of a representative few of the earlier defenses of Church history.[34]

Within the traditional American seminary "quadrivium," [35] each of the four fields has successively tried to "imperialize" over the others in its regnant period. For the most part in the period between 1900 and 1918, Church history did not have to justify itself; it was taken for granted as worthy of all esteem. It was rather in the immediately preceding phase, as we saw, that the newly developing discipline had to establish its claim over against (depending on the seminary) the previously dominant "exegetical" or, more commonly, "systematic" theology. Then in the phase following the First World War, Church history had again to defend itself, this time over against practical theology. In the spirit of the new functionalism, religious education, social service, and pastoral care were bulking large in the seminary curriculum,

[34] In the nineteenth century before 1888 there were, for example:

E. A. Park, tr., "Theological Encyclopaedia and Methodology: From the Unpublished Lecture of Prof. Tholuck," Sections 27-30 on Church history, *Bibliotheca Sacra*, I (1844), pp. 569-575.

Philip Schaff, *What is Church History?: A Vindication of the Idea of Historical Development* (Philadelphia, 1846).

Henry B. Smith, "The Nature and Worth of the Science of Church History," *Bibliotheca Sacra*, VIII (1851), p. 412.

William G. T. Shedd, "The Nature and Definition of Church History," *Lectures upon the Philosophy of History* (Andover, 1856), Lecture III.

Egbert Cotton Smyth, *Value of the Study of Church History in Ministerial Education* (Andover, 1874).

Joseph Henry Allen, *On the Study of Christian History* (Cambridge, 1878).

Ephraim Emerton (1883), above, n. 5.

John De Witt, *Church History as a Science, as a Theological Discipline, and as a Mode of the Gospel* (Cincinnati, 1883); reprinted in *Bibliotheca Sacra*, XLI (1884), p. 95.

For the epoch beginning with 1888 up to 1918 there are, for example:
Philip Schaff, *The Reunion of Christendom* (New York, 1893).
Arthur Cushman McGiffert (1893), above, n. 7.
John Fletcher Hurst (1897), above, n. 11.
Albert Henry Newman (1900), above, n. 9.
Walter Rauschenbusch (1907), above, n. 21.

[35] This is W. Barnett Blakemore's helpful re-employment and definition, "The Nature and Structure of the Practical Field," *Journal of Religion* XXIX (1949), p. 248. His introductory observations are particularly instructive.

while history was widely scorned. The comparatively large number of Church histories in the twenties, and thereafter, adapted to church schools and adult classes are evidence of the tribute paid by Church history to the new contender for hegemony in the seminary curriculum. Writings on the nature and function of Church history now appealed to the practical. We may instance Robert Hastings Nichols, "Aims and Methods of Teaching Church History" (1920),[36] John Alfred Faulkner, *On the Value of Church History* (1920), Ephraim Emerton, "History in Theological Education" (1920),[37] Roland Bainton, "Church History and Progress" (1922),[38] and Conrad Moehlman (who even from the early 'twenties was very much interested in schemes of popularizing history and who has continued to be especially interested in education), "Is the History of Christianity Practical?" (1926).[39]

Then, with the advent of the current epoch, efforts to redefine Church history become once again numerous, symptomatic of the readjustment and enforced re-evaluation of the discipline in the face of the world situation and the return of theology to her throne within the seminary curriculum. In this change of dynasty, "historical theology"—to perpetuate the older term for Church history for the moment—finds itself either a fierce foe of the new "systematic theology" or its enthusiastic ally while still carrying out a rearguard action against practical theology.

As representative of the lingering concern that Church history as a seminary discipline renew its credentials from time to time as a useful subject, we may take the inaugural address, "What is

[36] *Papers of the A.S.C.H.*, 2nd series, VII (1921), p. 39.

[37] See above, n. 5.

[38] *Education for Christian Service* by Members of the faculty of the Divinity School of Yale University (New Haven, 1922), p. 243.

[39] *The Rochester Theological Seminary Bulletin*, LXXVI (1925/26), p. 204.
  We may mention here as belonging to the genre but not illustrative one way or the other of the trend, William Walker Rockwell, "Rival Presuppositions in the Writing of Church History," *Papers of the A.S.C.H.*, 2nd series, IX. It is largely concerned with Catholic bias in ecclesiastical historiography.

the Value of Church History for the Minister?" [40] by John T. McNeill of Union Theological Seminary,[41] who in so many of his writings exemplifies that responsiveness, characteristic of many contemporary Church historians, to appropriate assignments suggested by the ongoing life and changing concerns of the Church.[42] "The Task of the Church Historian" [43] (1940) by Sidney E. Mead, Sweet's successor at Chicago, combines this high-level practical concern with the newer convictions about the special vocation of the Church historian in the academic community: to both tradition-bound and secularized students, he says, "in the final analysis the church historian is an evangelist." Mead significantly combines the older sociological emphasis of the Chicago school with the newer interest in the theological dimension of Church history. Utterly loyal to scientific methodology, he is pleased to observe that " 'Objectivity' is not indifference to the outcome for the historian any more than for the detective." And while pointing to the important function of history in the emancipatory process of developing personal and communal "self-consciousness," he puts one on guard against any fundamentalism or catholicizing, which would obtrude a creed or an institution into the relationship between man and God in the present attempt to check secularism.

Mead's colleague at Chicago, James Hastings Nichols, is prepared to go further. Nichols' emphasis on the Church and his ascription of almost epistemological importance to committed

[40] *Anglican Theological Review*, XXVII (1945), p. 41.

[41] Formerly of Chicago (1927–44) and before that of Knox College, Toronto.

[42] To mention only some of his books, around which could be clustered a very much larger number of related books and articles: *Unitive Protestantism* (1930) pointed up the survival of conciliar catholicity among sixteenth century Protestants, to which the ecumenical movement could appeal for historic support; *Christian Hope for World Society* (1937) provided historical perspective and inspiration for Christian social action and indirectly threw considerable light on contemporary debate on Church-State relations; his editing of *Medieval Handbooks of Penance* (1938), while it grew out of his earlier doctoral interest in Celtic Church history, provided historical specimens of their art for those concerned with pastoral care.

[43] *The Chronicle: A Baptist Quarterly*, XII (1949), p. 127. The introduction is given over to a helpful identification of four meanings of "history."

membership therein for a completed understanding of its history are all the more significant for the reason that this Church historian, son of a distinguished Church historian, served for a while in teaching and in writing on general cultural history.[44] His conception of Church history has found expression in two essays, "Church History and Secular History" (1944)[45] and "History in the Theological Curriculum" (1946).[46]

In the former article he shows the dependence of secular historiography on Church history not alone in the chronological sense but also in the profounder sense of its basic concerns, noting that it was precisely Augustine, the first to write an extended interpretation of all history, who also wrote the first real biography. "Christianity revealed a new *man* quite literally, as well as a new type of human *community* for such men, and modern secular history is inconceivable without these presuppositions." Then, noting how nineteenth-century historians advanced beyond the rationalist historians of the Enlightment in their appreciation of what might be called the sacramental aspect of history (culture) he observes that *Kultur* itself "becomes the holy church of modern secular man, and the historian becomes his priest." Nichols notes the way general cultural history was progressively nationalized[47] and Christian categories of history were secularized. But Nichols goes on to deplore the further particularization of history with the consequent loss of universal perspectives leading to the present crisis in history and concludes:

Surely there is a particular vocation for church history, especially modern church history, in this crisis, a church history broadened beyond ecclesiastical and doctrinal considerations to include the whole moral and spiritual life of those called to Christian loyalties, even at

[44] His first teaching position was at Macalester College. Some of his ideas on history are expressed in his Introduction to Jacob Burckhardt's *Weltgeschichtliche Betrachtungen*, tr. as *Force and Freedom: Reflections on History* (New York, 1943).

[45] *Church History*, XXXI (1944), p. 87.

[46] *The Journal of Religion*, XXVI (1946), p. 183.

[47] "Ranke was practically the last of the great historians who could comprehend the variety and intransigence of the new secular national states from the catholic perspective of a humanist church historian."

second hand. With the rapid decrease of the number of humanist historians of good will (of Judeo-Christian derivation), secular society is losing interpreters with insight for the values of universal humanity, universal moral standards, individual moral responsibility and a humble sense of the imperfection of all earthly institutions. Even secular society then may be served by historians based, not on a demonstrated theodicy, but on a wager and prayer to the Revealer of these truths that the destiny of mankind be indeed hidden in Christ and the God of Abraham, Isaac and Jacob.

Turning from the office of Church history for culture to its function for the Church, Nichols becomes more explicit about taking a stand avowedly from within the community of faith. He breaks explicitly from the school of Church history that in concentrating on environmental factors had "put second things first." Deploring the impoverishment of the sense of history in America, a legacy of the eighteenth-century rationalism and individualism which has shaped the contours of the American mind more than that of any other major people, Nichols rejoices in the ecumenical movement which has at length obliged us to think genetically about our denominational differences and has thus indirectly helped American Christians recover a sense of history, "not so much in the sense of knowing, as *belonging*." He points out, moreover, that Christianity properly "insists on its historical origins . . . because the initiation of the Christian faith was, itself, not a communication of a theology or ethics but a dramatic intrusion of God in Christ"; and thus in the profoundest sense "the Christian communion with God is not possible without a minimum of historical knowledge. . . ." And since history like autobiography ("history is the autobiography of a community") is usually written "from the vantage point of some decisive turn in life," Nichols expects that some of the best Church history will be composed in our time.

With convictions allied to those of Nichols, the Episcopalian Cyril Richardson of Union Theological Seminary declares in "Church History Past and Present" (1949) [48] that history has a

---

[48] *Union Seminary Quarterly Review*, V (1949), p. 3. The larger part of the inaugural address is given over to an attractive account of the history of Church history at Union.

prophetic function, alluding here to the inclusion of the historical books among the Prophets, and that the Church historian "cannot, if he tries to write sacred history in its fullest sense, be content to confine himself to that bare record of events which we know as *scientific* history [italics mine] . . . he has to tell the story against the background of ultimate meanings. He has to recognize that he stands on the boundary between symbol and fact, between myth and history, because the events with which he deals are transfigured by the holy." And like several other historians mentioned, Richardson holds that "Church history is inevitably the fountain from which reformation springs," instancing, for example, the many reformations which have appealed to some freshly rediscovered aspect of Augustine.

It is clear from this sampling of what might be called the self-conscious reflections of strategically located contemporary Church historians that Church history, where it is in league with the new theology, is conscious of a fresh sense of vocation after the aimlessness or self-apology in the presence of the practical field common during the history-debunking 'twenties. Moreover, as "theological history" it has fully recovered both the self-esteem and the outward respect within the seminary curriculum which as "historical theology" it had formerly enjoyed during the period from 1900 to 1918, when it had been, as we can see in retrospect, somewhat over-confident in the redemptive role of scientific method.

But this theologizing has not gone on unchallenged. As an opponent of what he pillories as "the revival of historical dualism" we may mention Shirley Jackson Case, sometime head of the Chicago school of religious history, who expressed his alarm at the new trend in *The Christian Philosophy of History* (1943). And in an essay [49] in the same year, the sometime Catholic priest George La Piana, Church historian at Harvard Divinity School (1917–1947), quite properly distinguished between the philosophy

[49] "Theology of History," *The Interpretation of History*, edited by Joseph R. Strayer (Princeton, 1943), p. 149. Cf. also his sensitive and at points almost vicariously "autobiographical" address "Ernesto Buonaiuti," *Harvard Divinity School Bulletin*, XLIV (1947), p. 47.

and the theology of history, isolating the four pillar myths of the latter, whether it be the Augustinian, the Democratic, or the Fascist "theology of history." He takes no notice of the currents astir in Protestant thinking. More obviously irritated than alarmed by the orthodox trend, is the New Testament scholar Chester C. McCown of the Pacific School of Religion, expressing thereto hostility in his article "In History or Beyond History" (1945).[50] These random outbursts are probably representative of a much larger, as yet inarticulate or perhaps as yet unaffected body of Church historians, than these few writings would indicate. But it is clear that there is among Protestant Church historians nothing comparable to the debate raised in academic history circles, for example, by Carl Becker's rarification of supposedly hard historical facts (1926)[51] and particularly by Charles A. Beard's address, "Written History an Act of Faith" (1933).[52]

Turning now from the contemporary expressions concerning the nature and function of Church history, we may, in conclusion, take note of the topics and issues of greatest current interest and of the prospects for achievement in the field.

American Church historians are increasingly concerned with collecting and editing New World source materials. Old World sources are being translated apace. Of interest here is Campbell Bonner's important addition to Patristic sources in his editing from the fourth-century Michigan-Beatty codex, Melito's *Homily on the Passion* (1940), and A. J. F. Ziegelschmit's editing of *The Greater Chronicle of the Hutterian Brethren* (1943), a capital source long believed to be lost, which came to light in an American settlement. In 1949 the American Society for Reformation Research assumed joint responsibility with its revived German counterpart for the ongoing publication of the old *Archiv* as an international series under the title *Archivum Reformationis Historicum.*

[50] *The Harvard Theological Review*, XXXIII (1945), p. 41.

[51] "What are Historical Facts?" Presidential Address before the American Historical Association in Rochester, N.Y.

[52] See above, n. 31.

The exploration of the left wing of the Reformation, already greatly stimulated by the work of Roland Bainton of Yale Divinity School, will be further extended with the mounting scholarly interest in their own sources among the numerous representatives of the Old World sects, notably the Mennonites. New classifications and fresh categories of interpretation, suggested by sociology, economics, and psychology, have already clarified the field.

We may expect also extensive exploration in the historic concepts of the Church of which Cyril Richardson's *The Church Through the Centuries* (1938) is undoubtedly a harbinger. Nor is it ecumenicity alone that will promote such studies. A full-length history of ecclesiology has never been written; it is only as institutions are gravely imperiled that we seek to define and defend them. Liturgical history and liturgy as a source will become increasingly prominent.

We may expect fresh research into the role of the foreign language churches in the process of acculturation and especially into the tensions both within the individual immigrant and between the first and second generations—tensions in which, by a reversal of socio-psychological roles all too frequently overlooked, it is the melting-pot democracy which becomes the community of *rebirth*, venturesome commitment and hope while the foreign language church serves in effect as the community of *birth*, protective cohesion, and memory. The half articulated feeling for America as at once a gathered Church and the Kingdom of God in process of fulfilment invites continued exploration into the relationship of Christianity and democracy with special attention in the future to the relationship of the Church to labor. Henry F. May's *Protestant Churches and Industrial America* (1949) and before it C. H. Hopkins' *The Rise of the Social Gospel in American Protestantism* (1940) belong in this line. Studies of the religious sources of democracy like those of Parrington and Gabriel will be succeeded by studies critical of the often too easy conflation of Christianity and nationalism recently probed by Koppel Pinson, *Pietism as a Factor in the Rise of German Nationalism* (1934), and Salo Baron, *Religion and the Rise of Nationalism* (1947). One may observe, incidentally, in connection with these writers, that the cultural ethos of America is such that American Jewish scholars feel utterly free to carry their researches into the Christian field with no religious self-consciousness and often, indeed, with extraordinary perception of the subtleties of Christian theology: witness e.g., the foregoing writers and Harry A. Wolfson of Harvard on the ongoing influence of Philo in the Fathers.

The present year has seen the publication of a three-volume climax to a mounting series of monographic and general studies on a theme of ever increasing interest and concern, *Church and State in the United States* by Anson Philips Stokes. Magnificent achievement that it is, we may expect numerous other studies freshly examining the more ancient sources and exploring also the bearing of changing Christologies and ecclesiologies on the historic relations between Church and State with a view to ascertaining the viability of the present doctrine of strict separation. Paul Tillich in his distinction between "autonomy" (in this context, secularism) and "heteronomy" (in this context, ecclesiasticism) and his clear definition of the middle position so difficult to perpetuate, "theonomy," has introduced a new set of theological categories that will prove especially valuable in guiding American research into the history of Church and State.[53]

As contemporary concern with Church-State relations invites or rather compels historical inquiry, so it is possible that the newer practical disciplines which are currently undergoing redefinition (religious education, church management, pastoral care, the interest in healing) and the older but undermined disciplines (preaching, for example) will press for historical exploration, documentation, and inspiration—as examples R. C. Petry's edition of medieval sermons, *No Uncertain Sound* (1948) and Carl J. Scherzer's *The Church and Healing* (1950).

[53] Paul Blanshard's *American Freedom and Catholic Power* (1949) is a splendid example of the strength and the limitations of the attack upon "heteronomy" from the vantage point of "autonomy." A "theonomous" inquiry remains a desideratum.

As far as geographical areas go, given the stimulation of La-tourette's magnificent history and the general American interest in the Pacific, we may reasonably expect substantial local and national histories of the younger churches of the Orient to make their appearance soon. If written by Americans in the cultural-historical mood, these histories will undoubtedly give prominence to problems of cultural interpenetration, ethical compromise and syncretism and, incidentally, will throw further light on the expansion of Christianity in the Greco-Roman and the Barbarian worlds.

As to epochs or periods of Church history, it is quite probable, given the fateful contraction of German scholarship and academic means, that New World scholars will feel emboldened to explore Germany in the Reformation century, the more so for at least three reasons: the extended Occupation, the maturation of the immigrant churches on the American scene pressing forward to wider academic interests, and finally the renewal of interest in the Reformation induced by the new theological emphasis. Roland Bainton's clear and discerning *Here I Stand* (1950) and E. G. Schwiebert's massive *Luther and his Times* (1950) are the rich first fruits in the line of Preserved Smith. Another period for which revisions are in store is Christian antiquity. Robert M. Grant in his recent survey entitled "The Future of the Ante-Nicene Fathers" [54] describes the recent gains and declares that the Golden Age in this area lies just ahead. The maturation of American biblical scholarship and the skills and achievements of American archeology will make up for the decline in classical studies and in conjunction with the extensive textual preparation underscored by Grant, insure great advances in the history of the Ancient Church. The monumental *Christianity and Classical Culture* (1944) by the Canadian C. N. Cochrane is an example of the kind of bold revisions we may expect in this field.

And finally, if we follow James Hastings Nichols' suggestion as to the relationship of crisis, catastrophe, and momentous decision

[54] *Journal of Religion*, XXX (1950), p. 109.

to the writing of autobiography and history, perhaps we may expect some comprehensive (I should like to say, momentous) historical interpretation of the nature and destiny of American Christianity. It is quite possible that it will be written by an American Negro historian of the Church, reaching back for basic categories of interpretation to the Judaeo-Christian experience of redemptive suffering and to the concept of God's Covenant with His ongoing Israel of history.

BIBLIOGRAPHY

Mode, Peter, *The Frontier Spirit in American Christianity* (New York, 1923)

Niebuhr, H. Richard, *The Kingdom of God in America* (New York, 1937)

Schaff, Philip and David, *History of the Christian Church* (New York, 1882–1910)

Walker, Williston, *A History of the Christian Church* (New York, 1944)

Latourette, Kenneth Scott, *A History of the Expansion of Christianity* (New York, 1937–1945)

McNeill, John T., *Christian Hope for World Society* (New York, 1937)

Hardy, E. R., Jr., *Militant in Earth* (New York, 1940)

Hurst, John Fletcher, "The Science and Literature of Church History," *History of the Christian Church* (1897/1900), I, pp. 15–57.

MacCracken, Henry Mitchell, "The Place of Church History in the College Course of Study," *Papers of the American Society of Church History*, III (1891), p. 217.

Rauschenbusch, Walter, "The Influence of Historical Studies on Theology," *The American Journal of Theology*, XI (1907), p. 111.

Schaff, David, "The Movement and Mission of American Christianity," *The American Journal of Theology*, XVI (1912), p. 51.

Nichols, James Hastings, "Church History and Seculary History," *Church History*, XXXI (1944), p. 87; "History in the Theological Curriculum," *The Journal of Religion*, XXVI (1946), p. 183.

PASTORAL THEOLOGY
AND PSYCHOLOGY

Seward Hiltner

SEWARD HILTNER was born in Pennsylvania in 1909, and he was educated at Lafayette College and the Divinity School of the University of Chicago. Prior to taking up his present position as Associate Professor of Pastoral Theology in the Federated Theological Faculty of the University of Chicago, he was for twelve years Executive Secretary of the Department of Pastoral Services of the Federal Council of the Churches of Christ in America. In this capacity he organized many research groups and spoke at numerous conferences in almost every state in the union. He is the author of several well-known books and numerous articles and pamphlets on counseling, the relations between psychology and religion, co-operation between doctors and ministers, etc. His best-known books are *Pastoral Counseling* and *Religion and Health*, and he edited *Clinical Pastoral Training*. He also serves as consultant for *Pastoral Psychology* magazine.

VIII

THE TITLE of this chapter is a kind of recent history in minia-
ture. If we referred only to "pastoral theology," we should be
attempting to link the pre-scientific formalism of the nineteenth
century with current dynamic thinking, and largely ignoring the
intervening stages of development. If our term were only "pastoral
psychology," we should be emphasizing a basic period of development, but implying that it had no antecedents or no future as an
inherent part of the Protestant Christian enterprise. Both terms,
and their relationship, are needed if an accurate assessment of this
field is to be made.

In 1900

By the end of the nineteenth century, pastoral theology in the
United States was a combination of formalism, dedicated intentions, and assiduity. The formalism was little in evidence in the
great evangelical churches like the Methodist and Baptist, but
was important in the liturgical or doctrinal churches like the Episcopal, Lutheran or Presbyterian. The former groups, although
settling down in a more settled country, were still basking in the
afterglow of the frontier movements with their revivals, their feeling of prophetic expansiveness, and their general itch to be up
and moving. They had little time for or interest in the laborious
and formal analyses of pastoral, moral and ascetical theology which
had been developed in Great Britain and Germany. Their theme
was evangelism, not edification. The "interviews" that accompanied revival meetings were not sufficiently individualized to
lead toward a pastoral theology.

Pastoral theology in the formal sense had been developed as a
study by an established priesthood or ministry. When the line
between minister and layman became hard to draw, educationally

as well as sacramentally, it was natural that there should be little interest in formal studies developed in a different context. Besides, these churches simply counted on the group itself to perform the edifying or sanctifying function. Growth in the Christian life was to come about through association with one's brother pilgrims. Since no priestly intermediaries were necessary, the practical conclusion often drawn was that no professional assistance was likely to be helpful. In short, these churches were not only uninterested in pastoral theology; they were even disinclined to ask the questions out of which a pastoral theology might have emerged.

The more liturgical and doctrinal churches were in a different position. Their closer emotional relation to the more settled churches of Britain and Germany was reflected in their tendency to stick closer to the eastern seaboard or, if they moved west as did the great German migrations of the nineteenth century, to become settled societies as rapidly as possible. We now see a fairly obvious connection between their urge to establish social stability and their interest in liturgical or doctrinal correctness, a marked need for order being the requisite in both instances for feeling at home. This was in contrast to the more ebullient churches which captured the frontier, where vitality was more important than order, and expansiveness than stability.

The orderly churches continued to insist on an educated ministry. The patterns of theological education reflected little of Emerson's American scholar, and were largely taken over from those of the respective mother countries. Study was liberal arts, stressing languages and literature, plus a continuation of the same patterns into theological education itself. Indeed, the most striking fact about the theological seminaries at the turn of the century was that they conceived their task to be chiefly an extension into a particular content of the procedures of liberal arts education.[1] The notion that professional education ought to analyze operations as well as content, the people as well as the gospel, was not firmly

[1] See "The Nature and Structure of the Practical Field," by W. B. Blakemore, *Journal of Religion*, Vol. 29, No. 4 (October, 1949).

grasped. The very business of having a seminary and insisting on formal theological education seemed against it.

There were in the seminaries some courses on practical or pastoral theology. Those in the Reformed tradition were almost entirely about methods of preaching. Those with Anglican ties studied moral and ascetical theology, which were in their turn descendants at long range of the penitentials and at briefer range of clear-headed British casuistry. The English penchant for common-sense moral thinking was clear. They did not, however, have a "case-work" point of view as we would think of that today. Moral theology, so far as it dealt with individuals, dealt with their offenses. Ascetical theology was procedural, but on the basis of a generalized Christian man.

The seminaries in the Lutheran tradition had, thanks to the German pastoral theologians of the early nineteenth century, a more comprehensive theory and framework than did the others. They recognized the unity of the ministry, and attempted to analyze pastoral operations so as to stress that unity while approving the obvious diversity of activities. But they were, from our contemporary point of view, lacking in content. They had the form and structure and order of a pastoral theology, but little to say within it.

In general, therefore, the pastoral theology of 1900 was formalistic where it existed at all. It was also compounded of dedicated intentions and persevering "art." The books of this period which were not purely formal in character tended to exhortations, to the pastor or theological student, to love people, spend time with them, call upon them. We would have a parallel if the clinical textbooks of medicine should consist mainly of urging that the physician value clinical practice, make home visits, not rely on people coming to his office, and be devoted to serving his patients. In either event, such books have a valuable place. But in medicine they were not at that time confused with clinical texts.

Thus, most of the writing on pastoral theology in that period was either formalistic or anecdotal or both. Once a formal framework had been established, the assumption was that a pastor proceeded by art and assiduity. It was and is clear that there is always a personal element transcending not only mechanical procedures but also attempts at formal definition. But the emphasis on exploiting one's charm, and doing his duty by pastoral work, betrayed the assumptions that there was no body of knowledge on which to build and that pastoral work was a price one paid for the privileges of preaching or conducting worship. This meant that there was no intellectual challenge in pastoral theology except at the point of the purely formal and theoretical.

This analysis is not meant to suggest that no good pastoral work was being done. We cannot doubt that here, as throughout the history of the church, the thoughtful and sympathetic interest of pastor and congregation were immensely helpful to multitudes of people. Besides, the decline of group discipline over the individual church member during the nineteenth century tended to extend the range of human problems on which pastor and congregation felt an impulse to help and not merely to correct.[2] This humanizing trend undoubtedly extended the number of persons who were helped by the practice of pastoral theology.

But even when they did well, they knew not what they did. And they were certainly ignorant, when they failed, of the reasons for failure. In our current perspective, they were not wrong to be interested in the formal and theoretical at one end, and humanitarian anecdotalism at the other. They were wrong in not realizing that the area in between was being neglected, and that in it lay the hope of a new pastoral theology. This middle area we could characterize variously as psychological content, as the study of interpersonal and intrapsychic processes, or as the application of scientific method, broadly conceived, to understanding what is actually occurring in people as the pastor goes about his work with them.

Psychology gave no help on this during the previous century.

[2] See the forthcoming *A History of the Cure of Souls*, by John T. McNeill.

Until the time of Wundt, in Germany, after the American Civil War, psychology was pre-scientific, introspective, and a handmaid to any particular philosophy. It was structural in character, based on the faculties in terms of content. The first advance came with the creation of Wundt's psychological laboratory, with the consequent movement for attempting to understand psychological processes by observing them systematically. At first such methods, naturally enough, were applied to apparently simpler phenomena, which mean that they were relatively divorced from the totality of man's complex experience as man. Neither faculty psychology, which lingered on, nor experimental psychology, which was rapidly growing, could at that stage help put meat on the pastoral theological bones.[3]

In our modern sense, there was no pastoral psychology at the beginning of this century. Experimental psychology had not got far enough to become a general dynamic psychology, and hence offered no adequate background. Faculty psychology was being exploded at specific points by experimental work. Not until there should be dynamic trends in psychology, which nevertheless moved closer to man and not just some function of man, could there be a base upon which a pastoral psychology could be erected.

In this analysis of where we were, no mention has been made of the fact that William James, John Dewey, Sigmund Freud and George A. Coe began their work before 1900. Each of them, in his own way, was to be, however unintentionally, a stage designer for the new drama of pastoral theology and psychology which the present century would produce. But their influence, while beginning earlier, did not have such an effect until after 1900.

Psychology of Religion

There were four broad movements or currents of thought which seem to be chiefly responsible in the first part of the century for the developments which have led to pastoral theology and

[3] See *Historical Introduction to Modern Psychology*, by Gardner Murphy.

psychology as we now understand them. These are the study of the psychology of religion, progressive education and religious education, psychoanalysis and the development of the several psychotherapeutic professions, and the successive theological movements, to use the common labels, of the social gospel and neo-orthodoxy. We shall consider them in turn.

In America the psychology of religion was begun not by pastors or professional churchmen but by university scholars who sensed, in the broadly empirical method which psychology had begun to use, opportunities for understanding certain religious phenomena for which no previous process explanations had been offered.[4] By those who tended to be sympathetic to religion and the church, the analysis stressed religious phenomena of the more extreme type, not practiced by the respectable. In those with an antipathy toward religion, notably J. H. Leuba, the tendency was to debunk even the religious theory and practice of the respectable.

The great American classicists of the psychology of religion were Edwin D. Starbuck, J. H. Leuba, G. Stanley Hall, Irving King, E. S. Ames, George A. Coe and, pre-eminently, William James.[5] Hall, Leuba and Starbuck began with adolescence and the relation of that developmental age to sudden religious conversions. This set a pattern for many followers, so that the most frequently discussed subjects under the rubric of psychology of religion came to be conversion and mysticism.

King and Coe made the first attempts to link the incipient process knowledge of religious phenomena with the normal course of religious development in the individual, Coe's far-reaching contribution being second only to that of James in the whole field.[6] Ames attempted to link patterns of social understanding with psychological knowledge. The greatest work was of course by James. Perhaps most important among his many contributions

[4] For a general survey, see my "The Psychological Understanding of Religion," *Crozer Quarterly*, V. 24, No. 1 (January 1947).

[5] *Varieties of Religious Experience.*

[6] *The Religion of a Mature Mind* (Revell, 1902), and *The Psychology of Religion.*

was at that time his demonstration that religious phenomena could be understood through analysis of their development, and that such understanding did not necessarily detract from their validity. Pastors and theologians were wary of James's pluralism; but his positive emotional tone toward religion was often more convincing than his pluralistic ideas.

Except through his writings, however, James did not teach pastors or theological students. George A. Coe did. In the tens and twenties, one citadel after another of heretofore psychologically unstudied religious phenomena was examined by him, his students, and others. The way religion operates—any religion, in any kind of person—was susceptible to examination. Nearly all the theological schools introduced at least one basic course in the psychology of religion. If its purpose was in many instances chiefly apologetic, to prepare students against this new source of theological attack, it could not remain wholly at that level, but became also positive.

During the twenties there appeared many new texts on the psychology of religion, most of them simply building on the work of the classicists without any new orientation. During the thirties and forties there was very little writing which called itself the psychology of religion, and but one significant new general text in the field.[7] The single genuinely original contribution was by Anton T. Boisen in the mid-thirties, who successfully challenged the contention, made even by James, that a fairly clear line could be drawn between understanding normal and pathological religious processes.[8] It has not been until 1950 that a new general avenue of progress for the psychology of religion has found its way into print, based on James but taking all of the intervening developments in dynamic psychology and psychotherapy into account.[9]

The fact is that the psychology of religion has won the point

[7] *Psychology of Religion,* by Paul E. Johnson.
[8] *The Exploration of the Inner World,* by Anton T. Boisen.
[9] *The Individual and His Religion,* by Gordon W. Allport.

which brought it into being. Religious phenomena are capable of being understood like any others. If the methods are complex, if analysis is sometimes made the cloak for reductionism, if our knowledge is mightily incomplete, still it is valuable even for religionists to learn what can be learned about the processes of religious development.

It is possible that the trend represented by Allport may result in the recrudescence of a study known as the psychology of religion, especially since psychology in general has become less scientistic in its philosophy and less attached to a laboratory point of view which would exclude reflection on meaning. Certainly there will be more work and studies. Pastoral theologians and psychologists of religion have now a basis and temper for work together which has not previously existed.

The significance of these developments in the psychology of religion for pastoral theology and psychology is plain. There could be no far-reaching pastoral theology unless there were a content in pastoral psychology. And there could be no such pastoral psychology if the processes of religious development in the individual were unexaminable. If they were to be examined for purposes other than general debunking, there had to be a conviction that whatever was found would in the long run strengthen the religion which ought to be strengthened. This is the permanent contribution of the psychology of religion to pastoral theology.

Religious Education

The second evocative movement was progressive education and religious education. The prophet and leader in secular education was John Dewey. Although Dewey remains incomprehensible to Europeans, and his permanent contribution is hidden under the bushel of turgid prose and metaphysical positivism, his fundamental influence upon education and religious education will remain as constructive. Dewey's basic point was that people learn in proportion as they recognize their interests to be touched.

If their interests are recognized to have some inherent worth, and they develop as contact is made with these, then there emerges a theory of education which refutes any authoritarian approach in education.

Because Dewey's philosophy and psychology were evolved around education, they did not partake of the fragmentation with which early twentieth century psychology was afflicted. Hence Dewey was close to a theory and practice of total personality years before the psychologists caught up.[10] It was his totalism and developmentalism which caught the eye of religious educators. They were trying to teach religion. But they became suspicious of Bible verses and homilies on love. They wanted not just to communicate knowledge about religion, but to bring about an inward appropriation of religion. It occurred to them that there was a difference between the intention of the educator and the performance of the pupil. This led to consideration of methods, and direct to Dewey. If they wanted children, and adults, to appropriate and assimilate meaningfully, voluntarily, and from within, they would do well to begin by touching existing interests or felt needs. If they were not imposing something external, they had better prove it.

It is difficult for us now to realize how radical this philosophy of religious education sounded forty years ago. For meanwhile the basic point has been won, to such an extent that we can not envision what it fought to conquer. It is true that Horace Bushnell had adumbrated such a notion as Schleiermacher had done still earlier for a psychology of religion. But Bushnell's point had been that children did not have to have life direction completely re-directed if it were rightly routed in the first place. The new point went further. Possibly children's needs, as made known in one way or another by children themselves, might say something about where they should go. It is true that reactionaries in religion and education have tried to make a mockery of the

[10] See article on Dewey's psychology by G. W. Allport, and Dewey's reply, in *The Philosophy of John Dewey*, edited by A. Schilp.

Dewey views. Yet the essential point in those views has won over every form of reaction. Education, secular and religious, is the beneficiary of the fight which Dewey and the religious educators waged against education in terms of the intention of the educator apart from the relationships involved in the educative process.

The immediate result of the Dewey trends in religious education was to create an educational group within the church but not of it, a group of educational leaders paralleling the ecclesiastical leaders but with a philosophy of development instead of a philosophy of transmission. The details of this development do not belong in this chapter. But the influence of the trend upon pastoral psychology's development does have a place here.

As soon as the religious educators took seriously the developmental idea, they found themselves with a point of view which plainly had as much significance for work with individuals as for work with groups, for pastoral work as for religious education. Along with this, in theological seminaries' departments of religious education, came a vital sense that here was the new against which the old could not stand, that here was a point of view which was relevant not alone to religious education in the narrow sense but to the work of the church as a whole. Consequently courses began to appear on religious education and worship, religious education and counseling, religious education and something else. Unintentionally, a powerful movement had been set in motion for breaking down the artificial lines of division in the operations of the pastor and the church. The fact that this was done imperialistically, as if religious education were the creditor and everything else the debtor, was inevitable but unfortunate.

The religious education movement became like the hospital chaplain who has seen the patient through a serious illness. The chaplain is remembered gratefully, even revered, so long as the ravages of illness persist. But so soon as his basic work has been done and the patient is again on his own feet, the last thing the chaplain can expect is gratitude. The fact that, in this case, the metaphorical chaplain insisted that he alone could help every patient did not add to his chances of receiving the gratitude due.

The fact is that the developmental point of view, which is the cornerstone of pastoral theology and psychology, was brought into theological education and church practice by the religious educators. Their concern was to study the processes of development, to find the norms from the study of process. Although this may at times have been placed in a naive philosophical framework, its permanent though partial value is beyond price.

Psychoanalysis

The third, and perhaps ultimately the most significant, trend which has evoked pastoral psychology has been psychoanalysis and psychotherapy. Freud, trained in the thought processes and assumptions of nineteenth-century medicine and therefore the positivistic philosophy of physical science of that age, nevertheless broke through this in discovering the meaning of what he called "unconscious" psychic processes and therefore of the powerful reality of dynamic and conflicting psychic forces.[11] We cannot question today the great positive significance of his essential discovery. It was he who found the key, in a systematic way, which has unlocked the dynamic meaning of the life sciences, that is, which sees man's psychic life in terms of forces, energies, pressures and values which affect and conflict and liberate him though his head be ignorant of the process.

Freud's findings in themselves tended to controvert all rationalistic or purely conscious psychologies. As has often been noted, they were, in the psychological realm, as threatening to idealism as were Marx's ideas in politics and economics. Whatever their detailed errors, both insisted on something more than intentions, and asked instead: What are the real forces operating here?

No doubt this fact would have produced religious reaction to Freud in any case. But when Freud attached to his findings a reductionist and positivistic philosophy of nearly everything including religion, the reaction became certain. So it was that the

[11] *The Basic Writings of Sigmund Freud.*

first response of churchmen to Freud was negative, and that his philosophy prevented them from proper assessment of his findings. Even the religious educators, whose views we now see should have made them congenial to Freud's findings, were very slow to take them into account. Indeed, it was not until the late twenties that a good beginning was made at disentangling the Freudian findings from the philosophy which had become attached.

It may be true, as some believe, that Freud would never have got a religious hearing if it had not been for Jung.[12] Joining himself with Freud in the first decade, Jung found himself after some years increasingly at odds with Freud's therapeutic rigidity, sexual theory, opposition to religion *per se*, and other things. Dissociating himself to found a new school, Jung seemed to many thoughtful religionists to be forming a dynamic psychology which permitted more positive affinity with religion. There are controversial issues here. While welcoming Jung's acceptance of religion as a fact of psychic life, often as a positive fact, some of us have considered that Jung's mystical tendencies, his creation of a new mythology of the psyche, and his resort to a collective unconscious make him an unsafe guide along theoretical lines. With others of more tender-minded spirit, as for example, the Guild of Pastoral Psychology in England, he has become the patron saint.

In any event, Freud's central principle of psychic dynamics has become so widely accepted that even those who criticize him fail to realize that they are indebted to him for it. The "unconscious" may be an unsatisfactory term; yet the notion that there are forces in the psyche which influence behavior and thought, but which are nevertheless unwitting in their operation, is widely accepted. It is indispensable to a comprehension of inner psychic forces and interpersonal relationships.

So far-reaching has been the influence of this key concept that, for a time, it tempted even pastoral psychology to neglect conscious or "Ego" factors. Such a pendulum swing was probably necessary to achieve an eventually truer perspective.

[12] See especially *Psychology and Religion* by Carl G. Jung.

Psychoanalysis and the associated trends in psychiatry, medicine, social work and elsewhere, have influenced both the theory and practice of pastoral psychology in a large way. We have already indicated that the heart of the theoretical contribution was in what the unconscious implied. The practical contribution has been at the point of understanding a particular parishioner, and then suggesting broad leads whereby ways of helping him could be found.

With a few unfortunate exceptions, pastoral psychology has not attempted to take over the distinctive therapeutic methods of psychoanalysis.[13] But it has greatly profited from learning how to understand the parishioner, how to assess the relationship between pastor and parishioner, and how to see whether the attitude and approach of the pastor is leading in a therapeutic direction in performance as well as intention.

Theology

The fourth set of evocative forces which led to modern pastoral theology and psychology was theological, first the social gospel movement and more recently what is usually known as neo-orthodoxy. The most obvious initial effect of the social gospel movement on pastoral psychology was negative. If the church made its influence felt and its ideals were more nearly actualized in social practice, less attention would have to be paid to the individual. There probably was an undue note of social optimism which tended to produce impatience about the relatively slow processes required to change individuals.

But in later perspective, it seems likely that the net effect of the social gospel on pastoral psychology has been positive. Before there could be deep and serious study of psychic processes, the naive individualism embodied in movements like revivalism had to be transcended. Once the churches committed themselves unmistakably to attempts to "Christianize the social order," they had made a decisive step toward understanding all the kinds of

[13] See my *Pastoral Counseling.*

forces, psychic as well as social, which can impede or help such a movement. If they had to reach some new disillusionment about the limitations of what was possible, recognition of social limitations was bound eventually to compel new consideration of psychic limitations. This did occur.

In so far as neo-orthodoxy has been a deepening movement in theology, an attempt to find the meaning of the Christian gospel through a deeper social and psychological realism, it should have had a positive and wholesome influence upon the development of pastoral theology and psychology. Since much neo-orthodox thinking has been more than that, especially in the wholly-other European brands, it has often appeared opposed to any kind of pastoral theology which conceives itself to be analytical in character and to get some of its data from empirical observation. Continental theology has not only not produced a pastoral psychology in the American sense, but seems still so preoccupied with the apologetic problem that it actively prevents the development of such a study by ruling it irrelevant.

Current American theological trends, reaching such a brilliant climax in Reinhold Niebuhr, have until recently held back pastoral psychology. They first introduced large scale realism about social, economic and political forces. When they went on to discuss the parallels in individual life, they often read general conclusions, socially derived, into individual experience without adequate study of the distinctive individual factors. Such a tendency helps to create the notion that, with the enunciation of a distinctively Christian theory, the details are of secondary significance. Since pastoral psychology is, in this context, details, it may simply be ruled irrelevant or derivative.

If the trends mentioned above are considered as swings of the pendulum, and what is now emerging is a more centrist view, then the deepening effect of the American neo-orthodox movement may have positive significance for pastoral theology and psychology. That this is beginning to occur is shown in such recent books as David E. Roberts' *Psychotherapy and a Christian View of Man.* Its viewpoint transcends both liberalism and neo-orthodoxy, but would have been impossible without both of them.

Pastoral Psychology and Pastoral Theology

The first practical movement leading toward modern pastoral theology and psychology was, as we have noted, religious education. But it tended to be preoccupied with the normative and the group, at the expense of the therapeutic and the individual. For this reason, it was not responsible in a major way for developing current pastoral psychology, even though it did create indispensable conditions for such development.

The second, and most influential, movement was that for clinical pastoral training.[14] Formally initiated in 1923, this movement attempted to bring clergy and theological students into intimate and daily contact with people, under supervision from the pastoral point of view. The locus of such training has usually been health and welfare institutions, where human problems are thrown into bolder relief than ordinarily. Several thousand clergy and students have now had such training, and its direct influence has been to underscore the importance of a dynamic pastoral psychology as one of the foundations for all the pastoral operations. Its secondary influence, such as effect on the formal theological curricula, or the stimulation of more expert writing and research in the field, has been of at least equal significance. Most of the top American leaders in the field at present are the products, at least in part, of the clinical pastoral training movement.

The shifts of viewpoint within clinical pastoral training have largely paralleled the shifts in development of pastoral psychology itself. In the first days of clinical discovery, during the twenties and early thirties, concentration was on understanding the parishioner, out there, as from a detached point of view. The dynamics of the life history became the focus of study. Then Richard C. Cabot and Russell L. Dicks discussed methodology in ministry to the sick, thus presenting an incipient theory of

[14] *Clinical Pastoral Training,* edited by Seward Hiltner.

relationship between pastor and parishioner.[15] To the life history advocates, however, Dicks' interview analysis did not seem sufficiently dynamic. For a time it seemed there would be two groups—one accused of non-dynamic methodism, and the other of detached dynamism. Fortunately these began to come together in the forties, when it was clearer that relationship as well as parishioner had to be studied, and that both could be examined dynamically. This paralleled a similar trend in psychoanalysis and other forms of psychotherapy, and was especially aided by the psychological work of Carl R. Rogers.[16] The most recent emergent has been a concern to study the attitude and approach of the pastor as he tries to counsel or administer or perform some other operation. This means study of the congruence or discrepancy between his intention and, considering the whole situation and relationship, his performance. This is the third dynamic link in the chain which includes parishioner, relationship and pastor. Study of all is now recognized to be essential to an adequate pastoral psychology.

The new knowledge and insight which has made possible this development has been the result of the sciences of man or the life sciences, whether it be a fact or process turned up by a psychiatrist and taken over by the pastor or something which the pastor, through his own observations and reflections, has found out for himself. Thus it has been natural that the new pioneers have stressed their connection with and indebtedness to psychotherapy, psychology, psychoanalysis, psychiatry, and the other life sciences or technologies. The focus has been, and still is, mainly on pastoral *psychology*.

Of very recent date, however, a new pastoral *theology* has begun to emerge. This is apt to be thought of as having a different or conflicting content from pastoral psychology. Actually, the content is the same. But it has a different frame of reference and

[15] *The Art of Ministering to the Sick.*
[16] *Counseling and Psychotherapy.*

sees its content in a different context. It has begun to appear as two points have become clearer. First, we see that the content of pastoral psychology has begun to fill in the gap which has always existed in pastoral theology through the centuries. Second, we realize that any concern and enterprise of the church must have its chief focus as theological in the broad sense, and that adequate study of any such concern is not to be viewed as merely the application of the Christian faith, understood and assimilated elsewhere, but as also an avenue for better understanding and assimilation of the faith itself.

Most pastors still prefer pastoral *psychology*, for it sounds as if it had some content and were not merely formal in character. But as it becomes more widely recognized that the dynamic content of pastoral psychology is also the dynamic content of pastoral *theology*, it seems likely that the latter term will once again come into wide use.

The Future

There is already very widespread interest within the churches in pastoral psychology. If my judgment is correct, this is rapidly expanding into a pastoral theology context as well. An effective new monthly journal entitled *Pastoral Psychology* has brought to four the number of journals dealing significantly with this field.[17] If the general trend of theological thinking becomes more positive toward pastoral psychology, as it may do in the United States, this will help remove some of the barriers to proper development of the field.

There are a few things which it seems possible to say about future development of this field with reasonable certainty. It is clear that we can never return to mere formalism or mere artistry and assiduity, or to them in combination. The new dynamic

[17] *Pastoral Psychology*, monthly (Great Neck, N.Y.); *Journal of Pastoral Care*, quarterly (Cambridge, Mass.); *Journal of Clinical Pastoral Work*, quarterly (New York, N.Y.); and *The Pastor*, monthly (Nashville, Tenn.).

knowledge, not alone in detail but in the very fact that there is an explorable body of knowledge, has made any such return impossible.

A second point is that the scientific method, if understood generically, is in the field to stay. At any time the pastor observes his work critically, in the light of his dynamic knowledge, in order to improve his understanding and his practice, he is in some respect a scientist as well as a helper or an educator. This of course dissociates generic scientific method from any necessary connection with unconcerned detachment, lack of interest in outcome, etc.

A third point is that pastoral care and counseling of individuals is here to stay, that the rise of however many therapeutic professions will not succeed in depriving the pastor of some therapeutic obligation to his people. But the rise of these other groups means that his results are judged by standards never before available. Hence, good intentions without study and knowledge become increasingly impossible.

A fourth point is that we are likely to see soon some genuinely advanced work, on both an academic and a clinical level, in pastoral psychology. So far study and research has been on an introductory plane. The chances of merging the interests of the church, the clinic, and the university have never been greater than they are likely to be in the years immediately ahead.

Fifth, pastoral psychology and now pastoral theology have begun to reach a point of maturity when they may be able to make basic contributions to our understanding of the Christian faith itself. Every examined version of Christian faith and expression has had one foot in some kind of psychology; for study of the human psyche is psychology. Not a few of the great theological insights of past ages have emerged out of what is basically psychological examination. With superior psychological knowledge and tools, it would be strange indeed if we could not gain certain new and deeper appreciations of the faith through proper psychological study.

BIBLIOGRAPHY

Allport, Gordon W., *The Individual and His Religion* (New York, 1950)

Boisen, Anton T., *The Exploration of the Inner World* (Chicago, 1936)

Coe, George A., *Psychology of Religion* (Chicago, 1916)

Cabot, Richard C., and Dicks, Russell L., *The Art of Ministering to the Sick* (New York, 1936)

Freud, Sigmund, *The Basic Writings of Sigmund Freud* (New York, 1938)

Hiltner, Seward, *Pastoral Counseling* (New York, 1949)

———, *Religion and Health* (New York, 1943)

James, William, *Varieties of Religious Experience* (New York, 1903)

Jung, Carl G., *Psychology and Religion* (New Haven, 1938)

May, Rollo, *The Meaning of Anxiety* (New York, 1950)

McNeill, John T., *A History of the Cure of Souls* (New York, 1951)

Roberts, David E., *Psychotherapy and a Christian View of Man* (New York, 1950)

Wise, Carroll A., *Religion in Illness and Health* (New York, 1942)

PREACHING

Charles W. Gilkey

CHARLES W. GILKEY was born at Watertown, Massachusetts, in 1882. He graduated from Harvard in 1903 and from Union Theological Seminary, New York, in 1908, where he received a fellowship for two years post-graduate study in Germany and Britain. He served as minister of the Hyde Park Baptist Church in Chicago from 1910 until 1928, when he became Dean of the University of Chicago Chapel and Professor of Preaching in its Divinity School, also teaching some courses in homiletics at the McCormick Theological Seminary and Garrett Biblical Institute. Retiring under the rules of the University of Chicago in 1947, he now lives at South Yarmouth, Massachusetts, and teaches part-time homiletics at Andover Newton Theological School. He has received honorary degrees from eight colleges and universities; he was elected by his fellow-alumni to the Harvard Board of Overseers from 1946 to 1948; and he is a member of the boards of George Williams College in Chicago and of Union Theological Seminary in New York.

IX

THERE are two characteristics of Protestant preaching—its endless variety, and its limited accessibility—which make definite answers to the double question raised in this book—whence and whither—peculiarly difficult in this area of contemporary American Christianity. Most other chapters in this symposium survey and appraise specific fields of Protestant thought, in each of which creative leadership is exercised by a comparatively few scholars and thinkers, who group themselves into diverging schools. The distinctive characteristics of these individuals and schools of thought have been made quickly and definitely accessible by the publication of books which most of them have written and nearly all of them read—in relation to which their respective points of view have been defined and developed.

But every Sunday in the year, in thousands upon thousands of Protestant churches across this American continent, nearly as many ministers preach more than as many sermons—for many of them preach twice. The content and quality of each man's preaching is likely to vary considerably from week to week: only occasionally is he at his own best. Anyone who has had personal contacts, not only with denominational differences, but with sectional and theological traditions and homiletic habits in different parts of the United States—to say nothing of the wide variations in professional training and personal gifts among all these individual preachers—will have gained some sense of how next to impossible it is to generalize about American preaching with any accuracy, or to trace any trends in contemporary preaching that are not subject to endless exceptions and contrary local evidences.

Again, very few of these countless weekly sermons have any accessible permanence other than in the memory of their hearers (which in most of us is short at best for any kind of public speaking, and notoriously so for sermons)—or in the notes or manuscripts (if any) stored away in what before the days of filing cabinets used to be called the preacher's "barrel." Such sermons as get themselves into print, in clerical periodicals like the *Christion Century Pulpit*, or in annual collections like *"Best Sermons of 19 . . . ,"* or even in volumes of sermons by some one minister widely enough known to justify by their sale the mounting costs of their publication—all these represent almost as much the selective invitation of an editor, or the selective favoritism of the preacher himself, as any typical characteristics of contemporary preaching as a whole.

Some arbitrary and partial selection among the available data seems therefore inevitable for any survey of the last fifty years of American Protestant preaching; and the basis of this selection is best stated frankly in advance.

In 1924 *The Christian Century* undertook to "get at the mind of the ministry for the purpose of getting at the mind of the church," by sending out ballots to about 90,000 Protestant ministers in all parts of the country, asking them to co-operate in finding "the twenty-five most influential and representative living preachers of our time." Nearly 25,000 ballots were returned, and on them 1162 different names were voted for. These last were obviously the preachers to whom at that time their fellow-ministers, and through them their churches, looked for light and leading. The twenty-five who led that poll were then asked to submit one characteristic sermon for inclusion in *The American Pulpit*—a collection edited by Dr. Charles Clayton Morrison, at that time editor of *The Christian Century*. Included in this volume are theological points of view and homiletic techniques as different as those of Dean Charles R. Brown and Dr. William P. Merrill, on the one hand, and Dr. Mark A. Matthews and "Billy" Sunday, on the other.

A study of these twenty-five sermons, as a primary source for the earlier period under review, has been supplemented from various volumes of *Best Sermons of 19 . . .* that have appeared in many of the years since 1924, and from volumes of published sermons by such outstanding preachers throughout this period as Dr. Harry Emerson Fosdick and Dr. Henry Sloane Coffin, as well as by younger men like Dr. Harold Bosley. Some of the annual Lyman Beecher Lectures on Preaching, given at Yale, which tend to reflect and clarify contemporary pulpit standards and ideals, have provided background and perspective; and for these later years, the files of the *Christian Century Pulpit* have made accessible a much wider range of selected sermons by younger and less widely known preachers.

Hardly less valuable than these printed sermons have been my own vivid personal memories of outstanding preachers at the turn of the century—Lyman Abbott, Maltbie D. Babcock, Henry van Dyke, George A. Gordon—whom I began to hear as a college undergraduate. And even more valuable was my weekly chance to listen, as Dean of the University of Chicago Chapel from 1928 to 1947, to the best preachers we could invite from all over the country and all the major Protestant bodies, who through those nineteen years did much the larger part of the preaching in that Chapel. Most of these visiting preachers were liberal in their theological outlook and mindful of academic proprieties in their style: but at the same time divergent trends in current theological thinking and in ecclesiastical affiliation were well represented among them; and the men who were most powerfully influencing contemporary student and faculty attitudes toward religion were regular and usually annual guests in our university pulpit.

As one looks back across these fifty years of continuing effort to hear and to read as much as possible of the best contemporary American preaching, one is struck by the constantly close relationship between that preaching and the changing intellectual and spiritual needs, the shifting moods and changing climates within this cataclysmic half-century in human history; and conversely, with the difficulty of estimating at its true contemporary value the preaching of another period than that from which one now looks back. The "age of confidence" before 1914 (as Henry Seidel Canby called it), found it easy to follow and respond to Lyman

Abbott when he used to preach on the reign of law on all levels of human experience, or to expound in a college pulpit "the theology of an evolutionist." But that optimistic and complacent time would have little understood the eagerness with which in this present "age of anxiety" (as W. H. Auden calls it), students and faculty on any and every campus in either America or Europe listen to Reinhold Niebuhr on the inability of human nature to save itself except by the grace of God. Whether they fully understand Niebuhr or not, he "speaks to their condition."

Conversely, men of to-day who are deeply concerned and often almost hysterically anxious about the future of civilization, find it hard to believe that one of the most famous preachers of that "age of confidence" should have said early in this century in a university baccalaureate sermon—before Hitler and Mussolini and the Kremlin, and the atom bomb in our own American hands, had given their terrifying evidence to the contrary:

> The forces of civilization were then, as always, beyond the reach of violence. In ordained tranquillity, they moved majestically forward to shine on Athens as they had never shone on Babylon; to shine in deathless splendor on New York as they had never shone on Rome. And it was because of the war which their light made on all darkness that the woe of Rome's expiring Paganism was a long-drawn agony, which, please God! may we never know again. . . .
> The despotisms which hitherto harassed men are gone forever.[1]

The difficulties involved in any fair appraisal of the strengths and weaknesses of the preaching of other days than our own, and the changing canons of judgment from one generation to the next, are familiar in the realms of literature. Stevenson and Kipling are quoted as far below par in the contemporary literary marketplace, as in our youth they were both quoted above it—up where Melville and Kierkegaard for instance are quoted to-day. As RLS himself shrewdly put it: "Times change, and opinions vary to their opposite"—and this holds for preaching also.

And yet it also remains true that the greatest preaching, like

[1] *Great Sermons by Great Preachers*, pp. 589, 597 (John C. Winston Co., 1927).

the greatest writing and music, has something timeless about it that speaks convincingly to men of every age at the deepest levels of their common human capacity and need; and for Christian faith this is especially true of preaching which can catch and re-echo the authentic notes of the Christian gospel. Phillips Brooks' sermons "live" for us, as we read them to-day, only less than for our fathers as they heard them. Almost sixty years after his death, thirty of Brooks' best sermons, selected and edited by Bishop William Scarlett with the assistance of Dr. Harry Emerson Fosdick, have been republished by Macmillan in 1950, for the benefit of our own contemporaries.

In a discerning chapter on "Religious Life and Thought" in his recent book on *The American Mind* from the 1880's to the present day, Professor H. S. Commager of Columbia remarks that three hundred years of Calvinistic theology and evangelical Christianity, with their common emphasis on the sinfulness of man before God, have had strangely little effect on the characteristic optimism and complacency of the American outlook on life. He notes that American Christianity has on the whole been little concerned with the profounder theological issues, and has tended to be traditional rather than creative in its thinking; and even so, he expresses surprise that Fundamentalism has persisted so long and so late as a major force in American Protestantism. He emphasizes the degree to which both church membership and church attendance have tended during this period to become nominal and conventional, and notes the lessening influence of organized religion on the main currents in American life.

There is one among the symptoms noted in Professor Commager's diagnosis of our American religious case-history, little emphasized in his treatment, which has considerably greater importance for our own purposes in this chapter: namely, the widespread weakening and increasing breakdown during the last half-century of the *social habit* of regular church attendance—only less evident among nominal church members than among the half of our adult population who have no affiliation with organized religion. Those of us who have lived for successive decades in the same community, whether in northern industrial and commercial centers, in their more sophisticated suburbs, or in rural New England, as we have watched this process among our own neighbors and gathered statistical evidence on it in our own churches, have become convinced that the optimistic figures showing that church membership more than keeps pace with the growth of our population, are the less important part of the total religious picture. This is true except in the South (and also in Canada), where the northern visitor rubs his incredulous eyes on Sunday morning—and often again on Sunday evening—to see the high proportion of the community that still moves churchward. Except in such untypical local situations as that of the Riverside Church or the Madison Avenue Presbyterian Church in New York City, or the First Methodist Church in Evanston or Lincoln, or the First Congregational Church in Los Angeles, church members do not as a rule attend as habitually, or non-members as frequently, as they did in our own youth at the turn of the century. The preaching is often very much better than it was then: but the attendance is usually less—and its make-up considerably less regular.

By and large, even our ablest Protestant preaching speaks to the ear, and probably to the knowledge, of a smaller proportion of our population than at any earlier period within living memory. Brunner's remark was doubtless made first about his own Continental Europe: but it applies increasingly to our own changing America: "The traditional form of preaching as a part of the religious cult and the Sunday service in the church has become strange and remains strange to a great proportion of our contemporaries."

From these sources and against this background, our next concern is to try to locate certain major trends in the preaching of the last half-century, which—like the Gulf Stream in the Atlantic, and other well-marked ocean currents in all the seven seas—may help us to discern whither Protestant preaching is tending, through the influence of its leaders on their brethren; and to ask what influence it is likely to exert on the moral and spiritual climate of the second half of the twentieth century.

The Reinterpretation of Religion

Probably the most evident and certainly the most controversial trend in Protestant preaching at the opening of the century was that which sought to reinterpret and restate the Christian faith in terms consonant with the rapidly growing historical and scientific knowledge of the time. Those of us who received our education and began our ministry in that period, are carried swiftly back to the theological climate and controversies of our youth, when we find side by side among the twenty-five representative preachers in *The American Pulpit* in 1925, the militant Fundamentalist Mark A. Matthews, minister of the largest Presbyterian church in the United States, the First of Seattle, choosing as his theme "The Virgin Birth of Jesus," which he declared in his opening sentence to be "the most important subject that could possibly be discussed"; while in the very next sermon Dr. William P. Merrill, minister of the Brick Presbyterian Church in New York, set forth "Christ, Our Religion" in a warmly religious but theologically undogmatic statement of the centrality of Christ as "the way, the truth, and the life." The difference in tone and temper between those two sermons recalls, across the crowded years between, the sharp theological controversies within American Protestantism during and after World War I, controversies in which Dr. Harry Emerson Fosdick became an embattled figure.

The economic and international cataclysms of the second quarter of the new century, however, soon carried the attention of both preachers and congregations to more urgent issues than those of theological controversy. The Great Depression after 1928 raised searching questions about our social order, and the high hopes raised by a victorious "war to end war" were darkened by the gathering shadows of World War II. Disillusionment and cynicism about the capacity of human nature to manage its own more and more complicated affairs in a shrunken world, and to escape the inevitable consequences of the pride and the greed for gain and power, not only among its neighbors but within its own heart, displaced the earlier optimisms and complacencies, and deeply affected the tone as well as the content of Christian preaching. A younger generation that had never known anything but a world of uncertainty and danger, and college graduates who took for granted the freedom of faith for which their fathers had had to contend, began to protest against the vagueness and uncertainties of the optimistic liberalism in which they had been reared, and to seek, not only for firmer ground in their thinking, but for more positive and dynamic convictions about the centralities of Christian faith, and for more shared reality in Christian fellowship.

Meanwhile theological students in conservative and liberal seminaries alike were coming under the stimulating influence of new emphases in contemporary theology. Among Biblical scholars, Dodd in England, Dibelius in Germany, Craig at Yale and Drew, and Knox and Muilenburg at Union, were emphasizing the faith and shared life of the early church as prior to all the New Testament sources and writings, and the total historical "event" of Jesus' life, death, and resurrection as the central and fundamental fact on which the Christian gospel builds its faith and hope and love. With all their theological and philosophical differences, the far-reaching influence of Barth and Brunner on the Continent, of the two Baillies in Scotland, and of the two Niebuhrs and Calhoun in America, has struck a much more positive note of Christian assurance about the self-revelation of God in Christ, and the adequacy of the grace of God to redeem and transform even the pride and folly of self-centered and sinful men. There is no mistaking this more confident and dynamic note in the self-dedication of larger numbers of men of high intellectual and spiritual quality to the work of the Christian ministry since the close of World War II, or in the preaching and pastoral work of the younger ministry—no matter under what contemporary theological banner they may march—as in 1950 they face toward the unknown future.

Looking back over the half-century since 1900, we whose entire active ministry has been carried on within that period rejoice in the widening recognition that equally honest and earnest Christians have never used exactly the same forms of thought when they started to reflect on the faith in Christ they share, or exactly the same language when they tried to express it to others—either in our own lifetime, or during the Protestant Reformation, or in the early church, or in the New Testament itself. We rejoice still more that so many Christians the world around, of so many races and names and signs, including many Fundamentalists and more conservatives, are more concerned in these critical times to win new believers to their common faith in Christ than to argue with their fellow-Christians about their theological differences. We see heartening evidences of the presence and power of the Holy Spirit within the Christian Church Universal, wherever brethren not only of different races and names and signs, but of differing theological views, are drawn and held together by the God-given realization that they are "all one in Christ Jesus." We know from the experience of our own generation that our successors will face new problems for thought, and new challenges to action, under changing conditions which we cannot now foresee; and we pray that they may be given the guidance of that same Spirit, and so know how to maintain, on the one hand, "our liberty which we have in Christ Jesus" (Gal. 2:4), and, on the other, "to keep the unity of the Spirit in the bond of peace." (Eph. 4:3)

The Socializing of Christianity

After the two worst wars in human history, it is not easy even for us whose youth was set in the sunny and sheltered years before 1914, to recapture their crusading enthusiasms. We who were then preparing for and entering upon the parish ministry well remember, even across the tragic years and decades between, the impact of Dr. Charles R. Brown's *The Social Message of the Modern Pulpit*, followed by the successive books of Walter Rauschenbusch, and especially his *Prayers of the Social Awakening*, not only upon our own youthful thinking, but upon the leadership of American Protestantism. Our own opening ministry was released thereby from complete preoccupation with theological reinterpretations, into the immediate challenge of urgent social tasks. Our conscience was deeply stirred about social conditions which American complacency and optimism had too long overlooked. Our eyes were opened to the contemporary relevance of the Hebrew prophets, and our daily prayer, "Thy Kingdom come," suddenly came alive at the heart of our personal religious life. The "Social Creed of the Churches," adopted by the Federal Council in 1908, was not only a landmark in the history of American Protestantism: it was a lighted beacon.

This swelling stream of social idealism was by no means limited to the Christian churches. It was the heyday of progressivism in American politics, of Theodore Roosevelt's "Square Deal" and Woodrow Wilson's "New Freedom." Then—like the Niagara River at the brink of the Falls—all this social idealism was precipitated by World War I into a kind of Niagara Gorge of confusion and frustration, at new and deeper levels of relationship and responsibility. The white water of the Rapids below the Falls, and the suddenly emerging back-eddies down the long miles thereafter, inadequately symbolize some aspects of our American experience during the thirty-six years since 1914.

To one who has watched those eddies as they twist and boil up to the smooth green surface of the river miles below the Falls, and then disappear again further downstream as suddenly as they emerged, there is at least some light on the oft-repeated question as to what has happened to the "social gospel" in American Protestantism. It has reappeared in the strong pacifist reaction against both the horrors and the follies of war as "mankind's chief collective sin," and has echoed in the preaching not only of such outstanding leaders as Tittle, Buttrick, Scherer, Luccock, and Bosley, but of scores if not hundreds of other ministers less widely known; and even more compellingly, in the personal decision and conduct of Christian conscientious objectors. It is not less evident in the strong reaction of the Christian conscience, especially among students and the younger generation generally, against the racial discrimination and religious prejudice that are so deeply rooted in American traditions; and likewise in the many religious movements, including in some cities local churches, that are completely inter-racial.

Commager remarks in *The American Mind* that Reinhold Niebuhr is the spiritual heir of Walter Rauschenbusch: better understood he thinks and more influential in Europe than in this country. But though Niebuhr and the younger ministry whom he and others have so deeply influenced, hold a very different "theology for the social gospel" than that which Rauschenbusch proposed in pre-war days, they insist, as Rauschenbusch did, on the social relevance of the Christian gospel, not only as an essential part of their preaching, but as part of their Christian responsibility in the life of their community.

Other seminary teachers like Holt of Chicago, Bennett of Union, and Pope of Yale, have likewise combined a critical realism, in dealing with complex social facts and forces, with a deepened conviction that only the guidance and grace of God can show us the way through the anxious years ahead. Their teaching and example suggest that the next generation of Protestant preachers may be less disposed than were their predecessors to draw blue-prints on Sunday morning for a "Christian social order"—or even for the guidance of their laymen in the complicated situations they confront—much less to sit in judgment on those who may not agree with them on involved social issues as they suddenly arise. But even so, they will agree with those same predecessors that in these areas also (as John Robinson put it more than three hundred years ago), "God hath more light and truth still to break forth from His Holy Word."

The New Emphasis on the Church

The stress laid in present-day thinking on the *social* aspects of all human experience, would doubtless have led in any case to a new appreciation of the fact that Christian faith is given to us all within a shared fellowship—as we are born into a family, and achieve our personality within a society. But this current emphasis on the collective side of the shield, as our fathers had stressed its individual side, has been reinforced by two main currents in the Christian thought and life of our generation.

One of these is the stress laid by our best Biblical scholarship on the historical fact that the early Christian church preceded the New Testament. Before there were any gospels or epistles as we now know them, groups of believers were keeping alive and sharing with each other their memories of Jesus, their experience of his continuing presence in their midst through the Holy Spirit, and their knowledge of the work and writings of Paul. Historically speaking, the church gave us our New Testament and its gospel, and out of its fellowship down the generations our personal religious life has been born and sustained.

The other is the ecumenical hope and faith, which seems to so many of us God's best gift to the church through the dark years in which our ministry has been chiefly set. Out of this very "time of troubles," as a child of the missionary movement, has been born a new sense of unity between Christians of all nations and races and generations, and a new perspective on our differences of creed and ceremony and order, as far less important than the God-given realization that we are "all one in Christ Jesus." The Christian church has proved to be the one fellowship that has kept its inner unity of spirit and loyalty, even through the strains of worldwide war. And this, as Archbishop William Temple pointed out, has not been the result of any human planning or organization. "This is the Lord's doing, and it is marvellous in our eyes."

The impact of these two creative forces can plainly be seen

in the changing attitude of many ministers of our generation toward the church, both local and universal. In our student days many of us were decided individualists in religion, and quick to criticize the church, not only for its theological conservatism and religious formalism, but for its unawareness or time-serving on social issues, and for the timidity of its leadership. We were fond of quoting "More of the divine fire, and less of the ecclesiastical candle-stick," and also the story about the devil, who when his assistant reported that they couldn't make head against the Christian religion, replied, "Then *organize* it." In this we were reflecting the perspectives widespread among our college teachers, many of whom conceded that personal religion might well be an asset in individual cases, but maintained that organized religion had usually proved to be a social liability in human history—or at the very least a drag on progress.

But already in seminary the teaching, and above all the example, of devoted and constructive churchmen like Henry Sloane Coffin, was leading us toward a maturer attitude. When we found ourselves in a parish of our own, we began to repeat the experience of one contemporary who said, as he looked back on a long and distinguished ministry, "I have rediscovered the church." Our pastoral visitation gave us a new sense of the spiritual support given by the church to its members through times of stress and strain—a sense greatly deepened when we ourselves were in hospital. The terrible wars of our time revealed to us the social significance of the church as the defender of individual freedom against totalitarian prejudices and pressures, and as the one worldwide fellowship that was able to maintain its relationships across the gulfs and against the bitternesses of war. Meanwhile the historical relation of the early church to the New Testament, of the Bible to western culture and democracy, and of the missionary movement of the nineteenth century to the ecumenical movement and the inter-racial fellowships of the twentieth—these perspectives opened our eyes to the long-range significance of the Christian church as the carrier and sower of the seeds of a better

human future, the harvests of which will be gathered by generations later than our own—under the blessing and guidance of God.

These longer perspectives and deepened convictions have had
a profound effect upon our own preaching—turning it more and
more toward the building up of the local church. We know, at
least as well as their numerous critics, the faults and failures of
the contemporary churches—have we not lived with them seven
days in the week, and most of the waking hours of each day? Some
of our brethren have suffered cruelly at the hand of organized
religion, as did the Master long ago, and the prophets before him.
But we believe in the church as we believe in our family and in
our country, even while we know their faults and seek to correct
them; and even more deeply we believe in the church, because
she is what Paul called her, "the household of God." She has sins
of omisson and commission aplenty to confess; but she has also
resources beyond her own wisdom and strength, through her
faith in the God Who called her into being through Jesus Christ
her Lord.

We believe further that this trend in contemporary preaching
will increase and deepen, because to our joy we find this focussing
of interest and concern upon the local church to be apparently
stronger in our younger colleagues in the ministry than in ourselves, who had to outgrow our earlier individualism—and strongest of all in the post-war theological students we know at first-
hand. We are heartened not only by their greater numbers, but
by their individual quality: they seem to us on the whole an abler
lot intellectually, and a much deeper and warmer lot spiritually,
than we were at their age. We are the more impressed to find that
many of them hold a far more definite and "higher" doctrine of
the church than we ever had, in which there is emphasis on the
role of the church, over against the world and modern culture
alike, as a worshipping fellowship within a "house of prayer," and
also as the custodian of the "Word" from God which gives Christian preaching both its message and its authority.

With such a high conception of the church, it is small wonder that we do not so often find among them the same ambitious eye lifted in the direction of "big pulpits" in city churches, that was more frequent among us. We note among them too a concern for what they like to call "pastoral counselling," and in many cases a deliberate choice of smaller parishes and communities, because they provide closer personal contacts. Some of them seem to recognize instinctively what it took us time to learn by experience the hard way: that, as Hugh Black put it, "we who are critics of the past are also its children." We, their elder brethren in the pastorate, conclude from all this, that this increasing emphasis on the life and work of the local church, and this more understanding and devoted concern for the "cure of souls," which has begun in our own time, will be much more characteristic both of their preaching and of their pastoral ministry in the half-century ahead.

The Democratizing of Preaching

One Sunday morning well before World War II we welcomed as our visiting preacher at the University of Chicago Chapel a famous Scottish minister, whose sermon seemed a masterpiece to those who know and love the best traditions of that home of the homiletic art. It was a rich and colorful tapestry woven of Biblical quotations and allusions, in which Scriptural scenes and characters subtly emerged into a unified and cumulative procession as the well-planned sermon unrolled. But in the middle of the sermon a graduate student in physics got up and went out, sat down on the steps outside, and began to read the *Chicago Tribune*. When a passing fellow-student asked him why he had left the Chapel, he replied, "I will not stay and listen to a man who cannot talk about religion in a language which his contemporaries can understand."

The incident reflects the growing "religious illiteracy" which is so widely characteristic not only of college students, but of Americans generally. A present-day preacher cannot assume on the part of his congregation the knowledge of the Bible or of Christian history, or the sense of their significance, which his predecessors could take for granted. Such ignorance is wide-spread, not only among church members, but even among theological students!

Some of the most obvious trends in recent American preaching are directly related to this situation. Topical sermons advertised on the bulletin board and in the Saturday newspapers, problem-sermons, life-situation sermons, book-review sermons, have grown more frequent as expository and even textual sermons have become fewer. The prominence of illustration, whether in such masters of "picture-thinking" as Fosdick and Merton Rice and Halford Luccock, or in less skilful hands as anecdotes of doubtful relevance but sometimes of deliberate humor, culled from inexpensive collections thereof—this is in part adjustment to a national temperament much more responsive to story-telling than to abstract or logical thinking, and in part a recognition by the preacher that any congregation, religiously illiterate or otherwise, is far more likely to remember his illustrations than his text, his exegesis, or his theology.

When Charles Cuthbert Hall, himself one of the outstanding preachers of the opening century, returned in 1907 from his second series of Barrows Lectures in the university centers of India, he remarked to one of his students that the current religious crisis seemed to him even more acute in America than in the Far East. He felt that most American preaching was then falling between the Scylla of an unintelligible piety, and the Charybdis of an unreligious liberalism. It had too many men who had a gospel, but did not know the language of their time—and so men would not stop to listen; it had also too many men who knew the language of their contemporaries perfectly—but had no gospel for them! If American preaching fifty years later is to escape that same difficult dilemma, it must labor and pray to learn how to combine the solid substance and positive gospel of Edwards and Bushnell and Brooks, with the contemporaneousness and vividness of Beecher and Fosdick, and the "inevitable word" that George Buttrick so often finds.

And yet there may prove to be assets as well as challenges for the preacher, in the anxious years that apparently lie ahead. A generation that buys half a million copies of Rabbi Liebman's *Peace of Mind*, or that realizes how precarious is the prospect of its hitherto boasted civilization, may be more likely not only to come to church, but to listen with open ears and heart to a sermon on either the inner life or the social gospel, than a generation that thanked God it was not as other men, or races, or generations— or that knew not that in the sight of God it was "poor and blind and naked."

The very fact that so many people are getting their religion these days from religious books or magazine articles, or by sermons over the radio, suggests to the watchful preacher the existence of a potential congregation whom he may have to discover and enlist by personal contact and cultivation. And the evident interest and concern of the more thoughtful younger generation in the great issues of human life and destiny with which religion deals, suggests that preaching disciplined to deal with these deeper issues in language that this generation can understand, may not lack for hearing in the days ahead. Along some such lines "evangelism" may find its way forward, under the guidance of God, out of its nineteenth-century traditions that no longer fit our present needs, into the twentieth century where genuine religious revival is so sorely needed both within and outside the church.

The editor of a thoughtful religious column in the *Manchester Guardian Weekly* remarked recently that, with a few outstanding exceptions such as Fosdick, American preaching seemed to him to deal too much with "problems"—and to lack depth. There must be many of us who would admit in our franker moments, to our consciences even if not to our colleagues or our congregations, that both these shafts hit at least the periphery of the target. But we who listened hungrily as students to George A. Gordon, and read him to this day with a satisfaction that is partly intellectual but even more deeply spiritual, know that this has not been true of all American preaching since 1900, as it was not true of Edwards in his time or Bushnell in his. Professor Roger Hazelton in his recent book, *Renewing the Mind,* pleads for more serious grappling by the American pulpit with the central issues of human life and destiny, and the central faiths of the Christian gospel.

This is not to say that all the best American preaching, past or future, has been or ever will be alike—or ought to move on parallel lines. The mantle of Beecher and Gunsaulus and Quayle is not the same as the mantle of Edwards and Bushnell and Gordon; and there is besides a long tradition of "popular preaching" that has made its own contribution to American democracy and its own appeal to the American conscience. Ever since the Day of Pentecost, men have said of successive generations of Christian witnesses, "We hear them speaking *in our tongues* the mighty works of God." It is the agelong task of the Christian preacher to bear that witness in his own tongue to his own contemporaries.

Chrysostom and Augustine, Savonarola and Luther, remind us also that Christian preaching has reached some of its greatest heights in difficult times. As the nineteenth century turned into the twentieth, one of the great Scottish church leaders of the earlier era, Marcus Dods, said in his own later years: "I do not envy those who will carry the banner of Christianity in the twentieth century. . . . Yes, perhaps I do: but it will be a stiff fight."

That prediction has been already fulfilled; and it is not less timely to-day.

BIBLIOGRAPHY

Collected Sermons

Morrison, C. C., editor, *The American Pulpit:* by Twenty-five Representative Preachers (New York, 1925)

Coffin, Henry Sloane, *The Creed of Jesus* (New York, 1907)

Newton, Joseph Fort, editor, *Best Sermons, 1924* (New York, 1924)

Fosdick, Harry Emerson, *The Hope of the World* (New York, 1933)

Bosley, Harold A., *On Final Ground* (New York, 1946)

Books About Preaching

Coffin, Henry Sloane, *In a Day of Social Rebuilding* (New Haven, 1918)

Newton, Joseph Fort, *The New Preaching* (New York, 1930)

Buttrick, George A., *Jesus Came Preaching*, Beecher Lectures (New York, 1931)

Atkins, Gaius Glenn, *Preaching and the Mind of To-day* (New York, 1934)

Sperry, Willard L., *We Prophesy in Part* (New York, 1938)

Thompson, Ernest Trice, *Changing Emphases in American Preaching* (New York, 1943)

The Mind of the Twentieth Century

Commager, Henry Steele, *The American Mind:* An Interpretation of American Thought and Character since the 1880's (New Haven, 1950)

CHRISTIAN EDUCATION

H. Shelton Smith

H. SHELTON SMITH was born in 1893 in North Carolina, graduating from Elon College in 1917. He served as a chaplain with the American Expeditionary Force in France during World War I. After receiving the Ph.D. degree from Yale University in 1923, he joined the staff of the International Council of Religious Education. In 1929 he became Associate Professor of Education at Teachers College, Columbia University. He subsequently served on the faculty of Yale Divinity School and then took up his present position as Professor of American Religious Thought and Director of Graduate Studies in Religion in Duke University. He has been actively associated with the ecumenical movement both locally, where he was founder and first president of the North Carolina Council of Churches, and as a member of various committees of the Federal Council of Churches and the International Council of Religious Education. His particular field of scholarship is the history of American religious thought, but he is best known as an author for his book *Faith and Nurture*, which has had a wide and deep influence on Christian thought about education. Dr. Smith is a member of the Congregationalist Church, and for several years he was vice president of the Congregational Home Board.

X

RELIGIOUS education, as qualified by the adjective "progressive," is chiefly a development of the twentieth century. Strictly defined, it has always been a rather small current in the total educational movement of the American churches. Nevertheless, its leading exponents have written books in educational philosophy of rarely equaled competence.

The basic theory of progressives was maturely formulated by the close of the First World War. During the next decade progressive principles achieved considerable experimental application in the better equipped local churches. Since the later thirties, however, the foremost progressives have spent much of their energy in defending their positions against what they call "theological reaction." In the category of reactionists they usually include not only avowed Barthians, but all those who have seen fit to abandon or seriously modify the traditional thought-patterns of left-wing Protestant liberalism.

Some of them have even revealed a marked distaste for all theology, often implying that those who concern themselves with it are at least side-stepping the main issues in religious education. They not infrequently apply the epithet "authoritarian" to those who find any significant value in the new theological trends.

Does this mean, then, that progressive religious educators have no theology of their own? Frankly, no. For any careful analysis of their chief publications in educational theory will show that they operate upon important theological assumptions. Those assumptions, to be sure, are not always made explicit, but they are present nevertheless.

It is the purpose of this essay to demonstrate the truth of this affirmation, and then to indicate the possible future of the progressive educational movement in American Protestantism.

Considered historically, progressive theory of religious education is indebted both to educational philosophy and to Protestant theology.

On the educational side, the movement of thought that has contributed most to the progressive theory of Protestant nurture is that of which John Dewey has been the prime determiner. When the twentieth century opened, he had already won recognition as an educational philosopher of unusual magnitude. His compact little treatise, *My Pedagogic Creed* (1897), ranks as an educational classic. It contains most of the germ elements that have characterized the progressive current in secular educational thought. Some of the more significant ideas found in that *Creed* are these: The aim of education is the continuous reconstruction of experience; the condition of effective learning is purposeful self-expression on the part of the child; the creative and unifying center of the curriculum is the pupil's own social activities; the school is democracy's primary agency of social progress.

Close on the heels of the *Creed* followed two other small books: *School and Society* (1899) and *The Child and the Curriculum* (1902). Both were essentially elaborations of the *Creed*. In *School and Society* Dewey identified his philosophy with what he termed the "New Education."

Of particular importance in the new education is his view of the relation that should exist between the school and society. The ideal, said Dewey, is "to make each one of our schools an embryonic community life, active with types of occupations that reflect the life of the larger society and permeated throughout with the spirit of art, history, and science. When the school introduces and trains each child of society into membership within such a little community, saturating him with the spirit of service, and providing him with the instruments of self-direction, we shall have the deepest and best guaranty of a larger society which is worthy, lovely, and harmonious." [1]

Dewey's definitive educational thought is set forth in his epoch-making work, *Democracy and Education* (1916). Its phil-

[1] *School and Society* (Revised edition, Chicago, 1929), pp. 27–28.

osophical framework is Pragmatism, a doctrine that Dewey did not formally adopt until the early years of the present century. The pragmatic theory of ultimate reality is avowedly naturalistic, and therefore it is definitely inhospitable to a Christian world view. Pragmatists generally prefer to deal with specific values in their immediate natural and social contexts, rather than to concern themselves with the problem of ultimate origins.

While Dewey was in the process of formulating his own pragmatic views, he recognized a positive aid in Darwinian evolution. Thus in a lecture given at Columbia University, in the year 1909, he made the following highly significant observation with respect to Darwin's contribution to the new logic: "In the first place, the new logic outlaws, flanks, dismisses—what you will—one type of problems and substitutes for it another type. Philosophy forswears inquiry after absolute origins and absolute finalities in order to explore specific values and the specific conditions that generate them." [2]

Whether or not Darwin may be considered the prime factor in the rise of the new logic, it is well known that Dewey both firmly defends empirical method and sharply condemns any philosophy that concerns itself with absolutes and finalities. Dewey's attitude at this point is definitely shared by a good many progressive religious educators.

There is another feature of *Democracy and Education* that should be made explicit. Dewey here views both education and democracy from a common perspective of growth. Education, he observes, has no end beyond itself; it is "all one with growing." Democracy, considered as a mode of mutually shared meanings and purposes, also is all one with growing. Both education and democracy thus converge on the concept of growth.

In his emphasis upon progressive growth, Dewey further reflects the decisive impact of Darwin. It was an easy mental step from biological evolution to an evolutionary philosophy of democ-

[2] *The Influence of Darwin on Philosophy and Other Essays in Contemporary Thought* (New York, 1910), p. 12.

racy and of education, and Dewey took that step unhesitatingly. Here, in particular, his influence upon the progressive educational movement in the Protestant churches has been far-reaching.

The second historical source of progressive theory of religious education is a version of Protestant thought which has always been distinctly critical of all forms of theological orthodoxy. Important elements of this new theological trend were active in American culture long before the dawn of the twentieth century. For example, three anti-Calvinist currents had already infiltrated New England Protestantism before the year 1850: Arminianism, Rationalism, and Transcendentalism.

But a liberal movement of far greater influence emerged in response to the Darwinian theory of evolution. During the closing decades of the nineteenth century, this school of thought often characterized itself as "The New Theology." In the year 1883, Dr. Theodore Thornton Munger, an influential New England minister, set forth the major tendencies of the new theology in a very illuminating essay. Among other things, he observes that while the new faith "does not part with the historic faith of the church," it does hold to the idea of a progressive faith. For him, revelation is a process "which is to be evolved in the history of the world." The Bible itself "is a continually unfolding revelation of God; it is a book of eternal laws and facts that are evolving their truth and reality in the process of history." [3]

Munger drew a logical conclusion from this evolutionary idea of revelation: there can be no final formulation of the Christian faith; it must always remain in process of revision in order to keep step with a growing revelation. He writes: "It is a mistake to regard the truths of the Christian faith, even those that are called leading and fundamental, as having a fixed form. Were they revelations *from* God, they might perhaps be so regarded; but being revelations *of* God, they imply a process of unfolding." [4]

In fairness to Munger, however, it must be noted that he was

---

[3] *The Freedom of Faith* (Boston, 1883), pp. 8, 19–21.
[4] *Freedom of Faith*, p. 59. Italics in original.

not quite so radical as that assertion implies. For him, traditional statements of the Christian faith are not altogether obsolete; indeed, they contain at least a "germ or heart" of truth which persists under new forms of expression. Thus all historic Christian doctrine must be approached as representing an "intermingling of permanent and changing qualities." The history of theological thought will therefore reflect both continuity and change.

By the opening of the twentieth century Munger's New Theology had already gained a considerable following. The term "new" was soon superseded by that of "liberal," but the general emphasis remained the same.

The foregoing analysis of late nineteenth-century educational theory and of Protestant theological thought shows that the opening years of the twentieth century were ripe for just such a movement as the new religious education. Significantly, leaders in religion and education alike accepted an evolutionary theory of history. They also agreed that the principle of progress provided the central clue to the reconstruction of both educational theory and Protestant theology. When, therefore, the insights of these two movements were fused, they made possible what could rightly be called "progressive religious education."

The year 1903 is historic in the rise of the progressive educational movement in the churches, for it was in that year that a national conference was convened in Chicago with the expressed purpose of seeking a way to unite the religious and educational forces of America in a great forward movement. Outstanding leaders in both religion and education attended in large numbers. Though Catholics and Jews were present, liberal Protestants really determined the main emphases of the conference.

Doubtless the most decisive achievement of the conference was the launching of the Religious Education Association. It was prophetic that both John Dewey and George Albert Coe were foremost participants in the process that gave birth to the Association, for this organized fellowship did more during the first quarter of the century to integrate the insights of progressive secular education and of progressive Christianity than any other single agency. Free from ecclesiastical and dogmatic restraints, it nurtured freedom of expression both in its official journal, *Religious Education*, and in its annual assemblies. Those who spear-pointed its policies and programs became the major creators of the progressive theory of Protestant nurture.

While many able thinkers took part in this pioneer movement, Professor Coe was unquestionably *primus inter pares*. He entered the gateway of the new century with excellent academic preparation in both philosophy and theology, and he had the added distinction of having taken postgraduate work at the world-renowned University of Berlin. At the time that the Religious Education Association came into being, he was occupying the chair of Moral and Intellectual Philosophy at Northwestern University. From 1909 to 1922, he served as professor of Religious Education in Union Theological Seminary. Thereafter, until his retirement in 1927, he taught at Teachers College, Columbia University. Unlike most retired educators, he published three of his ablest books after leaving the classroom: *The Motives of Men* (1928), *What Is Christian Education?* (1929), and *Educating for Citizenship* (1932).

Professor Coe has had no superior in his creative fusion of just those intellectual tendencies that were most essential to the development of the new theory of religious education. He was among the first to perceive the value of the psychological approach to religion, and from first-hand research he published two pioneering works in this field: *The Spiritual Life* (1900) and *The Psychology of Religion* (1916). Even before the century began, he had fully accepted both Biblical criticism and liberal theological views. In his *The Religion of a Mature Mind* (1902) ideas from these areas are woven together illuminatively. The new social emphasis in Christianity met with his instant approval, and from this viewpoint he wrote one of the most provocative educational works of his generation: *A Social Theory of Religious Education* (1917). How readily he embraced John Dewey's doctrine of the New Education is indicated by the fact that his first major book in religious nurture, *Education in Religion and Morals* (1904), quotes him more often than any other educational philosopher.

In light of such multiple intellectual interest and versatility, no one should be surprised that Professor Coe became the ablest theorist in progressive religious education that America has produced. Because of his acknowledged preeminence this essay assumes that the most authoritative way to document the basic theological presuppositions of the progressive doctrine of Protestant nurture is to concentrate upon his own views.

II

Prior to the Chicago conference Professor Coe had published some notable essays on the new theory of religious education. The most significant essay is entitled "Salvation by Education." [5]

Professor Coe here clearly indicated, among other things, that the new teaching movement of the church must bridge the gap between religion and education. This could be done, he thought, by fusing the new educational and religious ideals that were then emerging. He wrote: "If . . . we compare the ideals of the new education with those of progressive Christianity, we discover no such gulf as is commonly supposed." Indeed, the two are "tending toward a higher unity." For, in the first place, both explicitly take the position that spiritual values are immanent in the total round of human events; secondly, both are definitely committed to a philosophy of history based upon evolutionary growth.[6]

In advancing these two basic notions, Professor Coe gave progressive religious education an orientation that has fundamentally characterized it ever since. What are their theological assumptions and implications? In answer to this question, let us begin with the idea of divine immanence, for it is that idea that is presupposed in Coe's claim that spiritual values are inherent in every aspect of the common life.

[5] *The Religion of a Mature Mind* (Chicago, 1902), pp. 293–396.
[6] *Ibid.*, pp. 299–302.

1. *An immanent God*

No one at the turn of the century was more alive than Coe to the idea that the new theology as well as the new education must dissolve the dichotomy that split existence into two realms, the natural and the supernatural. On the other hand, he did not, as did Dewey presently, try to solve the problem involved by adopting an unqualified naturalism. Instead, he sought relief in the philosophical principle of the divine immanence. That principle became deeply rooted in liberal Protestant thought in the late nineteenth century by the growth of the idea of evolution. Joseph Le-Conte's widely publicized idea that evolution takes place "by means of resident forces," was eagerly assimulated by theological Darwinists like Lyman Abbott, John Fiske, and George Harris, and translated into an immanental interpretation of God's creative working in nature. Even the more cautious liberal evangelicals, including William Newton Clarke, Borden Parker Bowne, and Henry Churchill King, made the idea of divine immanence basic in their schemes of religious thought.

As Coe correctly observed, the new theology entered the twentieth century "committed to the doctrine of the immanence of God." He made constant use of the principle of divine immanence in his own religious thought, especially while under the dominance of philosophical idealism. This principle is, indeed, a theological cornerstone of his book, *Education in Religion and Morals*. After pointing out that the idea of an immanent God is the logical deduction from the premise of an evolutionary view of God's creative action, he writes as follows:

This means, among other things, that material atoms are forms of divine activity; that the laws of nature are simply the orderly methods of his rational will, which is in complete control of itself; that evolution does not suffer any break when man, a self-conscious and moral being, appears, because the whole of evolution is, in reality, a process of realizing a moral purpose; that the correlation of mind and brain is just the phenomenal aspect of the real correlation of our mind with the divine power which sustains us; that the development, physiological and mental, that man receives through nature is part of an all-inclusive educational plan, and that, in our work as educators, God is working through our reason and will to carry forward the universal plan.[7]

No one reading that statement can escape the conclusion that Coe believed in God's immanence in the whole of nature, including man. Even when, as in his later writings, he leaned more heavily on a functionalistic psychology and philosophy, he still predicated the immanental activity of God.

One can easily disclose the operation of this postulate of immanence in Coe's theory of Christian nurture. To this end, let us analyze his thought in a two-fold context.

(a) Basic in Coe's educational theory is his claim that the religious growth of the child from birth "takes place entirely within the kingdom of grace." [8] This doctrine underlies his famous formulation of the aim of Christian education: *"Growth of the young toward and into mature and efficient devotion to the democracy of God, and happy self-realization therein."* [9]

We are not now concerned with Coe's Christian democratic criterion of growth, but only with his thesis that the child starts its growth from *within* the kingdom. It is this thesis that makes him repudiate the classical evangelical view that distinguishes sharply between the natural man and the spiritual man, the lost and the saved. Correlatively, it makes him repudiate also the evangelical tendency to view the nurture of the little child as a process that merely anticipates later religious experience, rather than as a process that involves actual religious experience from the outset. Unmodified evangelicalism, he argues, has "no workable conception of a present Christian life" for the young child.[10] Even the ritualistic type of Protestantism, he points out, can provide the basis for a present religious experience of the young child only by employing an artificial mode of infant baptism.

[7] *Education in Religion and Morals* (Chicago, 1904), p. 43.
[8] *Ibid.*, pp. 37–40, 44–49.
[9] *A Social Theory of Religious Education* (New York, 1917), p. 55. Italics in original.
[10] *Ibid.*, p. 326.

As against all such traditional notions, Coe begins on the explicit predicate that infant human nature is not a total moral vacuum. He holds that the infant possesses naturally the very life-germ of divine grace, and that this life-germ is the potentially regenerate seed out of which the spiritual life grows from more to more.[11] Thus there need be no moral break between the old life and the new.

But what about total depravity? The answer is that ever since Coe published his essay, "Salvation by Education," he has always sharply scored that doctrine on both theological and scientific grounds. If its logic were to be completely followed, says Coe, it would paralyze child nurture, since the little child would possess only Satanic impulses and inclinations. But empirical science, he observes, does not support any such dogma; for it discovers in the young child the love-impulse, and this is the very tap-root out of which the Christian life can grow.

A word of caution must be added here, lest one get the idea that Coe believes that the infant descends from above trailing clouds of glory. That, Coe would readily reply, is a sentimental illusion. Indeed, as early as 1904 he issued a note of warning at this point. "In every one of us the good has a struggle against evil; in every one of us the good is so modified by evil that ideal character is never quite attained. Before a child can form a moral judgment he displays tendencies which, if they develop without check, will issue in a bad character." [12]

In that statement Coe shows that he is no uncritical romantic; he perceives that the child manifests tendencies to evil as well as to good. But in spite of this element of realism, there is evidence to indicate that he leans, on the whole, toward an optimistic notion of human nature. For while he admits the existence of evil tendencies in the child, he apparently believes that those tendencies derive, not primarily from the child's own rebellious self, but

[11] "What Does Modern Psychology Permit Us to Believe in Respect to Regeneration?", *The American Journal of Theology*, XII (July, 1908), pp. 356–361.
[12] *Education in Religion and Morals*, p. 49.

from the morally warped mores of society.[13] Thus although the child's conduct manifests both good and evil, the child at the core of his being is really good.

Now this idea that the child is naturally good and is therefore in possession of the germ of divine grace is a logical deduction from the assumption that God is immanent in human existence. Coe's doctrine of human nature thus accords with his theology of divine immanence.

(b) The postulate of divine immanence is no less involved in Professor Coe's idea of the nature of God's relation to human society considered collectively. If, as we have seen, God is the indwelling germ-principle of the individual self, then it is logical to assume that God is also the indwelling germ-principle of the community of selves. The postulate of divine immanence is thus applicable to society as it is to the individual.

Now this postulate is basic to Coe's "social" theory of Christian nurture. As already indicated, his social theory holds that the kingdom of God constitutes the ultimate end of Christian education, and that growth is the process of attaining maturity within that kingdom.

But in order to apprehend the inner nature of the kingdom as Jesus understood it, Coe says that it is necessary to interpret the kingdom in terms of the idea of democracy. Jesus' desire for brotherhood, he observes, "leads on with the inevitableness of fate to the ideal of a democratic organization of society." In Jesus' "fusion of divine with human love," he "presents us with a divine-human democracy as a final social ideal." [14]

In unfolding this social ideal, Coe reveals his faith in an immanental God in various ways. To take only one crucial example, he fuses divine with human love so completely as to teach that there can never be any love to God that does not also include love to men. This is why he distrusts all so-called private relations with God. This is why, also, he makes fellowship with God con-

[13] *A Social Theory of Religious Education*, pp. 145, 171.
[14] *Ibid.*, p. 54.

tingent upon prior fellowship with men. Thus he writes: "In and through his growing participation in the creation of an ideal society the pupil will realize his fellowship with the Father." [15] It is upon this premise that Coe sharply protests against those who teach children to "get right with God" first, and then be brotherly.

Considered, then, both in its individual and in its social aspects, Professor Coe's theory of Christian nurture definitely presupposes an immanentist conception of God's relation to human nature.

2. *A progress-making God*

The idea of evolutionary progress is no less basic in Professor Coe's religious and educational thought than is his conception of divine immanence. For him, the very term "progressive" derives its ultimate significance from a dynamic interpretation of the world-order. Like progressive Christians in general, he conceives the cosmos in terms of *a continuous becoming*, including both structural and functional changes.

Coe accepts as a matter of course the idea that man is integral to organic evolution. But for him the most significant fact is not that man emerges from within, and crowns, the animal series, but that man is himself a self-transcending being. Just as the whole world-order is continuously growing, so is man, as a part of that world-order, continuously growing.

Significantly, the central clue to Professor Coe's theory of religious education is to be found in his conception of the nature, growth, and worth of persons. This inclusive idea he often summarizes in the phrase, "the personality-principle."

An extremely important feature of Coe's doctrine of the personality-principle is his belief in the capacity of persons to remake religion. This belief is vitally connected with his theory of mental dynamics. The human mind, he holds, is not a static and finished entity; on the contrary, if considered from a functional standpoint, the mind is actually undergoing dynamic evolution.

[15] *A Social Theory of Religious Education*, p. 56.

Growth in mental functions reveals itself in the fact that the mind is always achieving new desires or wants. The mind not merely repeats ancient wants; it creates genuinely unprecedented wants. In the human struggle for existence, novel mental functions lead on to a better existence. Now this element of mental variation constitutes mental evolution.[16]

The evolution of religion, says Coe, is intimately connected with this growth of mental functions. For mental evolution manifests the function of a selective or preferential principle at the very center of the personal self. By reason of the operation of this selective principle, the self is not satisfied with old values; it strives for genuinely new values. In this dynamic process of the revaluation of values religion itself undergoes evolution.

This conception of the continuous evolution of religion in and through the valuative growth of persons involves Professor Coe in important theological assumptions.

(a) First of all, Coe perceives profound theistic implications in the fact that persons have emerged within nature. This leads him to contest the straight naturalistic interpretation of reality. The naturalist's trouble, he believes, arises largely from a preoccupation with subhuman elements of the cosmos. Thus he writes: "What is known as naturalism seems to me to draw its conclusions about man, on the whole, from inquiries that do not deal as seriously with the phenomena of personality as with the phenomena of the sub-personal." [17]

As against this tendency to dwell almost exclusively on subhuman structures and functions, Coe himself grapples with the unique functions involved in the growth of human selves, including self-identification, self-valuation, and self-transcendence. From this critical analysis he is led to posit the existence of a Divine Person who is immanently active in those functions which characterize growing persons. Thus he writes: ". . . the phenomenon of human personality taken in the large manifests an

[16] *The Psychology of Religion* (Chicago, 1916), pp. 215-221.
[17] *What Is Christian Education?* (New York, 1929), p. 89.

interfused personality, or God. I know not how else to construe the history of human personality." [18]

This personalistic approach to metaphysics lies at the very heart of Coe's religious thought, and it separates him sharply from the John Dewey school of naturalism. It also distinguishes him from all types of theistic naturalism that de-personalize ultimate reality.

(b) Professor Coe clearly perceives that his theory of the continuous evolution of religion raises the issue as to whether Christianity contains within itself any element or principle of permanent validity. Is the Christian faith a passing phase of evolving religion, or is there in it something that is unchanging and therefore permanently normative for the Christian educator?

Forthrightly Coe faces this basic issue. There is, he admits, something in Christianity that will persist through all change and therefore can serve as a continuing criterion for progressive Christian nurture. But that permanent element is not, he urges, to be found in any sort of theological dogma, nor even in any special person. Where, then, is that permanently normative reality to be found? It is found, replies Coe, in the principle of worth that Jesus ascribed to persons.

But what about Jesus himself? Is he not, in his unique being, the finality of the Christian educator? Coe's unequivocal answer is no. Because Jesus both perceived and demonstrated in his own life the value of persons, he will always remain a permanent source of strength and inspiration to the progressive educator. But even if Jesus had never grasped the personality-principle at all, that principle would still be final for religious faith. Thus Coe writes: "We hold to it [the personality-principle] because of its inherent validity, just as he [Jesus] did; it is not secondary to anything or anybody . . . The loyalty of the Christian, accordingly, is loyalty not to one person, even Jesus, but to persons." [19] This remarkable conclusion represents the logical deduction of Coe's

[18] *What Is Christian Education?* p. 94.
[19] *Ibid.,* pp. 181–182.

evolutionary theory of history and of religion. Reasoning, as he does, from the premise of a continuously growing religion, he has to reject the classical Christian view of the finality of the Christian revelation.

(c) Professor Coe's belief in moral progress is a definite factor in his optimistic interpretation of the human predicament.

As already noted, Coe denied the doctrine of total depravity on the predicate that the newly-born child inherently contains the germ-principle of the Father's kingdom, and thus from birth only needs further growth from within that kingdom.

This view, as Coe himself pointed out, does not mean that the child has nothing to struggle against. For, indeed, on an evolutionary theory of moral growth, the revaluation of moral values always implicates the self in a conflict with traditional values. From this point of view, the struggle with sin is both a reflection of prophetic religious awareness, and is also, in one sense, a pre-condition of the achievement of new values. Nevertheless, Coe's faith in moral progress gives his notion of the human predicament an optimistic tone. In fact, he makes his optimism explicit in these words: "If we look at society in historical perspective, we perceive that it is, on the whole, an evolutionary process in which we are working out the beast, and training ourselves to have regard for what is humane." [20]

On this assumption the progressive religious educator may take courage as he faces the future. For even though sin is rooted in instinct, confirmed by habit, and propagated by social processes, brotherliness will triumph over selfishness. "Love of one another," says Coe, "produces a degree of cooperation, which is the massing of human energy, that is impossible to greed, licentiousness, and the lust of power. Selfishness tends to disorganization and ineffectiveness in the long run." [21]

Now if one adds to this belief in growing brotherliness the further belief in man's essential goodness, one must admit that

[20] *A Social Theory of Religious Education*, p. 167.
[21] *Ibid.*, p. 168.

Coe's view of the human predicament is considerably tinctured with optimism.

III

In light of the foregoing analysis, is it not evident that Professor Coe's progressive theory of religious education is governed by important theological assumptions? Furthermore, is it not equally clear that his assumptions are those usually associated with the more radical forms of Protestant liberalism?

But if there is any lingering uncertainty on this point, Coe's recent critical comments on the newer theological tendencies should dispel all doubt. Ever since the late 1930's he has lost no opportunity to speak out on the dangers of those tendencies. In pointing out their dangers he further clarifies his own theological thought.

Professor Coe holds that Christian education is imperiled not merely by the more extreme Barthian forms of thought, but also by those milder types that characterize much of the recent ecumenical thinking of Protestantism. For example, he says that the Oxford Conference of 1937 "united intense religiousness with theological reaction." He believes that the World Council of Churches, in framing its basis of fellowship in terms of a high Christology, has "reverted to an utterly dogmatic and authoritarian test." [22]

Professor Coe is not satisfied merely to generalize in his criticisms of the current "theological assault upon Liberalism," for he is convinced that "there is a life-and-death issue" at stake in the area of Christian education.

First of all, he observes that there is a basic conflict over what attitude the teacher should take toward historic Christianity. Specifically, is the teacher to regard Christianity as a finished faith, and therefore to use educational method merely as an authoritarian tool with which to force the young to accept it as it

[22] "The Assault upon Liberalism," *Religious Education*, XXXIV (April-June, 1939), p. 88.

is, or is the teacher to assume that Christianity is a constantly growing faith, and consequently to employ educational method as a means of reconstructing religion by releasing the creative religious experience of the child? According to Coe, the former assumption dominates the mind of the new theologians. They represent an "anti-scientific reaction" within Protestantism which "involves a reversion to authoritarianism." [23]

Progressive educational theory, on the other hand, challenges this static notion of Christian faith. It sees in the growing experience of the child the growing-point also of the Christian faith; and therefore its primary concern is not to transmit the faith of yesterday, but to create the faith of tomorrow.

At another point Coe is troubled over the educational implications of recent theology. He notes that there is "almost a scramble to get more of God into religious teaching." He does not, of course, object to including God as a part of Christian education, but he does seriously object to beginning the educational process with some *a priori* idea about God, for he thinks that this approach is not only usually dominated by a transmissive and intellectualistic conception of teaching, but that it short-circuits the very creative point of Christian nurture, which is the present relations of living persons. [24] Thus the educational weakness of the newer theology is that it wants to lug God in at the very beginning of the teaching process and will not let God grow out of an experimental pupil-teacher quest for growing values. In other words, to paraphrase Coe, it is too anxious about God and not anxious enough about men. In contrast, Coe believes that a really vital Christian nurture will lead the pupil to an experience of God in and through a creative process of re-valuing personal-social values.

Coe notes a third point of conflict over the role of theology. The newer theology, he contends, is monopolistic, since it pre-

[23] "The Assault upon Liberalism," *Religious Education*, XXXIV (April–June, 1939), pp. 87–89.
[24] See Coe's significant statement as incorporated in Professor Edwin E. Aubrey's article, "A Theology Relevant to Religious Education," *Religious Education*, XXXIV (October–December, 1939), p. 199.

sumes to furnish all the factual data that will be needed in Christian nurture. But, says Coe, religious education is itself an important source of theological data, for it explores the present religious experience of growing persons. Thus formal theology can furnish "only a part of the basic and controlling ideas of religious education." Besides, "a theology that springs wholly from outside religious education, if it undertakes to prescribe either the content or the procedure of religious teaching, becomes thereby a self-deceived interloper." [25]

Finally, Professor Coe observes that there is a crucial issue between educational progressives and the newer theology over the nature of man. In the Oxford Conference, he says, "The dogma of depravity was treated almost as if it were the corner-stone of religious metaphysics." [26] Nothing is more outrageous to Coe than the revival of the idea of human depravity.

This summary of particulars shows beyond question that there is a fundamental clash between the left-wing liberal theology in which Professor Coe's educational theory is rooted and the new current in Protestant thought.

IV

In observing the new theological scene, one may well ask, what about the future of progressive religious education? As I size up the prospect, progressives have three courses of action open to them.

One course is to continue to reaffirm their already established theological convictions. This is apparently the choice of some of the best known American educational progressives, including Professors Coe, William C. Bower, and Harrison S. Elliott.[27]

---

[25] "A Theology Relevant to Religious Education," p. 199.

[26] "The Assault upon Liberalism," *Religious Education*, XXXIV (April-June, 1939), p. 88. See also Coe, "Religious Education Is in Peril," *The International Journal of Religious Education*, XV (January, 1939), p. 10.

[27] See W. C. Bower, "Points of Tension between Progressive Religious Education and Current Theological Trends," *Religious Education*, XXXIV (July–September, 1939), pp. 164–172; *Christ and Christian Education* (New

This emphasis will continue to serve as a counterweight against such extreme types of Protestant orthodoxy as Barthianism. This form of service, to be sure, is not unimportant, for there are elements in ultra-orthodoxy which do really imperil a constructive and vital doctrine of Christian nurture. On the other hand, if the progressive merely contents himself with criticism of this kind of orthodoxy, his role will necessarily be a negative one.

A second alternative for progressive educators would be to align themselves with metaphysical naturalism and abandon the distinctive Christian tradition altogether. This tendency, as a matter of fact, has been implicit in much of the thought of those left-wing educational liberals who have adopted an extreme functionalistic view of religion.

It is the current distinction of Professor Ernest J. Chave of the University of Chicago to affirm a naturalistic religious philosophy without reservation. In his compact little volume, *A Functional Approach to Religious Education* (1947), he sets forth a theory and a program for "a new day" for genuine progressives. The religious education for the new day, he contends, must be frankly naturalistic in its theory of reality. While it will connect man with "personality-producing forces," it will not identify his origin with a Divine Creator, nor will it ask him to worship "a blurred image." It will frankly recognize that the only forces of redemption "are in the growth processes of normal life," and that religion "is but the discovery, exaltation, and use of these." [28]

This consistent naturalism has at least one merit: it makes possible the fusion of religious education with progressive secular education. The logic of Professor Chave's position should lead him to seek such a fusion. John Dewey and other educational pro-

---

York, 1943); Harrison S. Elliott, *Can Religious Education Be Christian?* (New York, 1940).

[28] For a brief statement of this same position, see Professor Chave's recent article, "Religious Education for Liberal Progressives," *Religious Education*, XLV (March–April, 1950), pp. 67–72. A variety of evaluations, *pro* and *con*, are given on pp. 73–100.

gressives could have no objection to including "religion" in our state schools on this basis. Since, however, precisely this sort of religion is already present in the better public school curricula, it is difficult to see how progressive religious education could make any unique contribution to the splendid ethical and social processes that are now operative in such curricula. Its role, accordingly, would be essentially that of strengthening and extending the values that are already present in secular education. But in following this course, the obvious price that progressive religious education would pay is alienation from the distinctive educational work of the American Protestant churches.

There remains a third possible choice for educational progressives. They could undertake to reconstruct their theological foundations in light of the more realistic insights of current Christian faith. In this direction, as I see it, would lie their greatest constructive opportunity.

Recently a growing number of Christian educators have come to see that left-wing Protestant liberalism has largely lost its power of compulsion. Like Professor Coe, they were at first definitely negative in their attitude toward the newer Protestant theological trends, but today they show a more hospitable spirit toward many of those trends.

This new temper is significantly reflected in a special study that was sponsored by the International Council of Religious Education and released to the churches in the year 1947.[29] One of the eight major parts of that study is a thirty-six page document that deals primarily with the Christian presuppositions that should undergird Protestant nurture in the new era.

The new emphases are striking. First of all, the older optimistic notion of human nature is missing. Instead, man is said to reveal a "dual nature." Man's duality consists in the fact that he "is a

---

[29] *The Study of Christian Education* (The International Council of Religious Education, Chicago, Illinois, 1947). The material of this study has been interpreted in more popular form by Professor Paul H. Vieth in a book entitled *The Church and Christian Education,* published by Bethany Press, St. Louis.

child of God" and "is also a fallen creature." Continuing, the study says: "Man is alienated from God by the rebellion of his sin; he denies his true nature by his sensuality and his pride; he is prone to make himself the primary object of worship, confusing the copy with the original." Furthermore, "man is not a problem to himself because of the world in which he lives but because of his own nature. The impediment is not outside but inside. . . . Our civilization may increase the basic conflicts, but it is not their ultimate source." [30]

A second major accent is upon the nature and special content of the Christian revelation, including the centrality of Christ and his Church.

This study recognizes that the term "revelation" may be interpreted broadly to include God's manifestation of himself in the works of nature and in the course of general history, past and present, but it uses the term chiefly in its Biblical connotation. As thus understood, revelation refers to that special series of historical Biblical events through which God has savingly revealed himself. The integrative center of that series of revelatory events is Jesus Christ, "who is the embodiment of the gospel, the good news of the saving grace and power of God." "God commended his love toward us in the death of his Son. Here was more than man's utmost devotion to the divine will. Here was the redemptive act of God himself through a human life in history." Faith in the Christian revelation involves faith in a community which centers in Christ. "It began with the group to whom Jesus promised entrance to the kingdom of God. After his resurrection it was the group who looked to him as Lord and upon whom he poured out God's Spirit." It is within the church "that our faith has been formulated and passed on through a living succession of believing witnesses. The church has been the mother of us all, and there is truth in the historic statement, *extra ecclesiam nulla salus.*" [31]

[30] *The Study of Christian Education: II—Theological and Educational Foundations*, pp. 10, 11.
[31] *Ibid.*, pp. 16, 18, 19, 24.

From this brief account, it is evident that the educational leaders in the International Council have already recognized the value of the new currents in Protestant thought. They are not, to be sure, uncritical of those currents; they rightly distinguish between those tendencies that are compatible with a vital theory of Christian nurture and those that are detrimental to it.

As a whole, this study is a good example of the cautious yet favorable attitude that progressive religious educators might well show toward the new theological awakening that is emerging. Were they to abandon their purely negative attitude and participate sympathetically in this new renaissance in Protestant thinking, they could again become a great creative force in American Christian nurture.

BIBLIOGRAPHY

Bower, W. C., *The Curriculum of Religious Education* (New York, 1925)

Case, Adelaide, *Liberal Christianity and Religious Education* (New York, 1924)

Coe, George A., *A Social Theory of Religious Education* (New York, 1917)

——, *What Is Christian Education?* (New York, 1929)

Elliott, Harrison S., *Can Religious Education Be Christian?* (New York, 1940)

Hartshorne, Hugh, *Character in Human Relations* (New York, 1932)

Miller, Randolph Crump, *The Clue to Christian Education* (New York, 1950)

Smith, H. Shelton, *Faith and Nurture* (New York, 1941)

Soares, Theodore G., *Religious Education* (Chicago, 1929)

Vieth, Paul H., *Objectives in Religious Education* (New York, 1930)

Wiegle, L. A., *Jesus and the Educational Method* (New York, 1939)

Williams, J. Paul, *The New Education and Religion* (New York, 1945)

REUNION AND THE ECUMENICAL MOVEMENT

Henry S. Leiper

HENRY SMITH LEIPER was born in 1891, and he is now one of the Associate General Secretaries of the World Council of Churches. For more than two decades he has acted as an ambassador from the American churches to many countries throughout the world. He took his undergraduate studies at Amherst College, and then he studied at Union Theological Seminary and Columbia University. He served in Siberia during World War I, and in 1946 he made a flying trip to India to survey famine conditions, consulting Mahatma Gandhi, Pandit Nehru and M. A. Jinnah, as well as numerous church leaders. Dr. Leiper is the author of several widely read books, and he is, in particular, known as the editor of *Christianity Today*—a unique symposium about the work of the Church throughout the entire world. He is an editor of *Christianity and Crisis*, and he contributes regularly to various journals on both sides of the Atlantic.

XI

THE MOST representative American theological books issued at the dawn of the century assume that progress is inevitable. They reflect little anxiety about the future of Christianity. Representative thinkers confidently hoped that by evolutionary processes the Christian movement was destined to attain universal spiritual ascendancy in a peaceful world. Freedom, it was assumed, would soon be achieved by all mankind and would be lasting. The eschatological note was almost entirely lacking. This complacency was bolstered by theological views minimizing the sinfulness of human nature, seeing religion as chiefly a personal concern, and neglecting the significance of the Church either as a world-wide fellowship or a supra-national institution.

Partly because of this lack of anxiety, little concern for Christian unity appeared except in the trenchant writings of such men as Josiah Strong, Philip Schaff and William Reed Huntington. There was manifested little corresponding to what William Temple calls "St. Paul's horror of Christian divisions." To most of those who were at all concerned with unity, it was thought of as capable of satisfactory expression along functional lines through the co-operation of individuals across denominational frontiers. This was shown in the working policy, if not in what might be called the philosophy, of the Evangelical Alliance, the student Christian movement, the Sunday School movement, the Bible Societies and the foreign mission enterprise. Significantly there was at that time no movement for *Church* as distinguished from *Christian* co-operation or unity.

Indeed, there had not at that time been any union of denominations in America for years and none seems to have been under discussion. Although the so-called "Chicago Quadrilateral" had been in existence since 1886, it was only after it was taken up as a basis of discussion by the Congregationalists in America and the

Lambeth Conference in 1910 that it attracted any general attention.

Even federal unity of a corporate sort, although it had been envisioned in some detail by Dr. Samuel Schmucker, the Lutheran from Gettysburg, Pennsylvania, in 1846, was far from the center of American Christian thought. It was considered at the Chicago meeting of the World Alliance in 1892. And it was defined with singular foresight by Dr. Philip Schaff at an earlier meeting of that same body. In discussing the "Reunion of Christendom" he said: "Federal or corporate union is a voluntary association of different churches in their official capacity, each retaining its freedom and independence in the management of its internal affairs, but all recognizing one another as sisters with equal rights and co-operating in general enterprises such as the spread of the Gospel at home and abroad, the defence of the faith against infidelity, and the elevation of the poor and neglected classes of society, works of philanthropy, charity and moral reform."

Dr. Samuel McCrea Cavert gives it as his opinion that the Evangelical Alliance, just referred to, deserves more credit than is usually assigned to it for contributing the Church emphasis which was lacking among those who at the turn of the century thought of Christian unity in non-denominational terms. Under the influence of men like Dr. Schaff, he—Dr. Cavert—sees the Alliance pioneering for what came to be the Faith and Order Movement more definitely than any other interdenominational body of the years before 1900. It was, however, largely pan-Protestant and its constituency was personal rather than ecclesiastically delegated.

When the followers of Dr. Schaff in 1900 used the term "federal union," they apparently meant what we now mean by federation or federal *unity*. Federal *union* today connotes some such organic merger as would come about if the Stanley Jones proposals were to be accepted, i.e., the formation of a single Church with parts or branches corresponding to the present denominations but with voluntarily limited sovereignty.

Since the Alliance was inclined, apparently, toward what came to be known as the Faith-and-Order (theological and ecclesiastical) emphasis, Dr. Josiah Strong, one of its dynamic leaders, had left it shortly before 1900 to form what was called the "Open and Institutional Church League." Out of a meeting of this body and the influence of the "Federation of Churches and Christian Workers" in New York City, there came a meeting of minds in 1900 at a special conference which called for a national expression of the kind of Christian unity broadly described by Dr. Schaff in the quotation above. Here, perhaps, we find the genesis of what became the Federal Council of Churches.

In this connection, it is important to keep in mind an observation made by Dr. E. B. Sanford, historian of the early days of the Federal Council which, while definitely not a direct approach to church union, marked a notable advance toward unity and differed from most of the earlier attempts in being directly concerned with the churches rather than simply with Christians as individuals. Dr. Sanford's view [1] was that "this movement is towards the unity for which Christ prayed—not a unity necessarily of organization, but a unity of spirit and of purpose in the evangelization of man, and in creating social conditions which shall make men as helpful and blessed as may be in this world." In an early conference of Josiah Strong's "Open Church League," just mentioned, Dr. Sanford dealt with the relationship between common Christian social concerns and church union.—"This League seeks in its fellowship to bring together believers of every name asking: what can be done to make the church of Christ a more efficient instrument in accomplishing His redemptive work in the world? Organic ecclesiastical unity we may hold as a dream of the future or dismiss with the interrogation, is it desirable? But Christian unity as a spiritual reality and as a practical factor bringing the denominations into federative relations through which they can work out the problems of Christian service in city, country, and abroad without the present waste of forces, who that loves the

---

[1] Sanford: _Federal Council of the Churches of Christ in America_ (Revell, 1909), p. 148.

Kingdom of our common Lord can but desire and long to see consummated? It is coming and in its coming I believe that the Open and Institutional Church League seeking in its counsels to exalt the work and mission of Christ in the life of the church is destined to play an important part." [2]

In his book, *Christian Unity in the Making*,[3] Dr. Charles S. Macfarland says: "The early leadership was by prophetic individuals and groups induced by practical objectives to meet certain demands of human life. There were no preconceived plans for ultimate organization. . . . This period was characterized by its simplicity of thinking and its practicality in action. There was a growing sense of freedom, an absence of abstract theorizing, much practice in prayer. These men accepted and assumed each other's faith in the fundamental verities of the Gospel and one another's experience of life in Christ." That they avoided theological approaches was due, Dr. Macfarland thinks, to the general "assumption that institutional Christian unity implied an identical confession of theological belief or a uniform mode of worship or a common theory of the church's ministry and ordinances."

Three main purposes were incorporated later in the Constitution of the Federal Council of Churches which was not actually launched until 1908. These were: the manifestation of the essential oneness of the Christian churches of America in Jesus Christ as their divine Lord and Saviour; the promotion of the spirit of fellowship, service and co-operation; and the prosecution of work that could better be done in union than in separation. Only at a later date were the churches of the Council prepared to add to the Constitution recognition of responsibility for promoting "the application of the law of Christ for every relation of human life." Co-operation and not competition would manifest to the world a new oneness in Christ, thus advancing the Kingdom. "Working together the churches will minister to human need as never be-

[2] Hutchison: *We Are Not Divided* (Round Table Press), p. 124.
[3] Macfarland: *Christian Unity in the Making* (Federal Council, 1948), p. 25.

fore, and in so doing prove that the Gospel is the supreme remedy for all evils."

It is worthy of remark that at the founding meeting of the Federal Council in Philadelphia, December 1908, a very special emphasis was likewise laid upon the idea that unity would strengthen the world mission of the Church. The report on "Co-operation in Foreign Missions," presented by Dr. James L. Barton, secretary of the American Board, Boston, stressed five things: enthusiastic support for co-operation abroad; fellowship at home in developing support for the world mission; "the closest possible federation of all Christian Churches in Foreign Mission fields"; union educational institutions wherever practicable in foreign mission areas; and interdenominational efforts to create an adequate Christian literature in the vernacular for the people in all mission fields.

This pragmatic thinking about the objectives of unity in the world mission was going on alongside of united planning for advances in home missions. A fivefold report and appeal to the supporters of the home mission cause went out from the Philadelphia meeting. It extended also to the social application in industry and commerce of the Christian Gospel seen as truly independent of denominational differences.

Bishop Hendrix, first President of the Federal Council, in closing this historic and truly creative Philadelphia meeting, said: "The Council fervently appeals to the churches to search out the common ways of united and unselfish ministry, to give sway to the holy passion of saving men, to demonstrate unanswerably, in complete surrender to their Lord, the permanent reality of this profounder sense of unity, by eager loyalty, intense, unswerving, to the mighty purpose of salvation which brought Jesus Christ to Humanity. . . ." [4]

There was, however, so much hesitation to deal directly with unity—meaning then organic union—that a proposal to include

[4] Sanford: *Origin and History of the Federal Council of the Churches of Christ in America* (S. S. Scranton Co., 1916), pages 271–272.

it in the stated objects of the Council was rejected, and even the proposal to favor local union churches was set aside in favor of the idea of federation.

In the thinking of those who led the movement, there was thus a threefold concern—the first for practical forms of unity; the second for evangelization; and the third for social betterment, i.e., the creation of conditions which "will make man as helpful and blessed as may be in this world."

The second of these concerns—evangelization—was likewise the dominant concern of the missionary leaders in 1900 but although they did describe their world conference in New York in that year as "ecumenical" it was not because they were to consider union or even unity, rather their world-wide evangelistic interest led to the selection of that name, particularly because of its connotation "having to do with the whole world-wide household of faith." At the center was emphasis upon evangelization as if it could be achieved with little or no reference to either social transformation or church unity. It must, however, be parenthetically observed that the actions of many of these persons and the organizations with which they were related indicated a consciousness of being members one of another, and this seems to have made inevitable their later expressions of concern for unity as such.

There was yet another current of thinking which even in 1900 was preparing many minds for new advances in unity. It was due chiefly to the World's Student Christian Federation, organized by Dr. Mott in Sweden in 1895, which had trained a considerable body of future leaders of the ecumenical movement. That has often been recognized. What is not so frequently noted is what might be called the prolegomena to modern ecumenical philosophy which was being worked out by many of those responsible for the literature and program of the Federation. Many expressions of their thinking appear in addresses at such student conferences as were conducted by the Student Volunteer Movement.

As Dr. Henry P. Van Dusen points out in his book, *World*

Christianity,[5] the bodies constituent to the Student Christian Movement "have been among the most potent, indeed indispensable, forces in furthering the advance of Christian unity on every front. Their contributions have been principally at three points: a) They have, by daring experiments congenial to youth, prospected the most promising routes toward Christian fellowship and cooperation, and have discovered the circumstances and terms under which progress may hopefully be expected. . . . Especially noteworthy has been their courage in probing the deeper issues which divide Christians, issues of theological conviction which some other ecumenical movements have been hesitant to tackle.

"b) They have raised up the great bulk of the ablest leadership for every branch of the developing Christian unity movement in almost every country. . . . The late William Temple, Archbishop of Canterbury . . . testified that it was in conferences of the British Student Christian Movement and later of the W.S.C.F. that he first experienced the reality of ecumenical Christianity and became converted to its possibility.

"c) These Christian youth movements have in their own life demonstrated the reality of that ideal to which all the various efforts for Christian unity are in principle committed."

Another contribution of lasting importance is stressed by Tissington Tatlow, in his *Story of the Student Christian Movement*.[6] It was the working out of a clear distinction between undenominational and interdenominational (cf. p. 138).[7] The latter is so familiar to this generation that it is hard to realize how definitely new it was and how radical a departure from the view that one left one's church behind when joining in a cooperative Christian enterprise of non-ecclesiastical nature such as the Y.M.C.A. On both sides of the Atlantic, the students and their leaders pioneered this transition so full of significance for the future of the unity movement.

[5] Van Dusen: *World Christianity* (Abingdon-Cokesbury, 1947), pages 89–91.

[6] Tissington-Tatlow: *Story of the Student Christian Movement* (S.P.C.K., 1933), Chapters VIII to XVIII.

[7] *Ibid.*, Chapters VIII to XVIII.

As direct confirmation of the views just recorded, we find in Clarence Shedd's *History of the Student Christian Movement During the Last 200 Years:* [8] "The tendency to eliminate all geographical, confessional, and racial barriers to the realization of brotherhood among the students of the world has characterized the student movement from the beginning." L. D. Wishard (a student secretary in the '90's) saw "one world-wide movement of Christ for the students of the world and the students of the world for Christ." [9] In the amazing spread of the movement into the United Kingdom, Scandinavia, Germany, China, Turkestan, Japan, India, Ceylon, Persia, Kurdistan, Syria and elsewhere in the last decade of the nineteenth century, Dr. Roswell Hitchcock remarked that the students' "witness to the essential unity of the Church of Christ is a mitigation of the deplorable effect of our too disintegrated Protestantism." [10]

Yet another important current of Christian thought about unity has already been mentioned. The Chicago Quadrilateral of 1886, later to be known as the Lambeth Quadrilateral, involved an approach radically different from that of the Federal Council, the various functional agencies of a non-denominational character, the missionary movement, and the student Christian movement. It was not concerned with the idea of federal union, or functional unity of a pragmatic type, nor even with the world mission of the church as ordinarily conceived. These, like the modern ecumenical movement, were extroverted. The thinking of the proponents of the Quadrilateral was introverted: it had to do almost exclusively with the specific doctrinal bases of ecclesiastical organic union. These four bases are well known, i.e., the Bible, the Nicene Creed, the two Sacraments, and the historic episcopate.

Yet it took an exceedingly practical missionary statesman in the dynamic atmosphere of the Edinburgh Conference to see how this emphasis needed to be correlated with the others which had

[8] Shedd: *History of the Student Christian Movement During the Last 200 Years*, page 321.

[9] *Ibid.*, page 324.

[10] Wishard: *A New Programme of Missions*, page 85.

emerged in the general advance towards something more rational and more Christlike than an atomized Christianity. The 1910 meeting followed that of 1900, the former being the eighth of a long series marking a rising tide of interest in co-operation functionally for the sake of the world mission of the Church. Before taking up the story of Bishop Brent's contributions, attention must be drawn to other more immediate aspects of the tremendous thing that took place in the Assembly Hall of the Church of Scotland on the famous Royal Mile leading to "the Rock"—Edinburgh's justly famous castle, where was born James VI, patron of the English Bible.

It may seem something apart from the development of American thinking on the matter of unity. It was by no means without its many intimate relationships to that thinking, for in part it owed its character to American leadership and in part it stimulated a series of remarkable advances led by American churchmen of whom Brent was one.

One distinguishing mark of the 1910 meeting in Scotland was the presence of *delegated* representatives of mission boards rather than persons who came of their own initiative and without representative capacity. The significance of this was, of course, that mission boards as related parts of the churches were beginning to think in terms of a corporate responsibility for more co-operation. At that stage, however, even a suspicion of technical involvement in anything pointing toward organic union would have frightened away a considerable number, if not the vast majority.

Next to the growing recognition on many sides that missionary advance called for a united approach, the most immediate practical thinking growing out of Edinburgh had to do with next steps in the technical process of developing functional co-operation. It led, under the guidance of Dr. John R. Mott, who chaired the conference, to the only official decision of the Assembly, i.e., the decision to establish "continuation committees" in all the major areas of foreign missionary activity. Although it could not have been realized by many at the time, this was to lead in due course to the establishment of bodies in most parts of the so-called "non-Christian world," which were in time to become the National Council of Churches (although at first composed of missions *and* churches). Here was the idea destined to produce the International Missionary Council which in 1950 links thirty-one autonomous councils of varying constituencies—churches and missions, Anglican and Protestant—all embodying the idea of federal unity in some form and many, in due course, producing indirectly significant organic unions among constituent bodies.

As has already been intimated, the 1910 Edinburgh meeting saw the beginnings of a transition from the idea of unity as non-denominational co-operation in various functional forms to a real concern for inter-church approaches to working unity. It also was the seed ground for ideas which led not only to "Lausanne 1927" but also to "Stockholm 1925."

Concern for the fulfillment of the "Great Commission" was acute in the heart of Bishop Charles Henry Brent, eminent American Episcopal Bishop of the Philippines. He brought a new idea to focus as he incisively stated the chief reason for his growing conviction that organic church union as such should be intensively studied and fearlessly faced. He wrote: "It is little short of absurd to try to bring into the Church of Christ the great nations of the Far East unless we can present an undivided front. For purely practical reasons we feel the necessity of the Church's realization of unity. It must be either that or failure in our vocation." [11]

To the other ideas current among advocates of unity such as sensitivity to "practical necessity," coupled with tremendous conviction as to the will of Christ for oneness among his followers, Brent set out to add the definite consideration of organic union.

When he came to undertake the launching of a movement, he found a readiness to respond among the leaders of his own communion. What more natural than that they should suggest the relevance of the "Quadrilateral" to the studies the intense mis-

[11] Zabriskie: *Bishop Brent* (Westminster Press), page 92.

sionary Bishop proposed to inaugurate? And as a leader in the
Federal Council of Churches, as well as in the Anglican communion, Brent easily found other companions ready to travel
the new multi-lane highway toward the much desired goal.

But the central emphasis in Brent's thinking was not tech-
nically theological although it had even more profound theological
significance than the Chicago Quadrilateral (by that time renamed
for Lambeth, as has been noted). The central emphasis in his
thinking was on wholeness. He repeatedly points out that *wholeness* is synonymous with *health*—both etymologically and ideo-
logically. To him lack of communion among Christians was a
lack of wholeness and hence a diseased condition; and that within
the very body set to bring healing—wholeness—to the nations.
For him "sectarianism in spirit and form is *par excellence* the cult
of the incomplete" so that "there is no graver offense than to use
a catholic garment to hide a sectarian heart." Indeed, in another
connection, he points out that "Catholicity has nothing to recom-
mend it unless it is the condition in which everything is measured
and considered in terms of the whole." With his wide experience
in the missionary tasks of the Orient, it was naturally clear to him
that world-wide unity was essential because only so could the
central message of the Church be incarnated in the life of the
visible Church. For him co-operation was first. But it was not
enough. The Christian fellowship to be achieved must somehow
make available to its members the heritage of all Christians—past
and present. And unless individual Christians became united first
of all in the will to obey Christ's command "that they be one in
love at all costs," they would never be able to end the sin of ecclesiastical disunity.

In the ten years between Edinburgh and the next great step
in specific unity consultations at Geneva in 1920, competition
developed between (a) devotees of the idea of working together
on the social applications of Christianity without discussing the
profound differences which all saw in the area of theological convictions; (b) advocates of missionary expansion as practically the

sole concern of the churches collectively; (c) proponents of united church approaches to the problems of international understanding; and (d) the faith and order group of which Brent was the natural leader. But it was characteristic of the real catholicity of Brent's thought that he was almost alone in being genuinely interested in all the different lines of approach to the thing he cared about so passionately. Many of those with whom he was closely associated did not have his breadth of vision. Even as late as 1935, it was regarded as a bold move to suggest the holding of two world conferences then in prospect for 1937 in adjacent cities and at a time when it would be convenient for members of the one to attend the other. By that time Charles Henry Brent had gone from the earthly scene: although his spirit made itself felt in those who most closely shared his vision.

But it is necessary in tracing the developing idea of Christian unity to go back to a point only four years after Edinburgh, 1910. In the fateful year of 1914, the approach listed under "c" above had been attempted. It was one which was not aimed at internal unity as such but at increasing the effectiveness of the churches in developing international friendship. Largely through American initiative, supported by the generous gifts of Andrew Carnegie, a meeting had been called at Constance when it was still hoped that war might be averted.

Like other aspects of the total unity movement, this was to have consequences which nobody foresaw. One, not often recognized, had to do with the ancient Orthodox Churches of the East. For the long centuries after 1054 they had held wholly aloof from Western Christendom. What brought about the new contacts between them and the leaders of the Anglican and Protestant communions? It was the result of the pragmatic thinking of the leaders of the World Alliance for International Friendship Through the Churches and the Federal Council, as well as the financial aid of the former. Personal approaches were made after 1918 by officers of both bodies to the Orthodox leaders in the Balkans. The result was the somewhat hesitant acceptance on the part of influential

Orthodox prelates of invitations to consult with the Christians of the West about world peace.

Limitations of space necessitates omitting even brief reference to the many following developments. But it should be noted that in 1920, partly as a result of the approaches just mentioned, the Ecumenical Patriarch in Stamboul issued a precedent-shattering call for the formation of a world consultative council made up of the leaders of the churches. He frankly stated that he felt the time had come for it; and seemed prepared to have it develop into a genuine council of churches.

From that point on, the participation of the Eastern Orthodox Church in all important steps toward greater unity was an increasing factor with important consequences not commonly appreciated by Protestant observers who, unfortunately, tend to write off the nineteen Eastern Churches as if they were without significance in any genuine approach to world-wide Christian community.

Stockholm 1925 and Lausanne 1927 saw the genuine sense of fellowship with these churches growing to the point where it was impossible to conceive of an ecumenical progress which did not take into account the great traditions of the East, however difficult and long might be the process of finding viable solutions to the problems raised by them for the West. Fifteen of the nineteen Eastern Orthodox Churches were represented at the two conferences.

It was not until after the Jerusalem Conference of 1928 that a few Americans, notably John A. Mackay, then a missionary returned from Latin America, began to give the term "ecumenical" a new currency among Protestants and a somewhat new significance. The term has, of course, always been used by the Eastern Church, by Rome, and by many non-Roman Western Churches of continental origin. But its coming into the thinking of Americans was more than an etymological process, more than an accidental circumstance due to broader contacts with the churches of the rest of the world.

At the Oxford World Conference of Church, Community and State in 1937, Dr. Mackay, in his report on "The Church in the World of Nations," distinguished "interdenominational" or "international" from "ecumenical." The former terms were associated with the idea of separate units being assembled for co-operation in some form. The latter assumed an inherent or given unity. It started from the concept of wholeness as earlier stressed by Bishop Brent. His own later definition of "ecumenics" brings out the full meaning. He writes: "Ecumenics is the science of the Church universal conceived of as a world missionary community—its nature, its functions, its relations and its strategy."

The distinctive things only foreshadowed in earlier writings about the theme of Christian unity and the ecumenical movement were the emphasis upon the dynamic missionary character of the Church universal, its inherent God-given oneness, and its character as a community. The latter is the least commonly understood even in 1950! In this concept of fellowship, familyhood and *koinonia* lies the key to an understanding of this element—hitherto unprecedented—in the ecumenical movement as it has developed in the last decade. But it is important to look at the other two concepts with some care. The movement for Christian unity has been in America—as the earlier parts of this chapter amply reveal—accompanied by a recurring stress upon the need of unity in order that the evangelistic task of the Church may be performed. Yet all too often the idea has somehow gotten abroad that enthusiasts for unity had in mind only the merging of existing churches in some technical or organic way. The conception of God-given inherent oneness, on the other hand, is as old as the Church though it has been left too long in the background. Disunity has seemed normal. To desire unity—not to say union—struck many as abnormal. In the greatest crisis of His life, the Lord of the Church prayed for unity. In our inverted scale of values, it gets put off to a more convenient season.

Dr. Van Dusen has listed eight different types of Christian fellowship and co-operation all springing from the urge for more unity.[12] All of these were much in evidence in the two decades prior to the provisional launching of the World Council of Churches of which they were, many of them, anticipatory. These eight are: (1) associations of individuals of different denominations; (2) conferences of individuals of various denominations; (3) nondenominational associations; (4) interdenominational conferences of official representatives; (5) interdenominational organizations; (6) denominational world associations; (7) federations of churches; (8) church unions.

It appears that by emphasizing co-operation in common tasks rather than organic union a tide was set in motion which actually resulted in more organic unions with each passing decade until the number becomes little short of astonishing to the uninformed. On merely empirical evidence, there appears to be a correlation between the advance in various kinds of co-operation and the achievement of the full organic union. Unity in foreign missions lands grew perceptibly between 1927—following Lausanne—and 1936. In that decade, according to a report entitled "Unity in Foreign Missions," (a report of a joint committee of the Federal Council and the Foreign Missions Conference), of the twenty-three significant negotiations looking toward possible unification, thirteen occurred between two or more younger churches." In this period, of the ten unions fully consummated, six concerned younger churches. . . . In seven areas where missions have planted Christian churches—in China, in North India, in South India, in Siam, in the Philippines, in Puerto Rico, in Japan—unification of churches which in parent lands are still separate has been sufficiently extensive to warrant the title 'United Church.' " [13]

The same alert observer tells us that in the past two decades—1937 roughly to the present time—the number of unions of related and those of unrelated churches are exactly equal. With the consummation of the United Church of South India, mergers have now involved Baptist, Congregational, Christian, Evangelical,

[12] Van Dusen: *World Christianity*, pages 84–100.
[13] *Ibid.*, page 104.

Methodist, Presbyterian, Reformed, United Brethren, and Angli-can bodies. Commenting on what this has meant for the witness of the Church, Dr. Van Dusen adds: "In every area of severest testing (particularly during World War II)—in occupied Europe, in Germany, in China, in Japan, among the youngest churches—fidelity in witness and effectiveness in action have been in direct ratio to the unity of all Christian groups. . . . Nothing less than the *whole* Christian community has proved able to 'withstand, and having done all, to stand.' "

Dr. Van Dusen and Dr. John Bennett see forms of church unity classified as follows:

1. Unofficial organizations and fellowships that have a specific purpose.
2. Mutual recognition involving:
   a. Interchange of membership;
   b. interchange of ministries;
   c. intercommunion;
   d. comity arrangements in missions and church extension.
3. Federation for co-operative witness, teaching and action.
4. Federal union which presupposes mutual recognition and adds to it a federation to which is committed responsibility for missions and other selected activities of the churches.
5. Full corporate union that involves a single church government as well as the forms of unity previously mentioned.

But these representative free churchmen—Presbyterian and Congregational—agree in adding an important observation: "Christian Union which does not imply and make possible what-ever degree of church union may be held to be the ultimate de-sideratum is something less than genuine and true Christian unity." [14] They would insist, as do other free churchmen and a considerable number of Protestant Episcopal leaders, that what Canon Wedel has called *The Coming Great Church* must make "room within itself for the freedom to pioneer and to criticize that characterized the sects at their best." John Bennett, whose words I have just quoted, adds: "If it fails to do this, the radical ferment in the Christian Gospel will break through the carefully wrought,

[14] Van Dusen: "The Issues of Christian Unity," *Christendom*, Spring, 1946.

unified structures of the Church, and a new sectarian protest will have to find its home outside the united Church." [15]

It is now time for some brief summaries. Unlike the thinking of the opening years of the century, contemporary Christian thought in America is burdened with the sense of great reversals of what had seemed established trends. The "ground swell" of the time is against Christianity; and indeed against all that most enlightened men have regarded as progress. Science is for the first time afraid of its own powers of destruction. Instead of complacency, there is general alarm lest the world now so obviously one in a physical, scientific and logistic sense, destroy itself because of its failure to become one in any spiritual sense. The achievement of world community has become a life and death issue. The relevance to it of the only existing world fellowship—that of the Christian Churches—is becoming clearer to many minds.

It is notable, in view of these facts and what they imply that the ecumenical movement has more and more stressed community after the pattern of familyhood as the norm for Christians concerned for world order. The very fact that the movement has been so widely misunderstood, as Kenneth S. Latourette points out, is evidence that it is something new. Old analogies do not fit the new facts.

American as well as European and Asian Christians shared in the formulation of a 1950 statement of the World Council's Central Committee on "The Church, the Churches and the World Council of Churches." In that contradictions are held within larger agreements and centrifugal tendencies are resisted or overcome by stronger centripetal forces.

This document, which reflects much American thinking, makes a very clear distinction between church unity and church union. In contemporary ecumenical theory, the latter is solely the con-

[15] Nolde: *Toward World-Wide Christianity* (Harper & Brothers, 1946), page 74.

cern of the autonomous churches themselves. The former is the concern of all who know the compulsion of the will of the great Head of the Church toward more adequate expression of the community of interest which He has inspired in a growing number of Christians. While the World Council is not a Church and is emphatically not a super-Church, and while there are churches in its membership which do not even recognize other member churches as being "true" churches, there is manifest a bond of fellowship which has grown stronger as the need for unity in a divided world has become more tragically evident.

The statistical method of approach to measuring such a growth in the movement for ecumenical advance is open to objections, but it has some value, nevertheless, and what it shows is revealing. Many Christians on being confronted with the facts are so amazed that they exclaim: "We did not have any idea such things were happening." Well did Will Rogers—who had some insight denied to many theologians—remark on one occasion: "Everybody is ignorant—but on different subjects!"

What does the record show? Since we are considering a world movement, a glance at the world scene seems justified even though our immediate concern is with developments in America. Whereas at the dawn of the nineteenth century there were about 240 denominations in what is now the constituency of the World Council of Churches, at the dawn of the twentieth century the number had been reduced by organic unions to 200—at a rate of not quite one union for each two-year period. At the midpoint of this century, the number has gone down to 160 as a result of an increasing acceleration in the process of uniting organically. The rate was about one per year. From 1800 to 1910 the roster of outstanding events manifesting the growth of unity among Christians totalled 102, less than one per year. But from 1910 to 1940 the number was 215, a six-fold increase. The number of such events in the last ten years was 252. And organic mergers continued to be consummated at the rate of one per year on the average.

It hardly seems true that the thinking of those concerned with this matter has failed to register in outward and visible signs of change in the actual structure of the Church!

As for certain other contrasts between 1900 and 1950 in the matters related to the theme of this chapter, consider the following: In 1900, despite the influence of men like Schaff and Huntington, no churches were formally discussing unity—not to speak of union. In 1920 only 70 in all the world were willing to discuss the subject informally at the call of the American Churches. Today, 158 denominations (30 of them American with a membership of over 30,000,000 in the U.S.A.) are now officially a part of the World Council of Churches and have gone on record with the affirmation: "We intend to stay together." They have affirmed their conviction that God wills unity and have dedicated themselves to try to manifest more fully the unity which he has already given them.

In contrast with what was true in 1900, no one in the ecumenical movement today thinks that progress is inevitable. No one feels that co-operation between individuals undenominationally is full ecumenical co-operation. No one feels that interdenominational co-operation which does not commit the churches as such is ecumenical in any genuine sense although it may be helpful and lead in the right direction.

In contrast with what was true up to 1937, the Life-and-Work emphasis is now inseparable from the Faith-and-Order emphasis. Part of the reason for this is that the leaders of the latter have recognized more clearly the place which non-theological factors have in the experience of the churches and in their relationships. Progress in actual achievement of full organic union, as we have just seen, has been phenomenal. More progress has been made in this respect than in any previous period in a like space of time.

There is less willingness to salve the Christian conscience about the divided state of the Church merely by talking about the "Church Invisible." More and more Christian thinkers deny that there is any authority in the early tradition of the Church for such an idea. The Church, many insist, is a historic community which has certain marks and exercises certain functions. Most agree that its supreme function is to witness to the revelation of the redeeming love of God in Christ who incarnated a new covenant with the community of the faithful.

Again, Christ cannot be the head of each denomination as if he had many bodies. He is head of the whole Church. The objective of the ecumenical movement, as Charles Morrison puts it, is "the restoration of visible and functional unity to the body of Christ which is the community of Christian believers throughout the world."

For such a view, the authentic character of the ministry is always clear if that ministry witnesses to the central fact of Christian history—God's sacrificial self-giving for man in Christ. The true succession is to be found by the application of that test rather than any formula having to do with the form of ordination or the sacerdotal theory of any priest, minister, or bishop.

It is interesting to discover in the work of Charles Morrison, in his Lyman Beecher lectures at Yale, published under the title *What Is Christianity?* a return to very much the same position as that taken by Dr. William Reed Huntington, first in his volume on the Church Idea published in 1869 and later in the second edition of the same work brought out in 1899.[16]

Dr. Huntington saw as marks of the idea of the visibility of the Church evidence of the indwelling spirit of God, unity and capability for perpetual renewal. "Rome exaggerates the idea, Puritanism diminishes the idea, liberalism distorts the idea." The object of those concerned for the health of the Church should be to restore all four of the marks of the Church, and for him it could be done through acceptance of the Quadrilateral (which he has been credited with first giving wide currency in American Church circles). Under such a formula he hoped to incorporate Congregational, Presbyterian and Episcopal ideas or order. His argument for the historic episcopate is not so much on a sacer-

---

[16] "Christian Unity in 19th Century America," Bulletin of Franklin and Marshall College, Vol. 4, No. 3, May, 1950.

dotal as on a pragmatic and practical basis grounded in human experience with the problems of group government. And the Church is to him "a family, a brotherhood, a household, to whose guardian care the archives of the faith have been entrusted."

For Morrison, as for Huntington, although with different overtones, the problem is the restoration of the lost catholicity of the Church. Morrison puts it thus: "This means primarily that the community shall recover to itself the structure which has been stripped away from the body (by being) set up as sectarian structures in the denominational order."

The curious thing about the progress that has been made by churches in uniting structurally is that about as many of unlike types have merged as of types that are closely related theologically. The detailed study of causes of division which has gone on intensively since 1927 has revealed two areas: in the doctrine of the Church and in the nature of the ministry.

Although it took place in India, the merger of the Anglican with the Reformed Churches to form the United Church of South India was the concern of many Americans and has affected the thinking of many. Here for the first time the typical Catholic and the typical Protestant traditions—one seeking continuity in the historic episcopate and the other seeking it in the body of witnessing Christians, were blended despite many difficulties.

In general, however, the antinomy is marked and the clarification of the issues awaits further study and spiritual growth. It may well be that the Anglo-Catholic opposition to the South India Union, which has delayed inter-communion between that great new Church and the mother Church of Anglicanism, may undergo some considerable change as a result of the apparently deliberate recent action of the Vatican in widening the gap between Rome and all other parts of Christendom.

Although not definitely in the area of Faith and Order, the consummation in the closing weeks of 1950 of the merger of eight co-operative Christian bodies of an interdenominational character to form the new National Council of the Churches of Christ in

America has very great relevance for those interested in the progress of Christian unity. It is not in any strict sense ecumenical because it is without direct relationship to the rest of the church world. (Unless one thinks of the relationship between the Council and the International Missionary Council whose United States link—the Foreign Missions Conference—now becomes an integral part of this new body.) But the indirect effects of this action, taken officially by so significant a cross section of the Protestant and Orthodox Churches, will be very great. It is too soon to make any prediction as to just what these effects will be, although it seems safe to anticipate that they will further the cause both of national unity and of ecumenical co-operation on every stage.

The fact is that in areas of practical co-operation even the more aloof of the denominations find a way of participating. The Southern Baptists and the Missouri Synod Lutheran have taken part in the work of Church World Service, a body set up by the Foreign Missions Conference, the Federal Council and the former American Committee of the World Council (now the Conference of U.S.A. Member Churches). As this relief agency becomes a part of the new National Council the way seems open not only for the continuance of co-operation in this one area but for the development in due course of more co-operation and consequent closer relationships of a general character.

"History is stronger than logic," and the history of Christian co-operation, as we have noted, turns out to be in many instances the history not only of unity but of union. No one is wise enough to predict just what the Spirit will say to the Churches of the second half of the twentieth century. But they can ill afford to be lukewarm to the promptings of sensitized consciences with respect to their duty to take ever more seriously the desire of their common Lord for oneness among them all.

It is helpful to keep in mind the words of William Temple: "In a sense it is required that every existing Christian communion should die in order to rise again into something more splendid than itself." This is certainly no harder to accept than the view of some that there already exists the perfect form of Church and that all others must conform to it if there is to be not only unity but union in the fullest sense. Yet a third view sees organic union as not of itself a necessity, since variety in unity is possible and desirable, and "The Coming Great Church" need not be envisaged as organizationally integrated any more than the various parts of the Anglican communion are integrated organizationally today—yet see themselves, as they are seen by others, in a framework of undeniable unity.

It requires both faith and insight to labor in the cause of unity. But that faith feeds on the insight many American thinkers have shared with William Temple who said: "In the end the reunion of the Church will not be something fabricated by us at all; it will be the work of God resulting from a deeper devotion in all parts of the Church, and all members of all parts of the Church, to the one Lord of the Church." Not skill in debate or negotiation, not the power of philosophical analysis or theological insight, but devotion to the will of Christ is the utterly essential element. We cannot too often be reminded that Jesus said: "Follow me"—not "find the perfect theology and the ideal Church order." More and more the ecumenical movement in the first half of the century has demonstrated the truth of the statement frequently on the lips of its leaders: "The closer we come to Christ, the closer we come together." The primary loyalty which will unify in the future that which is now divided is not institutional but personal and the resulting sense of spiritual community is what gives and will give reality to the dream of "The Coming Great Church."

BIBLIOGRAPHY

Brown, William Adams, *Toward a United Church* (New York, 1946)

Dun, Angus, *Prospecting for a United Church* (New York, 1948)

Horton, Walter M., *Toward a Reborn Church* (New York, 1949)

Hutchison, John Alexander, *We Are Not Divided* (New York, 1941)

Leiper, Henry Smith, editor, *Christianity Today* (New York, 1947)

Macfarland, Charles S., *Christian Unity in Practice and Prophecy* (New York, 1933)

Morrison, C. C., *What Is Christianity?* (Chicago, 1940)

Pittinger, William Norman, *Historic Faith in a Changing World* (Chicago, 1950)

———, *Sacraments, Signs and Symbols* (Chicago, 1949)

Van Dusen, Henry P., *World Christianity, Yesterday, Today and Tomorrow* (New York, 1947)

Wedel, Theodore O., *The Coming Great Church* (New York, 1945)

Zabriskie, Alexander C., *Bishop Brent* (New York, 1948)

CHRISTIANITY AND
OTHER RELIGIONS

John A. Mackay

JOHN A. MACKAY was born in Scotland in 1889. He studied at the University of Aberdeen, the University of Madrid, the University of Bonn, and Princeton Theological Seminary. He spent several years in South America as principal of the Anglo-Peruvian College in Lima, Peru, where he was also Professor of Philosophy at the National University. After living for several years in Montevideo and Mexico City as a continental lecturer under the auspices of the Y.M.C.A., he became Secretary of the Presbyterian Board of Foreign Missions in the U.S.A. in 1932. Since 1936 he has been Professor of Ecumenics and President of Princeton Theological Seminary. Among the many offices which he now holds in the world-wide movement of the Christian Church are those of President of the Presbyterian Board of Foreign Missions, U.S.A., and Chairman of the International Missionary Council. He is also a member of the Central Committee of the World Council of Churches and the Editor of the quarterly review, *Theology Today*. His published contributions, both in Spanish and English, have been considerable; his best-known books, perhaps, being *The Other Spanish Christ* and *A Preface to Christian Theology*.

XII

WHAT is the essential nature of the Christian religion, that which differentiates it from the other religions of mankind? What should be the attitude of Christians to other religions and towards the people who adhere to them? What constitutes the justification, and what are the prospects, of Christian missions in the non-Christian world? In the course of the twentieth century, these questions have engaged the thought of some of the most virile and representative minds in Protestantism. They have also been the subject of pronouncements of world gatherings of Protestant churches.

At the turn of the century, two books of symbolic significance were published in the United States. The author of the first, which appeared in 1899 under the title *A Handbook of Comparative Religion*, was Samuel Henry Kellogg, an American missionary to India. The other book was published in 1900 by John R. Mott and entitled, *The Evangelization of the World in This Generation*. The former of these volumes is important because it was the first "handbook" of comparative religion printed in any country which was specifically designed to promote popular interest in the subject. That the book should have appeared in the United States is significant for, as has been pointed out by Louis Henry Jordan, a British authority on the literature of comparative religion, it was in America that the science of comparative religion was born.[1] The second book is significant because it constituted a resounding call to the Christian churches and, in particular, to youth, to carry forward the great task of world evangelization which had been the most significant spiritual feature of the nineteenth century, and in which American Christianity had played an important part. Its

[1] *Comparative Religion. A Survey of Its Recent Literature*, by Louis Henry Jordan. Second Edition. Oxford University Press, London, 1920. Vol. 1, p. 25.

author was destined to become the century's dominant statesman in the promotion of the Christian religion throughout the world.

1. World Forces which Affected the Status and Relations of All Religions

During the period which has elapsed since the above-mentioned books were written, great world forces have affected every religion, both as to its outlook and the conditions of its existence. These forces have been represented mainly by applied science or Technology, and by basically conflicting views of life, that is, by one ideology or another. Technology made the world a global physical unity, a planetary world, an "ecumenical" organism. During the same period Ideology caused two world wars, accentuated differences between peoples and nations, divided mankind into three major political systems and produced an unparalleled revolutionary situation.

Technology and Ideology affected the non-Christian religions, as well as the missionary thought and activity of Christianity. Because of the new global unity it became possible for Christian missionaries to reach the whole world as never before. It also became possible for Islam and Buddhism and the theosophical derivation of Hinduism to take on world significance. Scientific skepticism had an opportunity to propagate its doubt and negations in all the centers of ancient religion and culture. Because civilization tended to become one, there grew up in certain circles the illusion of a common world culture, of a "grand cultural synthesis." But the new physical unity in whose development millennia had been packed into decades, and as a result of which, all men had become neighbors and contemporaries, was held together exclusively by technological advancement. There existed a common civilization, but the basis for a common culture was lacking.

Ideology has brought about unprecedented disunity in this physically united world. Secularism, spear-headed by scientific skepticism, had emptied human life of all spiritual content, and produced a total emptiness. But men and nations had to live. The

double urge for spiritual meaning and for daily bread created
in the void new positive forces, which were religious in character.
When God and the transcendent were banished from life, new
"gods" appeared to take their place. Out of the depths of the human
soul, out of the national soil where people lived, out of the historical tradition of which they were a part, new divinities emerged.
In the absence of a common transcendent loyalty, a spiritual
loyalty was provided by some concrete heritage. God was banished and the "gods" returned; the whole polytheistic litter of
deities returned whose exorcism from human life the poet Milton
had described in his "Ode on the Morning of Christ's Nativity."

The rampage of the new "gods" seeking world dominion produced the Second World War. The struggle lasted six years. The
eventual destruction of militant Fascism left Russian Communism,
with its theory of a Messianic Proletariat, sponsored by a Messianic
people, as the strongest and most integrated world force. A nihilis-
tic spirit became rampant, which Russian Communism was interested in promoting, both in the lands of democracy and in the
lands where the ancient religions had their seat.

As the first half of the twentieth century draws to a close,
several things become plain. We witness the passing of the European world hegemony. Europe, where for nearly two millennia,
the traditional centers of Western culture and of the Christian religion had been located, occupies now a secondary position. Asia
is resurgent. The time-honored relativism, native to the East, has
succumbed to new secular absolutes. Under the influence of these
absolutes, Confucism and Shintoism tend to disintegrate. Challenged by them Islam, Hinduism and Buddhism make basic adjustments, and by every means in their power, seek to rehabilitate
themselves and strengthen their ancient position. Russia, the home-
land of Communism, and the United States, the chief center today
of both Protestant and Roman Christianity, have emerged as the
two leading world powers. Added to these, as the brightest single
feature of the contemporary situation, is the reality of the Ecumenical Church, a world-wide fellowship of Christians who are

united in faith and love across all the dividing frontiers of a revolutionary epoch.

II. The Sources of Protestant Thought on the Relation of Christianity to the World Religions

The study of Protestant thought during the five decades of the present century, upon the subject of Christianity and its relations to the other religions, is best undertaken in close connection with a series of international conferences which were held during this period. Those gatherings, convened between 1910 and 1949 to consider the missionary responsibility and task of Christianity in relation to the non-Christian religions and to the world as a whole, are landmarks in the realm of missionary policy and theology. They became occasions for the crystallization of thought on many important issues. Not a few of the studies written in anticipation of those meetings were the work of eminent Christian thinkers who took part also in the actual conference deliberations. For that reason the printed reports of the gatherings in question constitute a primary source of information regarding representative Protestant thought on the theme of this chapter. It is important, therefore, that I should begin with a panoramic view of those uniquely significant meetings.

In 1910 a great international missionary gathering was held at Edinburgh, Scotland. Its chief objective was to formulate Christian missionary strategy on a world scale. The vast majority of those present were representatives of the Western churches, for the new Christian churches of Asia and Africa had not yet sufficiently developed to send many representative figures. Quite apart, however, from that circumstance, the idea was latent in the mood and deliberations of this epoch-making assembly that the East was destined to be permanently dominated by the West. Out of the Edinburgh Conference grew the International Missionary Council which became the first ecumenical body of modern times. Four years later the First World War broke out.

Ten years after the War came to an end, that is in 1928, the Protestant missionary forces of the world met again, this time in Jerusalem, on the Mount of Olives. Nearly half of the delegates to this gathering were Christian nationals from the "younger" churches. The message of the Conference, familiarly known as the "Jerusalem Message," was drafted by a Committee whose chairman was the late Archbishop Temple. The meeting was dominated by the conviction that secularism was the most sinister and potent force which affected the spiritual life of mankind. It, therefore, called upon the non-Christian religions, as well as the Christian churches throughout the world, to combat the sway of the secularistic spirit. Taking place in the heyday of optimism regarding the possibility of a true international order, the Jerusalem Conference lacked somewhat the intensity and the tragic sense of life which its successors were to reflect.

When it was already clear that a Second World War was inevitable, representatives of Protestant and Eastern Orthodox Churches came together at Oxford, England, in 1937, to consider the topic, "Church, Community and State." It was at Oxford that thought began to be focussed upon the Church and its great importance in the witness and expansion of the Christian religion. At this conference, too, came into contemporary vogue a new use of the term "ecumenical." After Oxford, Protestant Christians began to speak of the "Ecumenical Church," that is, of the Church which is "coextensive with the inhabited globe." This conference, meeting as it did so shortly before the outbreak of the Second World War, prepared the Christian forces in thought and in life for the six years of world struggle that were to follow. Its spirit, moreover, and the decisions to which it came regarding the indestructible bonds by which Christians are bound together in Christ, made possible a speedy resumption of relations between Protestant Christians in the warring nations, as soon as hostilities came to an end.

During the Christmas season of 1938, not many months before the War actually broke out, another great gathering was convened in the Orient. It took place at Madras, India. The great majority of those present at Madras were representatives of the "younger" churches. Special consideration was given in the deliberations to a tension long latent in Protestant thought with respect to the true nature and function of the Christian religion in relation to the other world faiths. Two viewpoints had been expressed during the previous decade. One stressed the continuity between Christianity and the other religions. This view was associated with a book published in 1932, as the result of a study of the Missionary movement in the Orient by a commission of American Christians, mostly laymen, and entitled, *Re-thinking Missions*, or *A Layman's Inquiry After One Hundred Years*. The now famous report was closely linked with the name of the distinguished Harvard philosopher, Professor W. E. Hocking, who had been the Chairman of the Commission and the chief author of the resultant volume. The other viewpoint, the one which dominated thought in the Madras Conference, was that expressed in a book published in 1938 entitled, *The Christian Message in a Non-Christian World*. Its author was H. Kraemer, Professor of the History of Religions in the University of Leyden, Holland, and a former missionary to Indonesia. Dr. Kraemer, a layman like Dr. Hocking, had been specially asked to write this volume in preparation for the Madras meeting. The book, which reflected the movement in Protestant theology associated with the names of Kierkegaard and Barth, insisted upon the total discontinuity between Christianity and the non-Christian religions. Over against the universal fact of Religion it set the dynamic reality of Revelation.

Eleven years later, in the summer of 1947, that is, two years after the Second World War came to an end, representatives of the "older" and the "younger" churches met at Whitby, Canada. Made aware, by the experiences of the War, that the only spiritual force which is capable of weathering the horrors of war, revolution and persecution is a witnessing church, and deeply conscious that the world was in the midst of a new revolutionary era, the Conference set in high relief the "witness of a revolutionary church."

At Whitby a new slogan emerged: "partners in obedience." The representatives of Christian churches from the whole world pledged themselves to become "partners in obedience," so that, transcending all divisions, pooling all resources and working in perfect comradeship, they might make a common approach along a world front to the spiritual problems of the age.

A year later there took place at Amsterdam, Holland, the most significant ecclesiastical event of the century. A World Council of non-Roman Churches was constituted. One of the most significant constitutional actions which the Council took was to "associate" itself officially with the parent ecumenical body, the International Missionary Council, which had been organized some twenty-five years before. In this way the fact was symbolized that the whole Church in its official capacity now recognized the missionary obligation of the Christian religion. This obligation had previously been regarded as very largely the responsibility of missionary societies which might, or might not, be sponsored officially by the churches to which their members belonged.

The last of the great series of ecumenical gatherings which marked the first half of this century, was held in the city of Bankok, Thailand, in December, 1949. The new emergent region of East Asia was in a ferment. A Communist regime was in control in China from which no official delegates could come to this Conference. The gathering recommended the appointment of an Asian Christian to be an apostolic pastor-at-large for the Protestant Churches of East Asia, to function under the joint auspices of the two ecumenical bodies which had become officially associated at Amsterdam.

III. Interpretations of Christianity and Its Relation to the Other Religions

After this survey of secular world forces and of Christian world gatherings, we come now to representative answers that have been given during the present century to the question, What is Christianity? Wherein lies the uniqueness of the Christian religion?

a. *Christianity as one religion among others.* Comparative Religion as a special branch of study has veered between two extremes. As expounded by Dr. Kellogg, author of the first "handbook" on the subject, the comparative study of religion should chiefly establish the superiority of the Christian religion and so provide an apologetic for Christianity. Such an approach, however, is open to the criticism that it destroys the objectivity of Comparative Religion as a science and makes it merely an introduction to and a handmaid of Christian theology.

The other extreme is that represented by the new W. M. Birks, Professor of Comparative Religion in the Faculty of Divinity of McGill University, Montreal. In his inaugural lecture on the subject, *The Comparative Study of Religion*, Professor W. C. Smith recognizes that the study of religion is important, because as he says, different ways of worshipping God have very basic implications for the economic, the political, the agricultural, the medical, and the industrial life of peoples. Religious differences, moreover, affect cultural relations and human understanding between peoples. But Comparative Religion should neither define religion nor say what it ought to be. It is not interested in ascertaining the essence or essential structure of a religion, nor will it venture to formulate value judgments regarding the religions. To be a Christian from the view point of Comparative Religion, thus conceived, is simply to belong to the Christian tradition. What is important is simply the empirical historical reality of a religion. Such an approach to the study of religion, being hindered by considerations of scientific objectivity to seek the essence of a religion, and forbidden by the demands of academic neutrality, to show a marked preference for one religion over another, leaves untouched and unanswered all the great concerns which make people religious and make religious people want to propagate their faith.

We move therefore into a realm of interpretation where religious essences are sought, and where religious commitment is held to be indispensable for the true study of religion.

b. *Christianity as the highest religion.* That the Christian religion is the highest, though not the absolute religion, is the view expressed by Professor W. E. Hocking, in the book already referred to, *Rethinking Missions*, and in a subsequent volume by the same distinguished author, *Living Religions and a World Faith*. Religion is defined as "a passion for righteousness and for the spread of righteousness, conceived as a cosmic demand." It is religion's supreme role to establish a civilization and to keep the civilization sound. Thus the real absolute is culture whose servant religion is to be. *Rethinking Missions* was convinced that events the world around were moving in the direction of the emergence of a common world culture. Religion's task was to provide that coming world culture with a soul. For those seeking to fulfil this task, Jesus, the greatest religious genius who ever appeared, would become in spirit their "Companion and Master" in the great adventure. They who accepted His leadership would not be interested in displacing one religion by another, even by Christianity. They would not be interested either in a mere synthesis of religion, but would exercise a virile intolerance of all those aspects of religion which are unwholesome. This method would be one of "reconception," giving time for their faith to be considered under the most favorable circumstances by peoples of other faiths. Renouncing as futile all private proprietorship in truth, they would live and work for the expression of the final truth. That final truth, whatever it may be, is "the New Testament of every existing faith." This represents the so-called "liberal" view of the Christian religion.

From this viewpoint, Christianity, while being the highest religion which has yet appeared, as Christ is the greatest religious figure, is not the final religion. We must look forward to a still more perfect and adequate religion, which, as already stated, will constitute the soul and inspiration of a universal culture. But the expectation of an emergent world culture has proved, in the light of subsequent events, to have been purely illusory. To remove, moreover, from a religion the sense of being related to an absolute truth, and to divest it of an apostolic urge to make that truth known, has led, and can only lead, to religious formalism and spiritual stagnation. For the essence of a potent religion is not to believe that it has a truth, but that it is related to the Truth. For a religion to admit the relative into what it regards as its essence is to destroy its character as religion.

c. *Christianity as the absolute religion.* In striking contrast to the view that Christianity contains the highest truth is the view that it presents the *absolute* truth, because it presents Jesus Christ who is the Truth. During the first half of this century, the absolute character of the Christian religion has been set forth in "orthodox" Protestant thought under two forms or, one might say, with two distinctive emphases. For some, Christianity is the absolute religion because in Jesus Christ, who is the perfect revelation of God, the absolute meaning of life, and so life's absolute value, has appeared. Others in stressing the absolute character of the Christian religion put the emphasis upon the activity of the everliving God as that appears in the Bible. This view stresses not so much the quality of life which appeared in Jesus Christ, as the expression of the divine activity which became manifest when He appeared. In both views there is a high Christology. The one is impressed, however, by the significance of Christ as the supreme Value for life; the other, with Jesus Christ as the supreme Lord of life.

The former of these viewpoints was given classical expression in the Jerusalem Message of 1928. The Message said: "Our message is Jesus Christ. He is the revelation of what God is and of what man through Him may become. In Him we come face to face with the ultimate reality of the universe. He makes known to us God as our Father, perfect and infinite in love and in righteousness."

Those who met at Jerusalem were convinced that Christianity stands or falls with the conviction that the revelation of God in Jesus Christ is something unique. What we have in Jesus Christ is not simply the highest idea of God, but God Himself in His self-giving love. Inasmuch, therefore, as Christ is the Truth, a Christian must necessarily be missionary and pass on the Truth. When, however, we speak of the "superiority" of Christianity we are not saying that Christians have been more "religious" than the great men of the East. As a matter of fact oriental mystics have done much more spiritual climbing in a religious sense. The superiority of the Christian religion lies in the fact that God comes to meet man in Jesus Christ. The Christian, therefore, can glory only in this, that he owes everything to Christ. For that reason he must ever feel humble. It is by God's grace that he is what he is. The fact was emphasized at Jerusalem that the superiority of Christianity, for example, over Islam, could not be grounded in its culture or in its theology, but only in the fact that the "Spirit of God was in Christ." It was the manifestation of this living Presence which Islam lacked. For at bottom, religions differ not so much in their trappings as in their essence. When all is said and done they differ "in their view of the character of God." Or more concretely, the true division between religions is not between the East and the West, but, as Archbishop Temple expressed it in one of the Jerusalem documents, "between Bible and non-Bible." The inescapable fact is that "salvation is of the Jews." It is at this point that the Jerusalem emphasis passes into that which, in Christian thought on the subject of Christianity and the non-Christian religions, has become associated with the name of H. Kraemer.

Kraemer, then a missionary in Java, was present at the Jerusalem Conference. Several years before the Conference at Madras, and in preparation for it, he was asked to prepare a special study on the Christian Message. The fruit of years of thought and travel is the now famous and influential volume, *The Christian Message in a Non-Christian World.*

According to Kraemer, it is not enough to think of the Christian religion in terms of values, however great the values. A comprehensive view of life is needed. Such a view we derive from the Bible, or as Kraemer puts it, from "Biblical realism." "Biblical realism" is not interested merely in spiritual values, but in the dramatic saving events which the Bible presents. Christianity is essentially the religion of the Incarnation, of the fact that God became man for man's salvation. That being so, Christian truth is not eternal truth or the expression of eternal values, it is rather truth that *became*. Its central affirmation is that God became man. The most purely divine dimension of the Christian religion is the Resurrection. Because of this mighty act of God, Jesus Christ is Lord. That earliest Christian creed is "the pith of the Biblical revelation." In the Risen Christ, God began a new order of life of which Jesus Christ Himself is the center and head. Christianity is, therefore, not so much Religion as Revelation. Christ as the ultimate standard of reference becomes the crisis of all religions, not only of the non-Christian religions, but also of empirical Christianity, that is, Christianity as we know it in history. That being so, all natural religious superiority dies.

Thus Kraemer, under the influence of Kierkegaard and Barth, in stressing the special Divine activity of God in the Bible, affirms the discontinuity between Christianity and the other religions. The viewpoint takes issue with that viewpoint in Christian theology associated with the name of Clement of Alexandria, which, by stressing the principle of continuity, regards Christianity as essentially the supreme and ultimate wisdom. No, says Kraemer, Christianity is never a mere perfecting of what went before. The non-Christian religions are not schoolmasters which bring people to Christ. Christianity differs from them not merely in value but in the fact that the living God was active in Christ and in the drama associated with Christ, as He was not active in the leaders and the history of other religions.

IV. The Missionary Approach of Christianity to the Other Religions

What kind of missionary approach should Christianity make to the other religions? An adequate and representative answer to this question involves consideration of the missionary *objective*, the missionary *motive* and the missionary *attitude*.

a. *The missionary objective*. Two main answers have been made in the course of the present century to the question of the missionary objective. One is the view advocated by *Rethinking Missions* and subsequently enlarged on by Professor Hocking in

Living Religions and a World Faith. Christianity must ever maintain the point of view of world culture, which was believed to be emerging in the late twenties and early thirties of the century. A general desire existed in the world for the voice of Christianity to be heard. The authentic spirit of Christ would always be welcome. That being so, it should not be necessary to "sell" Christianity any more than it was necessary to sell the other wares of world culture. All that was needed was that the good things of Christianity be presented in order to be sympathetically received. Christian missionaries should, therefore, share with the representatives of other religions such certainties as they themselves had in the sphere of religion. Such an approach, however, should not involve any undue or embarrassing haste on the part of the preacher or of the philanthropist. Haste would be in order only when it appeared to the missionary that there was a danger of local customs changing too rapidly as the spirit of world culture loosened the sanctions and ancient customs of religion. He must never work towards the displacement of another religion, but towards the growing together of Christianity with it, or the continued existence of the other religion alongside Christianity. For, after all, the devotees of all religions are brothers in a common quest. It is for Christians, therefore, to share with the representatives of other religions the spiritual resources of Western civilization, those things which they have learned through Christ. This will be done best through a living philanthropy and education, rather than through evangelization in the traditional sense.

This point of view led to the organization in the U.S.A. in the mid-thirties of a movement called "The Modern Missions Movement," renamed soon after, "A Movement for World Christianity." It aimed to substitute for "Foreign Missions," a "Christian International," which would aim to build a Christian civilization. The rapid disintegration of this movement was a demonstration of the fact that its leaders had faced neither the realities of the world situation nor the realities of the Christian religion. The distinguished men and women who after a long period of close study of

Christian missions and the other religions in the Orient, wrote *The Layman's Inquiry*, seemed to be totally unaware that, quite apart from Christianity, there was a force present in many lands, namely Marxist Communism, which was bent upon the most radical transformation of ancient life and faith.

The other view, the view which is inherent in the nature of Christianity and responsible for its expansion in the world, has been that Christians should devote themselves to the evangelization of all mankind irrespective of nationality, religion, class, or race. The Edinburgh Conference of 1910 gave classical expression to Christian concern for world-wide evangelism. The Gospel, said the Edinburgh Convention, must be carried to all the non-Christian world. The world situation should be studied with a view to making the Gospel known to all men. The sense of urgency should be all the greater in view of the fact that the non-Christians were attempting to adapt themselves to modern conditions. Christians must make haste. It was a spectacle "of singular interest and grandeur," it was said, to think of the Christian Church advancing along many lines of action "to the conquest of the five great religions of the modern world." In these words becomes evident the tremendous crusading surge of missionary enthusiasm that dominated the great gathering in the Scottish capital. But it should be borne in mind that this conquest was to be the conquest of Jesus Christ who "fulfills and supersedes all other religions."

Some three decades later the Christian missionary forces, meeting at Madras on the edge of the Second World War, and representing the "older" and the "younger" churches, with the representatives of the "younger" churches predominating, made world evangelism the keynote of the gathering. It was pointed out that Christianity had come to a point in human history where it was in a fighting situation comparable to that in which the early Christians found themselves in the Roman Empire. In such a case the kind of missionary objective towards which Christians should look was not any goal inherent in the other great world religions. The true religious goal was no "return to totality," no "serene ecstasy or liberating gnosis," no "aristocratic mysticism," no "static conservatism," no "national self-deification," but a submission to the "Lordship and sovereignty of God, the Eternal."

b. *The missionary motive.* But granted that Christianity by its very nature must pursue the evangelization of the world, what is the motive of true missionary effort?

The motivation of Christian missionary activity was classically expressed in the "Jerusalem Message," which said, "Christ is our motive and Christ is our end. We must give nothing less and we can give nothing more." Christians, therefore, in their approach to other people, must be inspired by the "good news" of Christ. They must repudiate all ulterior purposes. They must eschew imperialism in every form. And never must they confer benefits on other people in order to be in a position to manage their souls. Let them reject "theological charity;" doing good to people must not be contingent upon their acceptance of certain theological ideas or their adoption of certain religious practices. To be a Christian and a missionary should be synonymous, for Christian witness is the supreme manifestation of self-giving love.

Pearl Buck in *Fighting Angel,* a book which describes her father, has a description of the intensity of the early missionaries: "To go forth, to cry out, to warn, to save others, these were frightful urgencies upon the soul already saved. There was a very madness of necessity and agony of salvation." Those who drafted the Jerusalem Message went on record as saying that, although they were as concerned as their fathers about the implications of men dying without Christ, they were still more concerned about the fact that multitudes were living without Christ. So they addressed themselves to the whole world; to all the Christian Churches; to all non-Christian religions; to all who enjoyed the benefits of Western civilization, that they might face the fact and its implications that "Jesus Christ is indeed the Saviour of the world."

It is an impressive fact that this sense of apostolic obligation towards God and the world has taken on new meaning and intensity in these last times. Those who attended the Madras Conference were aware that there was nothing left for many Christians save "purely religious and moral suasion." They were, therefore, being forced back to fundamentals. Impotent to use education or medicine, or to engage in philanthropy, nothing remained for many Christians but the simple proclamation of the Lordship of Jesus Christ over all life. As Kraemer has expressed it, "The former ideas of recommending Christianity as the bringer of enlightenment and freedom, as a capital, national and social tonic to make powerful nations, as the infallible guide to progress, had come to naught. . . . Sharing religious experience, even service to men, Christianizing the social order, or the economic and political order, though necessarily included in the living act of man's full missionary expression, cannot be the real motive and ultimate purpose. The real motive and ultimate purpose are not in anything that man or civilization call for. As Kagawa has said, 'The starting point of missions is the Divine Commission to proclaim the Lordship of Christ over all life.' "

A decade later, after the Second World War had ended, the men and women who met at Whitby, Canada, proclaimed two insistent needs: "The desperate need of the world for Christ; the unsatisfied yearning of Christ for the world." These together constitute the expression of the missionary motive in the best Protestant thought of the twentieth century.

c. But if evangelization is the missionary objective and if the Christ whom the world so desperately needs and who so yearningly loves the world, is the motive, what should be the personal attitude of the Christian missionary towards those belonging to other religions?

The missionary attitude. In the missionary thought of the nineteenth century it was not uncommon to regard any show of sympathy with the ethnic religions as a very great blunder on the part of the Christian missionary. The Edinburgh Conference, however, amid the surge of crusading passion which dominated it, and the world-wide strategy which it developed, advocated a sympathetic approach to the other religions. Missionaries, it was said, should proceed with knowledge and charity, looking always for the nobler elements in the other faiths. Such a sympathetic study would introduce them to "hitherto undiscovered riches in Christ who is the absolute revelation." Some considered that, in view of the fact that the Eternal Word had been active in other religions, they would find, as they penetrated within their structure, that Christ was no stranger there. Much would be found there which was expressive of His influence; people would be found there who would be responsive to His Lordship.

The ideal missionary approach has been finely expressed by Kraemer as the combination of "a prophetic, apostolic heraldship of truth for Christ's sake, with a priestly, apostolic ambassador-ship of love for His sake." The real point of contact with those of other religions would thus be the missionary himself. Everything depends upon the missionary's disposition and attitude. The foreign word must become indigenous flesh. Recognizing that he is not the possessor of a truth, but rather the witness to a truth which God has mercifully revealed, the Christian missionary can have no ground for pride or conceit.

When the problem was raised at the Bangkok Conference of 1949 as to the relationship between Christianity and the cultural heritage of East Asia, emphasis was laid upon the fact that it was the Christian, whether missionary or national, who was the true answer to this problem. The way to proceed, especially in the present situation, was not to formulate a theoretic statement of Christianity in relation to the Asiatic cultural heritage. What was required or suggested was that the true Christian working in those areas should sympathetically absorb and identify himself with all that was best in the cultural heritage of East Asia, and, thereafter, express in relation to it the unsearchable riches of Christ. The Christian who knows Christ and loves Him, and who desires to impart that knowledge and love to others, will relate himself sym-pathetically to other people and their culture. Then, in terms of that culture, and in a manner intelligible to those who belong to it, he will communicate the knowledge of Christ. He will study the Bible with representatives of other faiths not as if they were merely non-Christian, but taking into account that they are human beings he will treat them as such. A Hindu who experienced Christian love in a mission hospital in Fategahr, India, made the statement, "There is more healing in the dust of Fategahr than in all the waters of the Ganges." That expression was born out of the patient's contact with Christlike personalities, inspired and molded by the great Physician.

As a contribution to this point of view, and in illustration of it, the distinguished Indian Christian, P. D. Devanandan, made a remarkable contribution to the thinking of the Bangkok Conference. He showed how three of the central ideas stressed by Mahatma Gandhi could be realized adequately only by Jesus Christ. The sense of the sacredness of personality, expressed in *Ahimsa*, could only be secured by the belief that God had become manifest in the flesh. The soul force or passion for righteousness, expressed in *Satyagraha*, could only be achieved by a religion whose founder could say, "My Father worketh hitherto and I work," and which proclaimed that "God was in Christ reconciling the world unto Himself." An order of society in which all political and economic relationships between people would acknowledge the ultimate sovereignty of God, expressed in Gandhi's idea of *Ramrajga*, could only be realized by the worship of a God who was both omnipotent and actively concerned about righteousness.

V. The New Emphasis in the Christian World Outlook

What does the future hold for the Christian religion? Have the missionary days of Christianity come to an end? What does the emergence of the East in world politics, and the specter of Communist domination in the Orient, bode for a religion whose chief centers for nigh two millennia have been in the West?

These questions can only be answered when we consider the new status of the Christian Church in the world of today. We have witnessed in these last years the emergence, or better, the resurgence, of the Church both as a living world reality and as a principle topic of Christian thought.

In the early days of the Christian missionary movement the Church was taken for granted. It meant simply the local congregation or some form of organized Christianity. There was practically no theological thinking about it. But a new sense of the Church has been born; and the new reality of the Church has appeared. This new reality has come into being on a worldwide scale as the result of Christian missions. The Oxford Conference of 1937 gave birth to the slogan "Let the Church be the Church." Let it be itself and not something else. Shortly after Oxford, a new science, the science of Ecumenics, was formulated. Ecumenics has been defined as "the science of the Church universal, conceived as a World Missionary Community—its nature, functions, relations and strategy." Representatives of the Church universal have accepted and become committed to the new watchword, "partners in obedience," which involves the transcendence of everything in race, money, or administrative policy, which would prevent the fullest missionary cooperation between the "older" and the "younger" churches. It involves also the "association" of the two great Ecumenical bodies.

"Let the Church be the Mission." This is the slogan which is emerging. The Church was designed by God to be the mission and must take its calling seriously. World evangelism is its main task. It is "inherent in the nature of the Church as the Body of Christ, created by God to continue in the world the work which Jesus Christ began in His life and teaching, and consummated by His death and resurrection." So spoke the Madras Conference. "The Missionary Obligation of the Church" will be the theme of the next meeting of the International Missionary Council scheduled, world conditions permitting, to convene in 1952. Now that the Christian Church is "coextensive with the inhabited globe" it was never in a more favorable situation to evangelize the world, even "in this generation."

The Church must become the mission, because it finds itself everywhere in a missionary situation. It lives literally in a strange world. Many churches live in a post-Constantine situation where the Church has been deprived of privileges which it formerly enjoyed. In other countries churches live in a post-Christian situation where life is no longer dominated by the Christian ethos. In many regions of the modern world Christians have become in a wholly new sense "pilgrims and sojourners." That being so, the Church's missionary work must, therefore, be begun all afresh. The new situation gives significant meaning to the title of Kraemer's prophetic book, "The Christian Message in a *Non-Christian World.*"

As the mission, the Church is summoned to a new task. No longer can the representatives of the Christian religion think in terms of a global Christian strategy as was done by the men and women who attended the Edinburgh Conference in 1910. "To talk about global missionary strategy," says a distinguished Christian thinker and missionary statesman,[2] "is to surrender to the intoxication of verbiage. It is to fall a victim to Titanism. Decentralization of the missionary enterprise, not centralization is the clamant need of today." This means that the Christian churches in their great dispersion around the globe, while maintaining close ecumenical unity, must speak and act in their several national and regional situations as circumstances require.

In some parts of the world it becomes necessary for the Church to proclaim and to stand in a very special way for the dignity and integrity of man and of human nature. Never was it so urgent, in view of the enserfdom and debasement of man, to outline a true Christian anthropology. Beyond that the significance must be worked out for life of the living reality of Jesus Christ and of the "new man in Christ." This "new man" alone can meet the pagan dynamism of the new religions. He can meet it because the Comrade of his new frontier life is the Lord of the Frontier.

It is no less a part of the missionary task of the Christian Church today to manifest the meaning of true community. The Christian community, on the one hand, indigenous and national, and, on the other, loyally ecumenical because rooted in the Christian tradition

---

[2] Max Warren in *The Truth of Vision*

and related to other Christians throughout the world, has a missionary task of a communal nature to fulfil. "The Church herself is the leaven by which Christ transforms the life of society and nations. There can be no true Christian action which is not rooted in full participation in the worship of the Church and animated by zeal for the expression of true community in things both spiritual and material." So said the Oxford Conference, and Whitby added, "The Church alone offers the only concept adequate to furnish focal unity for corporate existence."

In his book *Living Religions and a World Faith*, Professor Hocking has expressed disdain of a plan of the ages. "The idea of a divine plan considered as a dated product of God's wisdom and goodness, wholly unimaginable to man, is, I fear, an ingenious invention of St. Paul. To take it up again today is to place a halter around the neck of Christianity for those to tug at who are disposed to work upon the more graven fears of the human heart. It is time for a robust and honest Christianity to have done with all this rattling of ancient moral chains." So writes the distinguished professor. Yet it is precisely the vision and understanding of this divine plan which is needed by the Christian Church today. Such a plan we find in Paul's Letter to the Ephesians, the greatest of all Biblical documents. It is the book of the Church Universal, the most contemporary book in the Bible. Here is found the only vision and theory of history which can match the Marxist dream.

Happily the vision of the "Mystery," the "Unveiled Secret" of God, is breaking upon the Church, which braces itself with militant faith for a wilderness life, on all the frontiers of the world. To build the Church, to make it a missionary instrument in God's hand is the great task of our time. For the Church is the one indestructible community which shall outlive the waxing and the waning of all political systems and religious organizations. Let the Church, therefore, be in a new sense the Mission, in the knowledge that Jesus Christ is Lord, and in the hope that all men everywhere shall one day acclaim His sovereign Lordship.

BIBLIOGRAPHY

Kellogg, Samuel Henry, *A Handbook of Comparative Religion* (Philadelphia, 1899)

Mott, John R., *The Evangelization of the World in This Generation* (New York, 1900)

The Missionary Message in Relation to Non-Christian Religions, Report of Commission IV, World Missionary Conference, 1910 (New York, 1910)

The Christian Life and Message in Relation to Non-Christian Systems of Thought and Life, Volume I, Jerusalem Meeting of the International Missionary Council (New York, 1928)

Hocking, William Ernest, Editor, *Re-Thinking Missions: A Laymen's Inquiry After One Hundred Years* (New York, 1932)

Kraemer, H., *The Christian Message in a Non-Christian World* (New York, 1938)

Hocking, William Ernest, *Living Religions and a World Faith* (New York, 1940)

Jurji, Edward J., Editor, *Great Religions of the Modern World* (Princeton, 1946)

Ranson, C. W., Editor, *Renewal and Advance: Christian Witness in a Revolutionary World* (London, 1948)

Ranson, C. W., Editor, *The Christian Prospect in Eastern Asia* (Report of the Bangkok Conference, 1949) (New York, 1950)